Blessings!

James Brewton

FROM
ꞬOOTMEN TO ꞬHORSEMEN

THE RISE OF COMMISSIONED,
KINGDOM-LEVEL LEADERS

KINGDOM HOUSE | PUBLISHING

DR. JAMES BREWTON

FROM FOOTMEN TO HORSEMEN
The Rise of Commissioned, Kingdom-Level Leaders
Copyright © 2016 Dr. James Brewton

First printing Sept. 2016. Published in the U.S. by Kingdom House Publishing, Lakebay, Washington.

Cover design by James Nesbit.
Interior design by Inspira Literary Solutions.
Library of Congress Control number 2016950704.
ISBN (Print): 978-1-939944-34-4
ISBN (Kindle/.mobi): 978-1-939944-35-1
ISBN ePub: 978-1-939944-36-8

Unless otherwise indicated, all Scripture quotations are from the New King James Version of *The Open Bible* Copyright © 1983, 1985, 1990, 1997 by Thomas Nelson, Inc.

Scripture quotations marked (AMP) are taken from *The Amplified Bible*. Copyright ©1987 by The Zondervan Corporation and the Lockman Foundation.

Scripture quotations marked (Message) are taken from *THE MESSAGE: The Bible in Contemporary Language*, Large Print Numbered Edition Copyright © 2002 by Eugene H. Peterson. All rights reserved. *THE MESSAGE* Numbered Edition Copyright © 2005.

Scripture quotations marked (NIV) are taken from *The New International Version* Copyright ©1973, 1978, 1984 by International Bible Society.

Scripture quotations marked (Passion) are taken from *The Passion Bible* Red-Letter Edition Copyright © 2004 by Holman Bible Publishers Nashville, Tennessee. All Rights Reserved.

Scripture quotations marked (GNB) are taken from the *Good News Bible* with Deuterononicals/Aprocrypha; The Bible in Today's English Version Old Testament: Copyright © American Bible Society 1976; Deuterocanonicals/Apocrypha: Copyright © 1979; New Testament: Copyright © 1966, 1971, 1978.

Scripture quotation marked (KJV) are taken from The Holy Bible, *King James Version* Copyright © 1981 and 1986 by Rainbow Studies, Inc.

Hebrew and Greek translations are taken from *The New Strong's Exhaustive Concordance of The Bible* Copyright © 1995, 1996 by Thomas Nelson Publishers. Also, Vine's Expository Dictionary of New Testament Words, Unabridged Edition, McDonald Publishing Company.

Certain definitions are taken from *Merriam-Webster's Collegiate Dictionary* 11th Edition Copyright © 2003 by Merriam-Webster, Incorporated.

Emphasis or italics have been placed on certain words and Scriptures at the author's discretion to amplify the meaning of the text.

To contact the Author: brewton4@atlanticbb.net; pastorbrewton@gmail.com; www.community-empowerment-ministries.com

DEDICATION

This book is dedicated to the Church – the Body of Christ. It is dedicated to the commissioned, kingdom-level leaders – kings and priests, commanders, kingdom enforcers and servant leaders who have surrendered their lives to Christ; endured the struggles, sacrifices and sufferings that accompany spiritual growth; submitted themselves to the process of transformation, which includes development and time; they have discovered their kingdom assignment; they have been fathered and mentored, trained and equipped for deployment into their specific field of expertise; and, they are walking in kingdom authority as ambassadors sent forth to impose the will of the King of kings upon the demonic systems of the world and subdue the nations for King Jesus. As they do so, they adhere to the standard of the Kingdom of Heaven.

The standard of the Kingdom of Heaven is the Word of God. God, His Word, and His kingdom are One. And, the Body of Christ is currently experiencing the Third Great Awakening of the Church. Some are referring to this time of transformation and reformation as the Kingdom Age Awakening. Whatever the best name for it, this is the season of the Church regaining her credibility, identity and authority. The Church is currently being transformed, from the inside-out, into her apostolic and prophetic identity. She will no longer substitute programs for power and ritual for purity of heart. She will no longer depend on charisma to define her. She will no longer seek power and influence being void of character. Rather, she will walk with royal confidence as she displays intimacy with the Father, love, faith, obedience, humility, purity, unity, stewardship, and the proper use of authority and power.

The Church is the victorious, glorious, Bride of Christ, who will present herself to the Lamb. She is without spot or blemish (Eph. 5:7); she will come in the unity of the faith (Eph. 4:11-13); she will be comprised of servant leaders, stewards of the mysteries of God (1 Cor. 4:1); and, she will do greater works than Jesus did (John 14:12). She no longer runs with the footmen, who once wearied her; she rides with the horsemen of the Armies of Heaven, led by the King of kings. She is finally prepared for her marriage to the Lamb. *"Let us be glad and rejoice and give Him glory, for the marriage of the Lamb has come, and His wife has made herself ready"*… *"Come, I will show you the bride, the Lamb's wife"* (Rev. 19:7, 21:9).

ACKNOWLEDGEMENTS

First, I thank the King of kings and Lord of lords! Thank You for granting me Holy Spirit revelation concerning the Kingdom of Heaven and its government. Thank You for calling and ordaining me an apostle and prophet to the nations prior to Your creating the world. You knew me in Your mind of eternity. And Your counsel stands, *"For the gifts and the calling of God are irrevocable"* (Rom. 11:29). Thank You for maturing me into the place of intimacy and discovery of my kingdom assignment. And thank You for pushing me and pulling me to the place of wholehearted acceptance. It is my good pleasure to serve the King of kings and the Lord of lords – my Commanding Officer, Jesus Christ!

I thank my wife, Pastor Margie, for her patience in allowing me time and privacy to complete this project. Thanks for standing with me over the years, especially the past 18 years of full-time vocational ministry. We have endured the surrender, struggles, sacrifices and sufferings together. Now the rewards are great. Much more, we receive the abundance of grace and the gift of righteousness, for we will reign in life as kings and priests unto God through Jesus Christ (Rom. 5:17). I love you.

Special thanks to my spiritual father, Apostle Dr. Gordon E. Bradshaw, a kingdom commander and mentor. I'm releasing in this book the things I have learned from you. May it accurately reflect my sonship.

Thanks to Dr. Bruce Cook, CEO and Board Chair of Kingdom Congressional International Alliance (KCIA), for continuously encouraging me and giving me opportunities to express my apostleship and writing through this global alliance of apostles and prophets – kingdom enforcers!

Thank you, Apostle Jon Grieser, for your consistent intercession and prophetic decrees declared over me and my wife as ministry leaders and our tribe. Thank you, Alexis Alexander, for keeping me "stable and in-check." You exude love and illustrate reality in a way unbeknownst to most people.

Finally, I thank my covenant ministry tribe at Community Empowerment Ministries, Inc. for their prayers and intercession covering Pastor Margie and me.

You are a joy to teach. You have matured into a company of servant-leaders, sons and daughters who are anointed to empower communities through revelation knowledge of the Word of God. You are no longer footmen, for you ride with the horsemen – the kingdom enforcers!

CONTENTS

ENDORSEMENTS

Wow!! Dr. Brewton's poignant description of the religious and legalistic principles we pick up as church goers, and how so many men and women of God find themselves undiscipled – therefore undisciplined in their spiritual walk, is a clear example of why many people leave the church and even in some cases turn away from God. Consequently, many prematurely postpone the call of divine assignment on their lives, and some even abort their assignments altogether. Without teaching and discipleship on the governance of God's Kingdom, we simply grow up with a "church going" mentality, remaining baby Christians – rather than experiencing the Kingdom of God right here on earth.

Your grasp of revelation and understanding of the power and authority of the Kingdom and how it relates to God's predetermined path for each of our lives from before the foundation of the world, resonates deeply within my spirit. For people to embrace this reality is not an easy task; for some it takes a lifetime; yet, once appropriated, it changes the very course of our lives. How exciting it is for us to know that we were planned and purposed before God even called the world into existence.

Dr. Brewton, I love the phrase you use, "life is a pursuit of discovery," indicating that when we're in right relationship or true fellowship with Christ, not only do we inevitably step into true and authentic identity as sons and daughters, but put ourselves on the divine path to destiny discovery. You go Dr. Brewton… I've known since we first met and sat side by side at a KEYS gathering several years ago, at first not even knowing one another's names, that you were/are one of the authentic Kingdom activists. Your apostolic pioneering & revolutionary spirit will indeed change the mindset of people of this nation and many others as we all learn to become "horsemen."

Gayle Rogers, Ph.D.
Forever Free & Apostolic Coaching For Empowerment
www.doctorgayle.com
Dana Point, California
Author, *The Whole Soul* and *Healing the Traumatized Soul*

Thank you, man of God for releasing this profound and insightful book, a message for the Body of Christ and particularly those who are kingdom-level leaders. Dr. Brewton makes it clear that "the Church is currently being transformed from the inside-out into her apostolic and prophetic identity." He also makes a valid assessment which has always been the heart of Jesus for the Church, and that is God's objective for the believer in Christ is not just simply to be "church folk" but become kingdom-level leaders who fulfill their kingdom purpose and predetermined assignments on earth (see Eph. 2:10).

In addition, Dr. Brewton brings enlightenment concerning the need for spiritual preparation. He says that "it's essential for spiritual maturity." Consequently, a lack of spiritual preparation will undoubtedly expose immaturity, impatience and questionable character traits in ministers. In short, many have not given much thought that spiritual development and God's timing are essential and as Dr. Brewton judiciously puts it, "the greater the call, the greater will be the preparation." What's more, this book will challenge spiritual leaders and laymen alike to move from religious protocol to embrace, encourage and promote kingdom agendas in their local churches.

From Footmen to Horsemen is a must read for those desiring to come out of and break free from mediocrity, tradition, legalism and lethargic mindsets. It is my prayer that after reading this book you will have a better comprehension and appreciation for the apostolic and prophetic ministry in the Body of Christ. I recommend *From Footmen to Horsemen* because it is absolutely an excellent spiritual textbook and resource for your spiritual library.

Apostle Donald M. Spellman
Author of *Christ Still Heals*
Overseer & Co-Founder of Living Word of Grace Ministries, Inc.
Baxley, Georgia
www.lwogministries.org

On occasion, one picks up a book that is so impactful and timely that the right words are difficult to come by. This is one of those books. Apostle James Brewton, in his latest book *From Footmen to Horsemen*, lays out a no-holds-barred challenge to the body of Christ to pursue the "something more" in order to discover, mature into, and operate in one's God-given identity and life's mission in order to unlock the kingdom servant leader within.

Written with vulnerable transparency along with the accountability of the spiritual son of excellence and the grace and truth of the spiritual father that is James Brewton, this book will encourage those who are searching for His mission statement for their lives as well as those in the process of preparation for their life's assignment. With keen revelatory awareness, Apostle Brewton also urges current kingdom-level leaders to transition into what he insightfully lays out as the 21st Century apostolic model.

From Footmen to Horsemen will irritate the religious and awaken the complacent. It will embolden us all to become the kingdom-level leaders – servant leaders and commanders – that we are designed to be in order to demonstrate the Kingdom of God in His character and His nature. On earth as it is in Heaven. This book is a must read. Be forewarned, however; once read, there are no more excuses!

Apostle Jon Grieser
Paga International
Wauseon, Ohio

We give a resounding amen to this amazing work by Dr. James Brewton. In this hour when we are told that statistically 1700-1800 pastors leave the ministry every month just in the U.S., we know there is a crisis. When we are told that over 3000 people per day left the Church last year in America, we know something is very wrong. There has to be a voice to rise above the storm. There has to be a prophet of hope. There has to be an apostle with a message that provides a solution. The cry rising from all creation is becoming deafening for the manifestation of the true sons and daughters of God to come forth. This will only come with transformed character and tears, with a message from the King of kings, who is calling out, "I am coming quickly; are you ready to stand before Me?"

Dr. James Brewton comes forward carrying the torch of truth and a light in these dark times. Now, when we need someone to step up with a banner to rally around, Dr. Brewton has responded to the call with his powerful book, *From Footmen to Horsemen*. There will be no transformation of families, cities, states, or nation without transformed character. The pressure is on and with this timely book we see there is hope and wisdom to accelerate this transformation. I lean into the truth revealed here and wholeheartedly give my endorsement and pray this book brings inspiration for the Body of Christ in desperate need of answers. There is time to get ready for the bridegroom and we fling wide our hearts and the gates of our cities and invite Him to take us from people who only run with horses to those who ride them. Dr. Brewton's book calls us to surrender to His loving hands to become the Apostolic and Prophetic leaders who are needed now more than ever.

Apostle Danny J. Dean
Overseer, Cascadia School of the Prophets
Author – *Poetry of the Dance* (Native American Centered Poetry)
Yakima, Washington

Dr. James Brewton has written a timely book on vital truths of the Christian faith. His life and ministry have reflected these deep understandings. I highly recommend *From Footmen to Horsemen* for all who are serious in maturing in their walk with the Lord!

Apostle Mark Henderson
The Glory House Ministries
www.gloryhouse.net
Austin, Texas

Several books have been written and published in recent years on the 'Kingdom of God', each with a fresh revelation. Every author has tried in their book to take the Body of Christ and the leadership from one level to the next with this continuous and progressive unveiling of truth on this subject. We are all in this great preparation as we continue our ministry and take our position by marching ahead with these revelations.

The recent book *I See Thrones* by Apostle Gordon Bradshaw is of great enlightenment on this subject, taking us all to a level of understanding and seeing the vastness of 'the coming Kingdom'. Apostle James Brewton in this book has distinctly challenged the leadership of the Body of Christ not to be dwelling in a stuck up situation, but to move forward from being 'Footmen to Horsemen'. I admire the challenge he has given to all of us in this book with further revelation and sharing of that truth.

I believe, if we are called to be 'kings and priests', then we have to position ourselves as a 'commander' in the present time 'kingdom church age' or '21st Century church age', and should have a victory mindset to rule with HIM, the King of Kings. It took 10 years (from 1996 to 2006) out of my 49 years of walking with the Lord to get this mentality. I pray and wish all those who read this book will be challenged and be prepared for His next move in the making of True Master Builders of His Kingdom.

Apostle Dr. Abraham Sekhar
Founder/President of Spirit Filled Churches of India and Global Apostolic Transformation Missions (USA)
KCIA Advisory Council member
www.kcialliance.org
www.globalatm.net,
www.spiritfilledchurches.net
www.globalmercyfoundation.in
www.indiahealingrooms.net
Mumbai, India

From Footmen to Horsemen is a powerful book that will challenge new Christians and seasoned Christians alike in their understanding of and application of the Word of God into their daily lives that will help them move forward in their God-given destinies. Dr. James Brewton masterfully weaves his personal life journey with Biblical principles that will inspire his readers to step into the fullness of all that God has prepared for them! The world desperately needs commissioned, kingdom-level leaders who will rise up to advance the Lord's kingdom in their spheres of influence. A new boldness from the Lord will arise in every reader of this book to become that commissioned, kingdom-level leader!

Ruth Lum
Leader, Right Hand Team
Executive Assistant to the President and Chairman/CEO
Secretary to the Board of Directors
Kingdom Congressional International Alliance (KCIA)
www.kcialliance.org
Fullerton, California

The ability to communicate deep biblical truths in a straightforward, easy to understand way that brings several "Aha" moments along the way, is truly a gift of God and Dr. Brewton certainly walks in this gift. This book, *From Footmen to Horsemen*, delivers these truths powerfully and motivates its readers to action and spiritual maturity as we are all on a journey through life with Christ.

Martin ("Marty") McClendon
Apostle and Elder
Gig Harbor Family Church
Real Estate Broker, Sotheby's International Realty
www.sothebysrealty.com
Gig Harbor, Washington

As a "wise master builder," Dr. James Brewton has presented an incredible blueprint for the implementation of a new apostolic model. This is not entirely new, but rather a return to the Kingdom apostolic model of the New Testament. It embraces not only the Church, but the marketplace and every sphere of culture as well. He has outlined patterns for transformation and reformation of the Church as it transitions to a "Kingdom mindset" from one that sometimes seems to be one of stale religion. The Kingdom Mindset is seen as the church returns to the basic foundation of saints being equipped for ministry, rather than just sitting back, watching and listening to "professional ministers." This results in greater maturity in the Body of Christ as saints become mature, multiplying, disciple-making, active "living stones," rather than passive observers. I recommend this monumental work without reservation.

Dr. Greg Linnebach
Marketplace Apostle, CEO, Business and Church Mentor
www.linnebach.com
Peoria, Arizona

Dr. James Brewton is a true Statesman of the Kingdom of God. In this book he shows the importance of passing on spiritual knowledge and revelation to others...a much-needed word for this day.

Amb. Dr. Clyde Rivers
Golden Rule World Peace Ambassador Representative to the UN – New York for the Interfaith Peace-Building Initiative
President, I Change Nations
www.ichangenations.org
Victorville, California

Ka-Boom!! Dr. Brewton's book *From Footmen to Horsemen* calls the Body of Christ to grow up! Grow-up-ology is defined as: The art and science of properly leaving the milk and sinking one's teeth into the strong meat of Gods' word. If there was ever a time we've needed such a book to encourage us to be strong, wise, steadfast, overcomers, filled with the Holy Ghost and power and always abounding in the work of the Lord, it is today! Thank you Dr. Brewton for showing us how to release and empower one another to use all the gifts God has given us. Ephesians 4:11-16 helps sum it up very well.

Charlie Fisher
President of Kingdom Economic Yearly Summit (K.E.Y.S.)
Bishop and Pastor of 25 years
Apostle to the Marketplace
Director of Guiding Business Transitions
Grande Prairie, Alberta, Canada
www.gbtiam.com

This book gives Christians an up close, personal look at religious laws and rules on display in the Church. It deals with many root causes of why many have left the Church in today's time. It takes you on a journey of soul-searching. Apostle James Brewton gives Scriptural proof of all he presents in this book. He makes the truth understandable by sharing life experiences. The church world is experiencing an Apostolic movement. God is restoring the real identity of His true disciples. This book will show Christians how to find themselves in Christ. Let the Scriptural truths and personal experiences shared challenge you to search for your true identity and soar to greater heights in Christ Jesus. As you read this book, allow the Holy Spirit to illuminate your mind concerning yourself and God's truth.

Dr. Sharon Billins
Founder and Apostle of Palm Tree International Ministries
www.sharonbillins.org
Columbus, Georgia

Dr James Brewton carries in his heart the embodiment of the heart of the father. He is a true Apostolic Father in the faith. *"For though we have ten thousand instructors in Christ, yet there are not many fathers: for in Christ Jesus he is begotten through the gospel"* (1 Cor. 4:15). He is bold in God to speak and not be silent.

Power, strength and energy is His nature. Dr Brewton is a prisoner for the Lord, urging the body of Christ to walk in a manner worthy of the calling to which we have been called. He walks with all humility and gentleness and patience, bearing with one another in love.

Dr. Brewton became a carrier of the glory of God and published the visions he coined as his truth. As a friend, my walk with him has been an experience of walking with truth. Dr. Brewton is not tossed by the storm but submitted to the mighty hand of God.

Dr. Brewton's heart is stirred by a noble theme as he recites his verses for the king; His tongue is the pen of a skillful writer (Psa. 45:1). *From Footmen to Horsemen* lays the foundation on how to maintain the unity of the Spirit in the bond of peace (Eph. 4:1-2).

He walks in the grace of God which was given to him, as a wise master builder, He has laid a foundation, providing us a path to build upon (1 Cor. 3:10). The road that he paved was not with words to impress but in demonstration and power as he learned from walking with the Father.

As Jesus came to be a blessing, He and His message were one. My friend reflects the nature and character of God. Dr. Brewton, humbled by the spirit of God, was strengthened to walk away from the religious systems of the church. He pressed into the power and authority of the living God. He is a reproducer in the body of Christ not from form and a powerless system of religion, but a restorer of hope and paths to dwell. He walks in foundational truth, characterized, and forged by the words of the King of kings. He trains and imparts with the tongue of a skillful writer.

He plows the path of salvation to the utmost. He skillfully reveals the demonic deceptions within the Church, while as an Intercessor, he binds the forces of darkness coming against the Church. He is built by wisdom and teaches from experience with the Father and His Word.

He builds the lives of others upon the foundations of the Apostle and Prophets.

His life mirrors what he teaches. He and the words of His mouth are one. James has paid the price to become a reflection of the glory of God. He was birthed in suffering, released in the glory.

He made the necessary adjustment in the spirit and taught others to seek after truth. He's aligned with the spirit of the living God. Mercy is His portion, working with God not to kill the religious system but to release its greatest spiritual potential. *From Footmen to Horsemen* releases the glory of God.

Alexis Alexander
N His Image
Prophet and Intercessor
Atlanta, Georgia

From Footmen to Horsemen delineates a clear path through the switchbacks of transformation, challenging footmen of faith to persevere through intentional, Holy Spirit, ruach-swept shifts. Dr. Brewton authentically and transparently leads the way with narratives and principles of humility, integrity, and godly character. With powerful anointing and passion, he calls leaders to move in sync with God's process and timing, and to steward our prophetic words and Kingdom assignments wisely. *From Footmen to Horsemen* is a call to the Church to fill the saddle of our assignment, to rein in the religious spirit, to lean forward into Spirit-led purpose, and to surge forward to the sound of thundering hooves, the cadence of an army of warrior spirits led by confident commanders and servant leaders.

Lynn Hare
Author, Prophet and Intercessor
Vice President, Telios Systems
Portland, Oregon
www.telios.com; www.lynnhare.com

From Footmen To Horsemen by Dr. James Brewton is a clarion call to RISE UP! The Church has settled for the weary march of faith too long, where there is no rest beyond the march, march, march of a never-ending journey toward breakthrough. The call to RISE UP provides an unapologetic sight line to God's call beyond where many in the Church have become accustomed to seeing.

From Footmen To Horsemen invites us to rise above the crowd with greater perspective on our kingdom purpose, while inviting the Church to a clearer view of the kingdom purposes we are called to. This book looks past and above the footmen and the endless march, never sure of where the march ends or if they'll ever get there, to the perspective of the commissioned horsemen who see clearly the path ahead, the purpose assigned and the clear Kingdom call they are to respond to!

Dr. Brewton has heard from the Spirit and been a careful scribe and faithful witness of what the Spirit is saying to the Church. I thank him for that.

Dr. Doug Atha
Assistant Professor of Graduate Studies
Trinity Western University
Langley, British Columbia, Canada
www.twu.ca

Dr James Brewton's new book, *From Footmen To Horsemen*, is a must read for anyone who wants to advance in the Kingdom of God. If you are looking for a way to break free from the norm or fear or playing church, and you are thirsty and want a change, then this book is for you.

This book will teach you to resolve to fight for justice (Micah 6:8), to live with integrity, to walk in obedience, and as you read, you will see what changes and commitment you may need to make.

There is too much at stake for us not to take integrity and maturity seriously (Eph. 5:15-16).

If you are reading this book, it shows that you want more. That is why you need to run your race and take your place as what God has designed for you to be as Kings and Priests on the earth!

Once you have decided, there are no excuses not to follow through. No turning back. Take dominion. Dr. James Brewton, thank you; the Church needs this timely word. You are a blessing, Man of God.

Rev. Dr. Paul Sene
Mentor and CEO
Founder of Shalom International Fellowship
www.sifds.org
Jakarta Pusat, Indonesia

I believe this book is a an eye opener to see what God has for those that seek Him and walk with Him. It's written from a place of passion seeking His will and understanding that His children must be more than just being born again, which is an entrance point and a key to qualify them into the kingdom now that they are engrafted and adopted in.

The kingdom life is loaded with many blessings. You can ride on the horse in the marketplace and in the area of your career and calling to provoke you to bring maximum impact and to influence the influencers in the high places and seats of power in culture.

You can't be just a footman; you are destined to reign with Christ, both in this life and the life to come. I recommend this book; it will inspire you to have a higher quality of Christian life and adding to your faith what you have been missing to be more effective and to be able to execute and steward what is already yours in Him. It will give you understanding of how to acquire the treasures of this earth and be of benefit to you and help you find the gold mine that is hidden in these pages you are reading and also it will reveal the importance of knowing who you are in Him and our place as kings and priests in this world.

Finding our identity in Him is what makes you successful. I pray that this book as you read and apply it is one of the best books in your library and it will bless you and also your family and friends. This book is MUST read. It will ignite the fire in you to seek His face and become a great horseman leader. Pick up a copy and enjoy it, join the journey, engage in the process, and receive the deep revelations in this book.

Dr. Gershom Sikaala
Co-founder, Zambikes
www.zambikes.com
Founder and Apostle, His Presence Fire International
www.gershomsikaala.org
Author: *You Shall Live in Breakthrough Thinking* and *New Dimensions of Glory*

Dr. James Brewton's book, *From Footman to Horseman*, is a "must read" for those God has chosen to be His kingdom citizens as we approach this important historic time. "The culmination of all things" is the time when those who are truly "God's horsemen" will be forcibly advancing His Kingdom on earth. As you read these challenging, life-changing truths you will picture yourself boldly fulfilling your destiny to be "a horseman" in this end-time kingdom age. You will see yourself like David, running through troupes and leaping over the walls of circumstances. We will all say together, "His Kingdom has come! His will is being done on earth as it is in heaven!" You will be saying with so many others who have read this timely and powerful book, "My life will never be the same!"

Dr. A.L. "Papa" Gill
Apostle to the Nations
Founder and President, Gill Ministries
www.gillministries.com
Big Bear Lake, California

"Elijah took his cloak, rolled it up and struck the water with it.
The water divided to the right and to the left, and the two of them crossed over
on dry ground. When they had crossed, Elijah said to Elisha, "Tell me,
what can I do for you before I am taken from you?"
"Let me inherit a double portion of your spirit," Elisha replied.
"You have asked a difficult thing," Elijah said, "yet if you see me
when I am taken from you, it will be yours—otherwise, it will not."
As they were walking along and talking together, suddenly a chariot of fire
and horses of fire appeared and separated the two of them, and Elijah went up to
heaven in a whirlwind. Elisha saw this and cried out, "My father! My father!
The chariots and horsemen of Israel!" And Elisha saw him no more.
Then he took hold of his garment and tore it in two. Elisha then picked up Elijah's
cloak that had fallen from him and went back and stood on the bank
of the Jordan. He took the cloak that had fallen from Elijah and struck the water
with it. "Where now is the Lord, the God of Elijah?" he asked.
When he struck the water, it divided to the right and to the left,
and he crossed over."
(2 Kings 2:8-14, NIV)

PREFACE

God's process toward spiritual maturity is usually slow and steady. The Holy Spirit is always moving "upon the face" of every single believer to bring forth the original plan of God that He intended in His eternal mind before He created the world. God is a God of order; therefore, He is very methodical. He moves us from one place to another place, which is always a place of higher standards and levels of surrender, struggle, and godly suffering. God never moves backward; He is always in forward motion. His steps toward spiritual maturity are deliberate; they are intricate; they are sure, and they are pure.

In each phase of spiritual growth, God tests our commitment, loyalty and character *"to humble you and test you, to know what was in your heart, whether you would keep His commandments or not"* (Deut. 8:2). His desire is for His children to fulfill the kingdom assignment and destiny that He ordained for us, where life is enjoyable and the rewards are great and abundant.

As an apostle, bishop and pastor of Jesus Christ, I am so blessed to share with you throughout the pages of this book what probably is the most significant scheme Satan has used to deter the saints' spiritual growth and keep them as spiritual babies. Satan knows that baby Christians cannot become wise master-builders. So, his deception involves keeping the saints busy with religious duties, but never embracing God's process toward spiritual maturity where saints become commissioned commanders – kingdom-level leaders.

These ones have discovered their kingdom assignment and have submitted themselves to the teaching, training, equipping and obedience that will meet the standard of the Kingdom, the lofty position of subduing earthly kingdoms that become the kingdoms of our Lord and of His Christ, according to Rev. 11:15.

Like many saints today, the prophet Jeremiah was deluged by a flood of complaints, questioning God's sovereignty. *"Why does the way of the wicked prosper? Why are those happy who deal so treacherously?"* (Jer. 12:1). How does a saint of God today come to this same place of complaint experienced by Jeremiah over 2,500 years ago? Partly, it is because many saints have conformed to the celebrity mentality of the world's system of greatness. They have been duped by the devil, living as if they are of this world.

Jesus prayed to His Father, *"I do not pray that You should take them out of the world, but that you should keep them from the evil one. They are not of the world, just as I am not of the world. Sanctify them by Your truth. Your word is truth"* (John 17:15-17). Yes, we live in the world, but we are not of the world. Jesus gave us the determining factor of how to distinguish between the two – the Word of truth.

Many members of the Body of Christ have succumbed to the devil's strategy, his quick fix, overnight sensation, personality-driven claim to fame. For many, when the name it and claim it doctrine and formula for success did not work, mostly because people weren't properly taught and never received revelation of God's process and timing for their manifestation, they lost hope and began to "make things happen" by their might and power rather than to patiently await God's perfect timing, *"who gives us richly all things to enjoy"* (1 Tim. 6:17).

Not abiding the process of spiritual maturity and God's timing for your kingdom commission will always result in spiritual immaturity. Saints of God want very much to be spiritual giants possessing the kingly anointing of Jesus with authority and power, but not many are willing to surrender to the process by which this level of anointing is attained, or to pay the costly price for God's promotion, whose *"blessing...makes rich, and He adds no sorrow with it"* (Prov. 10:22, ESV). So, like Jeremiah, they end up complaining and questioning God.

This is the place I found myself for so many years, in a backslidden state filled with complaints, and questioning God's love for me; at times, His reality. Then, one day as I was trying to make sense of it all, desiring to be restored to my heavenly Father, the Holy Spirit led me to this verse of Scripture. It was as if God was speaking directly to me face to face. *"If you have run with the footmen, and they have wearied you, Then how can you contend with horses?"* (Jer. 12:5)

My purpose in writing this book is to communicate through personal experiences the process towards spiritual maturity and how to endure it. It is a process that moves saints from footmen, spiritual babes, to horsemen – commanders – generals, officers, leaders and spiritual parents. Spiritual growth happens when a believer learns to trust God completely, obey, and submit to the God-process specific to that individual's kingdom assignment; the process is relative to the purpose, and the experience is unique to the believer.

I am very transparent in sharing some of the experiences I encountered and endured en route to spiritual maturity and becoming a commissioned apostle, spiritual father, and kingdom commander. Together, we will traverse the spiritual terrain in three stages or levels: 1) Salvation – footmen/babes; 2) Discipleship and mentorship – horses/sons/disciples; and, 3) Leadership – horsemen/fathers/command-level generals and officers. *"They shall be like mighty men, Who tread down their enemies In the mire of the streets in the battle. They shall fight because the Lord is with them. And the riders on horses shall be put to shame"* (Zech. 10:5).

The Church is now experiencing the Kingdom Age Awakening. She is being reformed from the inside-out as she embraces the new 21st Century apostolic and prophetic reformation model – the many diverse global networks, applications and expressions – the unity of the faith where the Church has matured to the measure of the full stature of Christ, speaking the truth in love and growing up in all things to Jesus Christ, her Head (see Eph. 4:13-16).

God is reestablishing and reaffirming the Church's credibility and viability, and the saints will indeed be known as a powerful and reliable apostolic and prophetic people who speak to the Seven Mountains of Culture with the authority of a king-priest. The Church has entered a pivotal season. She is now standing at the crossroads of the conclusion of the Age of Grace. The times are unique and she must recognize her mandate to advance the Kingdom of God in the earth.

The Church has come to the time and place in which she must divide between what she wants to do and what she actually does. There has got to be a difference between intention and performance. The Church must fulfill her obligation, her mandate, to subdue the kingdoms of the world as a fully-prepared bride adorned to wed the Bridegroom. *"Let us be glad and rejoice and give Him glory, for the marriage of the Lamb has come, and His wife has made herself ready"* (Rev. 19:7). *"Come, I will show you the bride, the Lamb's wife"* (Rev. 21:9b).

Apostle Dr. James Brewton
July 18, 2016

"Then I saw Heaven open wide—and oh! a white horse and its Rider.
The Rider, named Faithful and True, judges and makes war in pure righteousness.
His eyes are a blaze of fire, on his head many crowns. He has a Name inscribed
that's known only to himself. He is dressed in a robe soaked with blood,
and he is addressed as "Word of God." The armies of Heaven, mounted on white
horses and dressed in dazzling white linen, follow him."
(Rev. 19:11-14, MSG)

FOREWORD

As members of the greatest kingdom ever created, we take time to reflect on exactly how we arrived where we are today. Many of us have sown many decades of our lives toward this awesome kingdom experience, and that's precisely why we reflect on it. It was a valuable journey, both to ourselves and to those we have come to know and share with. It has cost us something and it will cost everyone something if they intend to press into the great and full measure of this kingdom experience.

We are part of the government or "Misrah" of God. This Hebrew word means: Power to prevail, government and empire. It impresses upon us the great responsibility of leadership that we have as part of the human race and as kingdom citizens. Isaiah 9:6 says *"...the government shall be upon his shoulder..."* This means our shoulders as well as the shoulders of Christ. He led us by example and through His experiences, namely, having citizenship in two realms - the realms of heaven and of earth. Mankind had not really known how to navigate those dual dimensions before Jesus showed us how it is to be done. He leads the kingdom of God as the King of kings, and without a doubt, His experiences on earth form an indelible pattern upon our lives as the kings who follow in His footsteps.

"And there are also many other things which Jesus did, the which if they should be written every one, I suppose that even the world itself could not contain the books that should be written. Amen." (John 21:25, KJVA).

The truth is, all of our lives are "open books" that serve to teach people valuable lessons. People can learn what to do or what not to do by observing us. 2 Cor. 3:2, GNB, says, *"You yourselves are the letter we have, written on our hearts for everyone to know and read."*

The "Empire" or government that Christ leads required Him to "live" a pattern and to "leave" a pattern for us to follow. It is no coincidence that the word "empire" relates to the personal experiences of those who lead and follow.

The word "Empirical," which means: Experience based on, concerned with, or verifiable by observation or experience rather than theory or pure logic, plainly reveals that experiences are powerfully connected to how we process our journey in this kingdom and in the other kingdoms of the world or in the Seven Mountains of Culture.

"...The kingdoms of this world are become the kingdoms of our Lord and of his Christ; and he shall reign for ever and ever." (Rev. 11:15, KJV)

How the mission and mandate of Rev. 11:15 comes to fruition will depend to a great degree on the "empirical" experiences we each have while being a part of some structure or system of power or authority or influence and whether we properly yield ourselves to the molding, shaping and configuring that we encounter over the years. There can be no true "empires" without the "empirical experiences" of those who serve in or over them.

*"Now all these things happened unto them for **ensamples**: and they are written for our admonition, upon whom the ends of the world are come."* (1 Cor. 10:11, KJVA, emphasis added)

*"And ye became followers of us, and of the Lord, having received the word in much affliction, with joy of the Holy Ghost: so that ye were **ensamples** to all that believe in Macedonia and Achaia."* (1 Thess. 1:6-7, KJVA, emphasis added)

*"Feed the flock of God which is among you, taking the oversight thereof, not by constraint, but willingly; not for filthy lucre, but of a ready mind; neither as being lords over God's heritage, but being **ensamples** to the flock."* (1 Pet. 5:2-3, KJVA, emphasis added)

All three texts shown here contain the word "ensamples" which translates from a Greek term - "Tupos," meaning: Model, die or shape. In each text it was an experience that the writer or others had that served to guide, encourage or motivate others toward success in their walks with God. They were being encouraged to know that their experiences would make a difference to those who were watching and learning along the way.

Every day of our lives should contribute in some way to our stature, character, identity, purpose, mission, mandate and motivations. We should not pass time simply growing older but we should also be growing in maturity, influence, skills, power, ability, wisdom, grace, prosperity, courage, and strength.

Dr. James Brewton has written a very valuable composition that will serve to encourage, inspire and instruct many who take notice of his journey. Many people are quoted in life as saying, "If I knew then what I know now, things would be different." The material found in this book will help people discover that while there are no shortcuts, there are definitely certain ways to do things. There are principles of spirituality, self-examination, realization, maturation, growth and determination in this book that none can afford to overlook. This book contains practical and powerful principles that lead to the discovery of one's purpose, true self, identity, mission, calling and assignment in life.

As a man who has had the pleasure of knowing Dr. James Brewton for many years, I can say that he exemplifies the character and spirit of a true spiritual son. His "son-ship" has in no way compromised his identity as a strong, capable, courageous, anointed, educated, spiritual and inspiring leader. Let it never be said that when one yields to spiritual covering or authority, he or she automatically loses autonomy and becomes a clone or puppet or one with no true sense of self-worth or identity. Dr. Brewton has proven over the years that nothing could be further from the truth. He is a man among men and a vessel of the highest honor. The spirit of this man cries out to please God and to do an effective work as a steward of what he has been given, both by God and those he serves.

His ability as a "*Tupos*" for others means that he will shape and influence believers for many, many years to come; both through his actual life and through his writings. His command of the text of Scripture and his interpretations thereof are profoundly sound, accurate and applicable to this day. His "ambassadorial" spirit gives him a reputation as a peace-maker and bridge builder and as one who can see the value in relationships even when they are not always clear. Dr. Brewton has laid a clear path for every reader who wants to know what "the price" is for greatness in the kingdom of God.

People often ask what the price is for accomplishment. He makes the answer clear in this book and he also makes it clear that advancement is not an option. He has made it clear that advancement requires dedication, faith and courage.

But, he has also made it very clear that this goal is truly attainable and that the reward is worth the journey. He is an astute "reproducer" of kingdom principles and practices and has an uncanny ability as an "expander and expounder" of truth.

I salute Dr. James Brewton as an apostle of apostles, a prophet among prophets and a true kingdom-level leader who is raised up for a time such as this! May the "Misrah" government of Christ forever rest upon his shoulders and may he forever be an example of one who has mastered the journey "from footmen to horsemen!"

Dr. Gordon E. Bradshaw
President – Global Effect Movers & Shakers Network (GEMS)
www.gemsnetwork.org
President – Kingdom Congressional Int'l Alliance (KCIA)
www.kcialliance.org
Author – *The Technology of Apostolic Succession, Authority for Assignment,* and *I See Thrones!*
Chicago, Illinois

FOREWORD

In the age and time we live in where the whole world has seemingly gone mad, and spirits of humanism, relativism, secularism, terrorism, radicalism, racism, universalism, liberalism, historical revisionism, globalism, and antichrist spirits abound and appear to be prospering, gaining ground, exerting undue influence and controlling the high ground of culture and societal beliefs, values, ethics and institutions, a book such as this one is refreshing, timely, and desperately needed by both the Church and those called to leadership and influence in the market-place and government--i.e., the Seven Mountains of Culture.

God has promised us that everything that can be shaken will be shaken, and so the present shakings, tremors, rumblings and aftershocks on planet Earth to the world's financial and political and cultural and legal systems, while alarming and even disturbing, should come as no surprise to those who are led by the Spirit and familiar with the word of God. According to Matthew's gospel, there will be wars and rumors of war until the time of Jesus' return. That being the case, the question presents itself: how should we as believers live so as to redeem the time, and to please the one who has called us unto Himself and into His body to a life of service to others.

Jesus is quite clear in the Parable of the Talents and other Scriptures that He expects and calls us to live as stewards of all that He has entrusted to us, and to be profitable servants as His sons and daughters who are kings and priests in the Order of Melchizedek, and joint heirs of eternal life with Jesus. Much of Matthew 13, for example, is devoted to providing various analogies of how kingdom citizens are to use their influence to bring change and/or make a positive difference or distinction on the earth to those around us in our spheres of influence.

Many Christians, unfortunately, appear to suffer from a common malady named Arrested Development (aka Stunted Growth). They are content and comfortable to stop at knowing Jesus as their Savior, when that is just the starting point of the Christian life, and not the finish line.

Knowing who I am in Jesus is the gospel of salvation. This informs me of the benefits I receive in the Great Exchange such as grace, mercy, forgiveness of sins, regenerated spirit, redemption, unconditional love, the indwelling of the Holy Spirit, and eternal life. But, that is not enough, according to scripture. Otherwise Paul the Apostle would not have had to write his numerous epistles to the churches and John the Revelator would not have had to write to the seven churches of Asia, with each apostle giving the churches correction, instruction, warning, admonition, and exhortation. The deeper work of the Spirit in producing spiritual maturity in the lives of believers, begins after salvation.

Sanctification is a lifelong process. Although you have been convicted of your sinful state or condition and have repented and asked Jesus into your heart, and your spirit has been regenerated at salvation, your soul – mind, will and emotions — remains in the same state as before your conversion to Christ. Therefore, you have to be willing to change and to enter into an ongoing process of transforming and altering your thoughts, speech, actions, attitudes, habits, dreams, will and desires by surrendering and submitting them to the Lordship of Jesus and the ministry of the Holy Spirit (Rom. 12:1-2; 2 Cor. 10:3-5). There is a vast difference in knowing Jesus as Lord than knowing him as Savior. Knowing who I am in Jesus is equivalent to elementary school and junior high school studies and curricula, to use an education analogy. Knowing who Jesus is in me is equivalent to high school and college or university studies and curricula. It is significantly more advanced training, and training for a specific purpose with tangible fruit and measurable results.

Spiritual training is for reigning, not complaining, feigning, abstaining, entertaining, gainsaying, or fainting. Knowing who I am in Jesus is membership. Knowing who Jesus is in me is citizenship. Both are important but obviously God, and the world, both need and would prefer we function as citizens also, and not just as members. *"So then you are no longer strangers and aliens, **but you are fellow citizens with the saints and members of the household of God,"** (Eph. 2:19, ESV, author's emphasis). Members can quit anytime they feel tired or unappreciated or discouraged or offended or bored, and either transfer their membership elsewhere, choose to isolate/hibernate and not to fellowship with other saints, or start a home fellowship which may or may not have authority structure or leadership accountability. Citizens, on the other hand, understand their duty and responsibility. They vote, work, pay taxes, engage in public discourse on public policy, run for elected office, and volunteer their time, talent and treasure to build and protect/defend their communities and nation. We are members of a local church or fellowship, AND citizens of a kingdom.

The global Church, and the broader Kingdom of God, need citizens who can bring ideas, creativity, experience, energy, passion, wisdom, discernment, leadership and other gifts, talents, abilities and attributes to the table. Members of organizations usually expect services and are used to being served. Citizens, on the other hand, serve others. Jesus is not one-dimensional, and neither are we. He is King of kings, Lord of lords, Prince of peace, Son of God, Son of Man, Emmanuel, the Christ, our Redeemer, our Chief Advocate and eternal High Priest, Savior, the Lamb of God, and so much more.

Dr. James Brewton has described in detail here a process or progression in spiritual maturity, from salvation to discipleship to leadership. Anyone who has ever served on a sports team, a corporate team, or in the military, knows that teamwork requires discipline, focused effort, humility, honor, respect for authority and character development. It is no different in living life as a Christian. Scripture says, *"What we do see is Jesus, who was given a position 'a little lower than the angels'; and because he suffered death for us, he is now 'crowned with glory and honor. Yes, by God's grace, Jesus tasted death for everyone.* **God, for whom and through whom everything was made, chose to bring many children into glory. And it was only right that he should make Jesus, through his suffering, a perfect leader, fit to bring them into their salvation"** (Heb. 2:9-10, NLT, author's emphasis).

Scripture also says, *"Though outwardly we are wearing out, inwardly we are renewed day by day.* **Our suffering is light and temporary and is producing for us an eternal glory that is greater than anything we can imagine"** (2 Cor. 4:16-17, God's Word, author's emphasis). *"And since we are his children, we are his heirs. In fact, together with Christ we are heirs of God's glory.* **But if we are to share his glory, we must also share his suffering"** (Rom. 8:17, NLT, author's emphasis). *"But rejoice insofar as you share Christ's sufferings, that you may also rejoice and be glad when his glory is revealed"* (1 Pet. 4:13, ESV, author's emphasis). *"And we boast in the hope of the glory of God. Not only so, but **we also glory in our sufferings, because we know that suffering produces perseverance; perseverance, character; and character, hope.** And hope does not put us to shame,"* (Rom. 5:2b-5a, NIV, author's emphasis).

Many Christians want God's glory without the suffering; they want God's promotion without the obedience and sacrifice and testing and discipline and faithfulness required for refinement and character development and becoming effective, accountable spiritual leaders. Joseph, Esther, Daniel, Moses, Joshua, David and so many others, patiently endured the process and were found faithful in their assignments, then were promoted into the fullness of their destiny from God. 2 Tim. 2:20-21, NLT, (author's emphasis) says, *"In a wealthy home some utensils are made of gold and silver, and some are made of wood and clay. The expensive utensils are used for special occasions, and the cheap ones are for everyday use. **If you keep yourself pure, you will be a special utensil for honorable use. Your life will be clean, and you will be ready for the Master to use you for every good work."***

Obviously, God will not force you to become ready for honorable use and for every good work, or to actually do such work when invited by Him. Those are intentional, deliberate, conscious decisions you must voluntarily choose to make. Spiritual leadership costs something, and the price is always some form of death (John 12:24).

It has been well said that whatever is worth doing is worth measuring, and that we tend to get more of whatever behavior or outcome we measure. The modern Church has measured and documented responses to evangelistic campaigns and soul-winning crusades with excellence and precision, but failed miserably at measuring or documenting discipleship, sonship and mentoring programs and processes to produce maturity and character and identity in future leaders by true spiritual fathers and mothers. This status quo is obviously out of balance and it's no wonder, then, that the Church has lost ground in its perceived influence, credence, and relevance to the broader culture over the last 50+ years.

Jesus did not focus on numbers; instead, He focused on discipling 12 men, and a small handful of other inner circle followers, including several women and the 70. He was faithful to both His assignment and His Father. As our churches and spiritual leaders begin to shift from a primary or exclusive focus on membership and numbers to a more balanced approach of both soul-winning AND producing kingdom citizens and disciples in equal measure, then we will see the Church regain lost ground and momentum, and the Kingdom regain and reclaim its distinctiveness and influence, and true leaders – not only commanders and generals but statesmen and ambassadors – emerge from our ranks.

Thank you, Dr. Brewton, for reminding and redirecting us of and to the "ancient paths" of our forefathers – both spiritual and natural. Your book *From Footmen to Horsemen* is a clarion call and clear trumpet sound to this generation to return to the ancient paths, and the ancient foundations of righteousness and justice. Then we can again expect and see reformation, transformation and a spiritual renaissance on the earth in our lifetime. This is what the LORD says: *"Stand at the crossroads and look; ask for the ancient paths, **ask where the good way is, and walk in it, and you will find rest for your souls**"* (Jer. 6:16, NIV, author's emphasis). *"If my people, who are called by my name, will humble themselves and pray and seek my face and **turn from their wicked ways,** then I will hear from heaven, and I will forgive their sin and will heal their land"* (2 Chron. 7:14, NIV, author's emphasis). **It's not too late Church, but it is time to wake up, stir up, suit up, show up, and grow up.**

Both the world and the Kingdom of God need and deserve your best. Jesus set the example, and modeled transformation for us. He purchased our freedom and redemption and victory and inheritance with His own blood, and His own life. **He gave His best; we can do no less. The Church is God's only plan for the earth; there is no Plan B.** We have everything we need to get the job done, so it's time to stop making excuses and feeling sorry for ourselves. As warriors and championship-winning teams know, the best defense is a good offense. It's time the Church plays offense again. And here's the game plan and heaven's winning strategy for that. *"So Christ himself gave the apostles, the prophets, the evangelists, the pastors and teachers, **to equip his people for works of service, so that the body of Christ may be built up** until we all reach unity in the faith and* *in the knowledge of the Son of God and **become mature, attaining to the whole measure of the fullness of Christ**"* (Eph. 4:11-13, NIV, author's emphasis). This sounds like discipleship training and mentoring to me and a functionally-diversified Church structure and government.

This passage of Scripture is every bit as strategic and important as the Great Commission for the mission and purpose and assignment of the Church, but receives far less attention, focus and resources, in comparison, for a variety of reasons. That needs to change. In fact, Paul told Timothy, *"You have heard me teach things that have been confirmed by many reliable witnesses. Now teach these truths to other trustworthy people who will be able to pass them on to others"* (2 Tim. 2:2). This again sounds like discipleship and equipping from a five-fold ministry leader.

Col. 2:6-7 (NLT, author's emphasis) says, *"And now, just as you accepted Christ Jesus as your Lord, you must continue to follow him. **Let your roots grow down into him, and let your lives be built on him. Then your faith will grow strong** in the truth you were taught, and you will overflow with thankfulness."* This sounds like developing spiritual maturity and stability is an active process requiring effort on our part. We have to grow before we can overflow.

In closing, I echo the words of Paul the Apostle, which are inspired by the Holy Spirit and reflect the spirit of Dr. James Brewton's latest book, which I encourage you to read, learn from and apply: *"My dear children, for whom I am again in the pains of childbirth until Christ is formed in you,"* (Gal. 4:19, NIV). It's time to become the army of God and the bride of Christ, not just the body of Christ. Make yourself ready Church. You are God's answer and solution and wisdom to the world's woes. It's time to shine even brighter as the darkness increases.

Dr. Bruce Cook
Chairman/CEO
Kingdom Congressional International Alliance (KCIA), www.kcialliance.org
VentureAdvisers.com, Inc., www.ventureadvisers.com
Kingdom House Publishing, www.kingdomhouse.net
Author: *Partnering with the Prophetic, Aligning with the Apostolic*
Lakebay, Washington

SECTION ONE:

THE PURPOSE OF GOD ACCORDING TO ELECTION STANDS

God's Selection is Just!

"What should we say then? Is there injustice with God?
Absolutely not! For He tells Moses:
I will show mercy to whom I show mercy,
and I will have compassion on whom I have compassion.
So then it does not depend on human will or effort, but on God who shows mercy.
For the Scripture tells Pharaoh:
For this reason I raised you up: so that I may display My power in you, and that
My name may be proclaimed in all the earth.
So then, He shows mercy to whom He wills,
and He hardens whom He wills."

(Rom. 9:14 – 18, The Passion Bible, author's emphasis)

CHAPTER ONE

GOD'S PREDETERMINED PATH

"You will show me the path of life;
in Your Presence is fullness of joy,
at Your right hand there are pleasures forevermore."
(PSA. 16:11, AMP)

I was born again in 1972 at the age of 12. A holiness preacher from the local Church of God of Prophecy organization conducted a revival at our church and many young people got saved as we tarried (called on the name of Jesus repeatedly) while kneeling on the altar. True salvation meant that a believer had to be filled with the Holy Ghost with the evidence of speaking in other tongues. Without this evidence, you were not considered to be saved by this denomination. The purpose for receiving the baptism of the Holy Ghost was so that He would keep, guide, sustain, convict, and comfort the believer. Because we "had the Holy Ghost," we were simply to "live holy." The mindset here was, "If you really did get saved, you won't sin anymore. The Holy Ghost is a Keeper; 'it' will keep you from sinning."

The church was my life. Can you relate? I am sure many of you probably can.

I was brought up within a strict environment of fundamentalism and emotionalism. The theology of the Holiness church was very condemning of adherence to any social activity, no matter how harmless it seemed. I grew up within this enclosure of church doctrine believing that Jesus Christ was the Son of God who was crucified, buried, and resurrected by God. Jesus died so that anyone who believes He is the resurrected Son of God can have eternal life. But, that was not the end of the story.

There was a long list of things we could not do and still be considered saved. Women couldn't polish their nails, wear pants, makeup, or jewelry. They couldn't wear sleeveless blouses or tops; dresses had to be worn to the ankles. Men couldn't wear shorts or expose their feet. We couldn't go to the movies, eat pork, or any kind of shelled seafood. We were forbidden to participate in social and school functions. We were erroneously taught that we should separate ourselves and come out from among sinners (see 2 Cor. 6:17). Apostle Paul describes all of the above as *"vain deceit, after the tradition of men, after the rudiments of the world, and not after Christ... Touch not; taste not; handle not... These are all destined to perish with use, because they are based on human commands and teachings. Such regulations indeed have an appearance of wisdom...but they lack any value in restraining sensual indulgence"* (Col. 2: 8, 21-23).

Now there is something about this message of separation from sinners, when it is belted out by a Holiness preacher, which would make some people who were supposedly saved from their sins, feel as if they were the worst people in the world. Feelings of guilt and condemnation frequently are the byproduct or result of this message for the audience, with true spiritual conviction optional. For a long time, I fell into that category. Like the overwhelming majority of our congregation, whatever our bishop said had to be true, had to be correct; he was a man of God. He would preach in a thundering tone that could penetrate even the soul of the Virgin Mary.

In the mid-1970's Bishop Welch was in his forties. He was a big man of dark chocolate complexion, standing 6'3" and weighing approximately 270 pounds, with an athletic build. Everything about this man's physical attributes represented strength, like a diesel-powered locomotive. His articulate speech complimented his charismatic personality. Whenever he spoke or preached, people could sense and feel his authority. He had become very successful during the late 1950's and early 1960's near the height of the evangelistic tent ministry. He had several large tents and tractor trailers to haul his equipment. His tent ministry was called, "Revival of Power." Many miracles and healings took place during the course of his ministry.

From my perspective, this man could look at anybody and discern whether or not that person was living a "sanctified life" or a life of sin. Many times I would have done some of the "wrong" things my friends did, had it not been for the fear that I had of Bishop Welch. I used to be afraid to do anything wrong for fear that he would single me out during one of his "prophecy sessions."

I had the highest respect for Bishop Welch. In 1976 he had taken me on as a member of his tent crusade to play bass guitar. The team traveled from Georgia to Albany, N.Y. for a two-week crusade. I was 15 years old. And, for me, it was an adventure because it was my first opportunity to travel up North, away from the South.

As I stated earlier, the church was my life. It was always church in some form. Church on Sunday was an all-day affair. It included Sunday school, a morning service, an afternoon youth service, and an evening service, which sometimes didn't end until well after midnight. On Monday evening, there was a one-hour prayer service. Tuesday and Friday evening services consisted of a devotional service (a form of praise & worship), along with open testimonies of God's goodness from anyone in attendance, with preaching afterward. Wednesday was reserved for Bible study and Saturday was reserved for choir practice – adult choir, junior choir, and youth choir.

Nevertheless, I enjoyed church, especially on Sundays when we would have a full house. My brothers and I enjoyed playing the music while all the "holy rollers" sang and danced. It was a thrill for me to see all the sisters and brothers, missionaries, deacons and ministers dancing the holy "shout" to the sounds of Rick James and K. C. and the Sunshine Band. They never even knew, nor did they seem to care, what type of music they shouted (danced) to, as long as they had music.

What happened in late 1976 was like a nightmare for me. Several months after my return from Albany, my parents decided to end their membership in the church our family had been attending since 1963. Like several of my sisters and brothers, I did not understand the circumstances that led to our parents' decision. Out of the 10 children born to James and Valliree Brewton, it seemed we were split down the middle concerning leaving the church. It was extremely difficult for me to come to grips with my parents' decision. But, despite our lack of understanding, all 10 of us were urged to stop attending Healing Temple Holiness Church.

My last two years of high school, 1976-77 and 1977-78, was a timeframe of personal transition and moral conflict. It was also a time of newfound freedom and exploration. I became a different person. Bishop Welch was no longer around to positively influence me and keep me in my place. And so my enthusiasm for church and my commitment to a life of holiness became less intense. It wasn't long before I lost my zeal for righteous living, and with it my interest in church attendance and activities altogether. By the end of my junior year in high school, spring 1977, I had backslidden.

A new world was before me. I began going to parties and clubs, something that I'd never done before. I began drinking beer and listening to "worldly" music, both of which were forbidden in the Brewton family. Let me tell you, it wasn't long before my once holy palate acquired an unholy savor. It wasn't long before I'd developed a dislike for church altogether. And, I felt ashamed, like I'd lost my respect and honor. What bothered me most is that I felt like my family had committed an unforgiveable sin. For the next year and a half I didn't care anymore. I decided to just hang out and have fun until I left for college. "Then," I'd said, "I'll make my own damn decisions."

How did I fall into this backslidden state? I believe it happened because there was no government in place in our holiness church to guide me into spiritual maturity, no spiritual fathers, and no spiritual foundation for maturity. And, for the next 15 years, 1977-1992, I lived in a backslidden state. During that time my life, if it had been a written novel, would have been an adult non-fiction consisting of high dramatic issues, and a stark narrative combining a religious and secular plot told in a practical and explicit tone — one which many Christians would consider "worldly."

But, how many backsliders do you suppose experience the same problems and vices as unbelievers, because, for whatever reason(s), they became alienated from Christ and never discovered their true identity? This is where I found myself. I did not know what God's predetermined path for my life looked like. I had no spiritual father or mentor to train me and give me the benefits of their experiences of how to grow in Christ and become a spiritually mature saint with the authority and power to carry out my divine assignment. So, I got stuck in the gospel of salvation – meaning, I got saved and did not know what to do or how to grow spiritually except go to to church and praise God and try to live a holy life. I was in a steady state of spiritual immaturity – a baby Christian – with no one to disciple me.

Many people have given their lives to Christ only to backslide or stay within the body of Christ postured only as a baby Christian. They hit the real world and opted for an easier, more self-indulgent lifestyle. The burden of religion, tradition, and legalism became too heavy to bear. Meanwhile, their sinful experiences are real and graphic. It is very dangerous to be born again into the body of Christ and remain a spiritual baby. Baby Christians are not wise masterbuilders.

The decision still confronting many believers today is whether or not to abide in the body of Christ as "church folk", who have embraced the gospel of salvation, or to become kingdom leaders, which is spiritual maturity developed by embracing the gospel of the kingdom. When anyone gives his life to Christ through faith in the gospel or good news that was preached, he has adopted the gospel of salvation. This is the beginning of a new life of trusting in God. He has been born again. A seed has been planted. But, seeds only grow and mature over time. *"Since you have been born again – not of perishable seed but of imperishable – through the living and enduring word of God...that was preached as the gospel to you. So rid yourselves of all wickedness, all deceit, hypocrisy, envy, and all slander. Like newborn infants, desire the unadulterated spiritual milk, **so that you may grow by it in [your] salvation**"* (1 Pet. 1:23, 25; 2:1-2, The Passion Bible, author's emphasis).

Being born again by incorruptible seed by the word of God is speaking of a nature rather than a person. We've been born again into the very nature of God. It is not the person who cannot sin, but it is the new nature that each believer receives through rebirth that cannot sin. **The nature of the seed determines the nature of the life that comes from the seed!** *"And have put on the new man, who is being renewed in knowledge according to the image of his Creator"* (Col. 3:10, Passion). Paul the Apostle teaches us that there is no condemnation to those born again believers whose lifestyle is totally dependent upon the Spirit (grace), and not upon the flesh (law). The Spirit of life in Christ Jesus makes us free from the law of sin and death (Rom. 8:1-2).

> *"But if Christ lives in you, [then although] your [natural] body is dead by reason of sin and guilt, the spirit is alive because of [the] righteousness [that He imputes to you].For if you live according to [the dictates of] the flesh, you will surely die.* ***But if through the power of the [Holy] Spirit*** *you are [habitually] putting to death (making extinct, deadening) the [evil] deeds prompted by the body, you shall [really and genuinely] live forever."* (Rom. 8:10, 13, AMP, author's emphasis)

Paul is referring to the process of growth by the believer through the power of the Holy Spirit, and not through the flesh. Clearly, salvation is an introduction to living in total dependence upon the word of the Lord which endures forever. The Word of God is eternal! As you give yourselves wholly to desire the unadulterated spiritual milk, consistently receiving the purity of God's word through revelation knowledge given by Holy Spirit, Who is the teacher of the truth of the Word, you will grow by it – in your salvation. If you are growing in it, you've got to be growing into something else. What you are growing into is the New Testament grace and truth, which is the foundation of the gospel of the kingdom.

We are to mature from the gospel of salvation, which is not relegated only to our deliverance from sin, "having church," and going to heaven after we die, but also is inclusive of our divine health, prosperity and protection while we live on earth. The gospel of the kingdom is about maturity and leadership, through our salvation, that will confront and destroy demonic systems – personal, social, global – and impose the will of the King of kings in the earth.

Apostle John said that the Word was made flesh, and lived among the people of Jesus' day. They saw Jesus' glory – the same glory that God Himself possesses because Jesus is His only begotten Son, Who was full of grace and truth (John 1:14). So then, what does glory look like and what did the people see when they had an encounter with Jesus? They saw an eternal abundance of grace and truth. *"And of his fullness have all we received, and grace for grace. For the law was given by Moses, but grace and truth came by Jesus Christ"* (John 1:16-17). Apostle Peter urges believers to grow in grace, and in the knowledge of our Lord and Savior Jesus Christ (2 Pet. 3:18). Jesus prayed to God that believers would be sanctified through the truth. Then He said, ***"Thy Word is Truth"*** (John 17:17, author's emphasis).

God never intended for His children to remain spiritual babies. He encourages us to grow in love, faith, unity and knowledge of His Son, Jesus, into a perfect man which is the measure of the stature and fullness of Christ. The word "perfect" does not imply that we are without flaws. It means that we are not stagnant, and we continue to press into the completion of becoming spiritually mature – kingdom leaders who embraced the gospel of salvation and grew because we were being fed the unadulterated spiritual milk of the Word into adolescents of the Word; then, teenagers, and young adults who were faithful stewards of the Word of God at each stage of growth. Finally, we have become spiritually mature adults advancing steadily towards the completion of our divine assignment, which is to advance the Kingdom of God in the earth according to Rev. 11:15 – *"The kingdoms of this world have become the kingdoms of our Lord and of His Christ, and He shall reign forever and ever!"*

Believers who are still babies in Christ cannot forcefully advance God's Kingdom. I'll say it again. Baby Christians cannot be wise master builders. We must grow from the gospel of salvation and embrace the process of suffering for Christ, being persecuted and hated, rooted and grounded in love, exercising our faith, walking in humility, being pruned, and waiting patiently for the manifestation of the promises of God. Through all of this, we must maintain an intimate relationship with our Father through praise and worship, abiding in His presence, reading and meditating on His Word, and praying in the Spirit.

9

This is the process for spiritual growth by which we are developed into kingdom leaders, commissioned to fulfill our divine assignments which include bringing heaven's government to earth. *"Thy Kingdom come, thy will be done, as in Heaven, so in earth"* (Luke 11:2, KJV). Apostle Paul said, *"We must through many tribulations enter the kingdom of God"* (Acts 14:22).

God has a predetermined path for His children. His Word is a lamp to our feet and a light for our path (Psalm 119:105). Each believer has to discover what has already been predetermined in the mind of God from before the foundation of the world concerning his assignment. God's purpose for each of His children is a mystery that He is very much willing to reveal to those who seek His will through His Word. God and His Word are One. And God, through His eternal love, has chosen us in Him before the foundation of the world – holy and blameless! He predestinated us according to His will and good pleasure to be adopted as sons through Jesus' death, burial and resurrection to Himself (Eph. 1:4-5). *"And He has made from one blood every nation of men to dwell on all the face of the earth, and **has determined** their preappointed times and the boundaries of their dwellings…for in Him we live and move and have our being"* (Acts 17:26, 28, NKJV, author's emphasis).

If then, believers are to embrace God's predetermined path for our lives, we must decide whether or not we are going to remain spiritual babies or grow in grace and truth, embracing and enduring the process of growth that will develop us into commissioned, kingdom-level leaders. We must become wise master builders. We must become violent in the spirit and exercise the resurrection power that God used to raise Jesus from the dead and take by force the Kingdom of God. We must apply and activate the faith of God, calling things that are not as though they are. We must learn to endure hardness as good soldiers of Jesus Christ. We must train our mental faculties through consistent use of the Word of God to discern between both good and evil. In short, we must decide whether or not we are simply going to be "church folk" or kingdom leaders.

> *"For even though by this time you ought to be teaching others, you actually need someone to teach you over again the very first principles of God's*

Word. You have come to need milk, not solid food. For everyone who continues to feed on milk is obviously inexperienced and unskilled in the doctrine of righteousness (of conformity to the divine will in purpose, thought, and action), for he is a mere infant [not able to talk yet]! But solid food is for full-grown men, for those whose senses and mental faculties are trained by practice to discriminate and distinguish between what is morally good and noble and what is evil and contrary either to divine or human law." (Heb. 5:12-14, AMP)

"THEREFORE LET us go on and get past the elementary stage in the teachings and doctrine of Christ (the Messiah), advancing steadily toward the completeness and perfection that belong to spiritual maturity." (Heb. 6:1, AMP, author's emphasis)

I believe that the Church, the body of Christ, has entered God's season of purging, the removal of impurities relating to spiritual sluggishness that have caused the church to become less violent in the use of its spiritual authority. Too many believers still have not grown beyond the gospel of salvation, and have yet to discover their purpose or divine assignment. When believers relegate themselves only to the gospel of salvation, they become spiritually sluggish, possessing little to no authority in spiritual warfare. They simply have a good time in church, try to live right, and hope that one day they will make it to heaven. There is so much more of God that we cannot even fathom. Paul prayed that all saints would comprehend what is the length and width, height and depth of God's love, which surpasses knowledge, so that we can be filled with all the fullness of God (Eph. 3:18-19).

Baby saints can never expect to experience the fullness of God on earth. They feel that this is something that can occur only in heaven. And in many ways, these saints become "church folk." They are steeped in religion – legalism. I'm not putting down or mocking any saint of God as much as I am attempting to expose the religious spirit of control that keeps saints from growing and discovering their assignment, which is a mandate to advance God's kingdom by utilizing the spiritual authority we've been given through Jesus' death, burial and resurrection.

> *"And what is the immeasurable greatness of His power to us who believe, according to the working of His vast strength. He demonstrated [this power] in the Messiah by raising Him from the dead and seating Him at His right hand in the heavens –far above every ruler and authority, power and dominion, and every title given, not only in this age but also in the one to come. And **He put everything under His feet** and appointed Him as head over everything for the church, which is His body, the fullness of the One who fills all things in everyway."* (Eph. 1:19-23, Passion, author's emphasis)

Church folk basically praise God within the confines of religion. "If God wants me to be healed, he'll just heal me." "What God has for me is for me." These are religious confessions. Basically these types of confessions keep believers in their comfort zone, where they don't exercise their faith and stand on their authority to use the Word of God and see positive results. And so, they pack the pews Sunday after Sunday, adorned in their best attire, looking a bit more "holy" than everyone else. They create the illusion of having joy, as they clap their hands and sing along with the worship leaders. Many of these saints will out-praise you; they will pray eloquently when called upon, and have lengthy testimonies about what God has done for them; they will probably give a large offering, being sure that everyone sees what was given. All of these kinds of things are done out of wrong motives – for an outward show as opposed to from the heart, and from the outside-in, rather than the inside-out.

But, the truth of the matter is that this is a display of religion – the acts of an immature believer. This religious spirit is bent on impressing people. Those under its control express an outward show of their holiness, having church protocol to a science, but there is nothing taking place where it counts – in their heart. These are baby Christians and a commissioned kingdom leader can spot them right away. They may be able to put on their façade and hide their spiritual immaturity from other church folk, but people of God who are mature can readily expose their religious cover. Some of them even take pride in seeing other saints fail because they believe it makes them look better and more powerful.

But, as I stated earlier, God is purging these religious spirits out of the Body. He is separating the tares from the wheat. He is removing the weeds from the principal seed. He is destroying the religious spirit that seeks its own and exalts itself against the knowledge of God (see 2 Cor. 10:5) apart from the Word of Truth. Many of these saints have zeal for God, but not according to knowledge (a Holy Spirit revelation of the Word). They are ignorant of God's righteousness, and have established their own, not submitting to the righteousness of God (see Rom. 10:2-3). They hold to a form of godliness, but deny the real power of God (see 2 Tim. 3:5). Immature saints have got to commit to plug in to where the real power is – a consistent life of faith in the word of God which indeed begins with the gospel of salvation, but matures into the gospel of the kingdom, the full measure of Christ which transitions believers from faith to faith. That sounds like growth and maturity to me.

"For I am not ashamed of the gospel, because it is God's power for salvation to everyone who believes…For in it God's righteousness is revealed from faith to faith, just as it is written: The righteous will live by faith" (Rom. 1:16-17, Passion). God wants to consistently reveal to us the supernatural path that will transition us from one level of maturity to the next – to the next – to the next. He knows that mature saints live by their faith; and as they consistently live by faith, greater measures of faith are acquired until it becomes like the faith of God or the God kind of faith. This is the faith of God that Jesus commands us to have. *"And Jesus, replying, said to them, Have faith in God [constantly]"* (Mark 11:22, AMP).

We might as well face it saints. Church as usual is static. It's not necessarily holding saints accountable to spiritual maturity, the place of spiritual growth where we are processed and developed to use our faith in the Word of God with the authority of God given to us by Jesus Christ. *"Behold! I have given you authority and power to trample upon serpents and scorpions, and [physical and mental strength and ability] over all the power that the enemy [possesses]; and nothing shall in any way harm you"* (Luke 10:19, AMP).

These are the end-times and God is positioning the Church for the fulfillment of her earthly assignment as kings and priests unto God, who are led by Holy Spirit, and use their authority to command the systems of the world (the Seven Mountains of Culture) to recognize God's Sonship in us. We are citizens of the Kingdom of Heaven – ambassadors for Christ, who make decrees concerning destruction of the demonic systems of the world according to the Word of the King of kings.

Therefore, believers must realize that we are not called to be church folk; we are called to be kingdom leaders. Our priority is to please the King. God desires a Spirit-led church, not a social club ruled by emotionalism and an outward presentation of godliness. The Church cannot complete its assignment in the earth without spiritually qualified people – kingdom leaders. Believers must commit to spiritual maturity by moving beyond the gospel of salvation and embracing the level of spiritual accountability and authority referred to as the gospel of the kingdom. Why haven't many church folk moved beyond salvation?

I suggest that the main reason they've not moved beyond salvation is that they have never been taught the gospel of the kingdom, although the Bible clearly teaches that Jesus came preaching the gospel of the kingdom of God. *"Now after John was put in prison, Jesus came to Galilee, preaching the gospel of the kingdom of God, and saying, 'The time is fulfilled, and the kingdom of God is at hand. Repent, and believe in the gospel'"* (Mark 1:14-15). When there is no Holy Spirit revelation of Jesus' statement, it can be misconstrued as mere rhetoric. But, what this adds up to is a religious mindset bent on the traditions of men, eventually leading Christians to reject the gospel of the kingdom through ignorance. As we study the Word of God, we must ask Holy Spirit to teach us and give us a divine revelation of the logos that we are reading. Revelation knowledge is simply the supernatural wisdom of God revealed to us by Holy Spirit, Who searches all things including the deep things of God (see 1 Cor. 2:10).

Saints of God must understand that the gospel of the kingdom is the gospel of grace (the kindness of God to man) predicated on the love of God, Who gave His only begotten Son to die on the Cross at Calvary for the sins of the world. It is the good news or gospel of good tidings having come. It is a present given, a gift of grace and truth for full and free deliverance from sin based on faith in Jesus Christ. Jesus preached this message prior to His death, burial and resurrection. The gospel of the kingdom is grounded in Luke 11:2 KVJ – *"THY KINGDOM COME. THY WILL BE DONE, AS IN HEAVEN, SO IN EARTH."* (author's emphasis)

As citizens of the Kingdom of Heaven, saints are ambassadors for Christ called to reflect the government of the kingdom in the earth as we reconcile the world back to God. This requires a spiritually mature mindset, one that has been processed, developed and trained according to divine purpose for the subduing of nations. These are the kingdom leaders whom God has commissioned to operate according to His divine pattern. These spiritually mature kingdom leaders pattern their lives after the life of Jesus; they believe, honor, respect and emulate their earthly spiritual parent, imitating their righteousness, godliness, faith, love, patience and meekness (see 2 Tim. 6:11). The Lord knows these to be His, for they do the work of advancing the Kingdom of Heaven in the earth. *"Nevertheless the solid foundation of God stands, having this seal: 'The Lord knows those who are His'"* (2 Tim. 2:19).

Those who are "His" understand that they have a set race to run, which is ultimately God's predetermined path for their lives. *"Let us lay aside every weight, and the sin which so easily ensnares us, and let us run with endurance the race that is set before us, looking unto Jesus, the author and finisher of our faith"* (Heb. 12:1-2). They have Jesus' example of endurance as He despised the shame and endured the Cross. He stayed on the path that God had predetermined for Him by focusing on the joy that would follow His suffering – seeing the devil's grip of sin and death being snatched away from anyone who would receive Him as Savior and Lord, and restoring all things back to His Father. *"Then I said, 'Behold, I have come – in the volume of the book it is written of Me – To do your will, O God'"* (Heb. 10:7).

The words **race** and set are the Greek words for ***agon (ag-one)*** and ***prokei-mai (prok-i-ma-hee)***, respectively. In their various forms they mean: To lead; a mode of living: a manner of life; a contest, an effort: conflict, contention, fight; something that is superior to; before or ever, laid up or made; to be present to the mind, to stand forth (The New Strong's Greek Concordance of The Bible).

Kingdom leaders who have been commissioned by God have the presence of mind to understand that God has set, placed, made, and laid up for them a superior position before the foundation of the world. He has a course, a career, a path, mapped out for them to complete. It is a manner of life that requires them to endure, without complaint, the contest of life which requires growth because it is a journey filled with conflict, contention, strife and violence sent from Satan to steal, kill and destroy the saints of God. In other words, the devil's desire is to separate the saints from their source of Light and spiritual maturity, keeping them inundated with "busy church work" containing no kingdom content; basically, this is the framework of religion which is also spiritual immaturity.

Baby Christians are not mature enough to fight violently in the spiritual realm against principalities, powers, rulers of the darkness of this world, and spiritual wickedness in high places (see Eph. 6:12). They have not grown in their identity as children of God, possessing the same resurrection power and authority God used to raise Jesus from the dead. The result is that the kingdom of God continues to suffer violent attacks by Satan through the immaturity of the saints. *"And from the days of John the Baptist **until the present time,** the kingdom of heaven has endured violent assault, and violent men seize it by force [as a precious prize – a share in the heavenly kingdom is sought with most ardent zeal and intense exertion]"* (Matt. 11:12, AMP, author's emphasis).

Even today, the Kingdom of Heaven is bombarded with violent assaults led by Satan. But, the good news is that the Kingdom of Heaven has endured! Why? God has raised and commissioned kingdom leaders who know who they are in Christ, and know how to deploy the resurrection power and authority of God in spiritual warfare. What could possibly stop us from subduing the nations and bringing the mountains of culture subject to the government of the Kingdom of Heaven if all of the saints walked in the authority and power that is available to us?

Like Apostle Paul, all of us should submit to God's predetermined path for our life and finish our course, making full proof of our ministry. There is no Scripture to support lay people in the body of Christ. We all have been given a specific assignment from God, a course that we must run and finish, even if it requires our life. Our primary concern should be to please our Father. And, He is purging the church and confirming it so that the body is completely joined with the Head.

God has declared a directive. From ancient times, He declared the end from the beginning – things that have not yet come to pass, saying, *"My counsel shall stand, and I will do all My pleasure and purpose"* (Isa. 46:10, AMP). God's predetermined path is one of consistent growth and spiritual maturity through intimacy with Him, which leads to the discovery of purpose. He has created each of us, ordained us, and called us from before the foundation of the world to be enjoined to Himself as we discover, accept, train, and are equipped to be deployed into our divine assignment.

CHAPTER TWO

DISCOVERING YOUR KINGDOM PURPOSE

"The Lord will fulfill his purpose for me;
your love, O LORD, endures forever –
do not abandon the works of your hands."
(PSA. 138:8, NIV)

The genius of God has planned every aspect of your life to conform to His workmanship and His will. Every fiber of your being, along with the divine assignment for your life on earth has been thoroughly inspected by the Creator and comes out of Him as His will. But, there is a discovery process involved. Too many believers still do not know their identity as a child of God, nor do they understand the process of self-discovery relative to who God intended them to become. Life is a pursuit of discovery. And, true relationship with God puts you in the place of discovery where you must pursue the "real you" in real time; seeing it in a vision is not a possession. God's genius always produces a Genesis – a beginning that will eventually become a revelation of something that was not fully known at the beginning. Every Genesis produces a Revelation.

Being made in God's image and likeness is of eternal proportions, yet it is a seed – a beginning encoded with the DNA of what it is to become. And, because God created man with an independent will, the original DNA of the kingdom can be altered or become degenerate. In other words, to degenerate means to undergo social or moral decline, to deteriorate. We can become degraded as we turn away from God's original plan and purpose for our lives. *"Yet I planted you a noble vine, a seed of highest quality. How then have you turned before Me Into the degenerate plant of an alien vine?"* (Jer. 2:21).

The genius of God produces capacity: more space for your place – the capacity to demonstrate His workmanship in us through Jesus Christ to accomplish the good works He planned for us before the foundation of the world (see Eph. 2:10). God lets us know that we were planted in nobility, a seed of highest quality. He has created us with a kingdom purpose – a standard of highest quality. God wants to confirm His calling in our lives, but we must establish a relationship of intimacy with Him. He wants us to discover the nature of the seed as it continues to germinate and grow. During real spiritual growth, we should see the nature of the nobility of our kingdom purpose emerge – the nature of the King of kings, Who subdues nations. Our kingdom purpose, in whatever form it comes, is to subdue nations. Remember, the nature of the seed determines the life that comes from the seed. The writer of the epistle to the Hebrews lets us know that the Old Testament heroes of faith *"through faith subdued kingdoms"* (Heb. 11:33).

So, what causes far too many believers not to discover their kingdom purpose? I like Eugene H. Peterson's translation of how believers can misinterpret the meaning of life and either not discover their kingdom purpose or discover it but end up degrading the nature of their kingdom purpose by becoming self-reliant and pursuing it without being properly processed and developed in godly character and spiritual maturity. *"God made men and women true and upright; we're the ones who've made a mess of things"* (Eccl. 7:29, MSG).

However, when you discover your kingdom purpose and say yes to God, thanking Him for encoding you with His original design and assignment for your life, He begins to process you. First, He gives you flashes or glimpses of a pictorial representation of who you are to become; then, He gives you a narrative content. Your devotion, loyalty and faithfulness to God and your kingdom purpose will determine how well you follow the narrative of God's preparation for the greatest assignment ever! It is your kingdom assignment of subduing kingdoms and bringing the Seven Mountains of Culture under the rule, authority, influence and dominion of the Kingdom of Heaven.

God desires for you to discover your original purpose and destination. Moreover, the value of who you are and what you are in the mind of God can only be found in the Original. Your value is your usefulness, importance, or general worth – the principal quality and nature of God placed in the original seed He referred to as "you". This can only be extracted by continuous movement and growth that is progressive and measurable. In the beginning – the Genesis of life – you are unrevealed. You are essentially a blank canvas for God to paint on. And, because God is sovereign and has predetermined your purpose, His story (not history) is significant to how your story plays out. Not seeing the picture of your life clearly can cause you to question the Creator. This is why God, once you accept the abstract version of who you are in your Genesis, gives you a picture of your destiny.

Let's take a look at the scenario of the Genesis or abstract version of Abraham's life. *"The Lord said to Abram, 'Leave your country, your relatives, and your father's home, and go to a land that I am going to show you. I will give you many descendants, and they will become a great nation. I will bless you and make your name famous, so that you will be a blessing'...When Abram was seventy-five years old, he started out from Haran, **as the Lord had told him to do**"* (Gen. 12:1-2, 4, GNB, author's emphasis). This is the abstract version of Abraham's discovery of divine purpose and the value that is inclusive in it because it comes out of God as His Will.

Anything that is abstract is difficult to understand; it is insufficiently factual, having only intrinsic form with little or no attempt at pictorial representation or narrative content. But, Abraham gives us probably the most important key to discovering purpose. He listened attentively to God. He understood that God was speaking to him concerning his destiny. He did not have all of the facts. He simply accepted the assignment. In other words, he heard God and obeyed. When Abram moved or did **"as the Lord had told him to do,"** immediately he was on his way to "becoming" a great nation. Abram simply had to extract (draw, pull or take out forcibly and willfully) from the abstract. What you **extract from your abstract** will eventually determine your destiny.

God said that Abram would become a great nation. God released to Abram his kingdom purpose. God was saying to Abram, "This is how I planted you in my mind from before the foundation of the world. You are a noble vine; a seed of highest quality. Now I can begin the process of growth, developing your full potential to become the father of many nations."

As Abram obeyed God, not knowing where he was going or what would befall him on his journey, God gave him a picture and a narrative content of his destiny. And, He did it through covenant.

> "After this, **Abram had a vision** and heard the Lord say to him, "Do not be afraid, Abram. I will shield you from danger and give you a great reward. "But Abram answered, "sovereign Lord, what good will your reward do me, since I have no children?"... Then he heard the Lord speaking to him again: "Your own son will be your heir." The Lord took him outside and said, "Look at the sky and try to count the stars; you will have as many descendants as that." **Abraham put his trust in the Lord, and because of this the Lord was pleased with him and accepted him... Then and there the Lord made a covenant with Abram.** He said, "I promise to give your descendants all this land."
> (Gen. 15:1-2, 4-6; 18, GNB, author's emphasis)

In the same way, God has made covenant with you. This is how He releases you into your destiny, and how you discover His kingdom purpose for your life. As you obey God, accepting His assignment for your life, He shows or gives you a vision, a glimpse of a pictorial representation; then, He gives you a prophetic word – a narrative of your destiny – from men and women of God, true apostles and prophets. Paul said, *"I was not disobedient to the heavenly vision"* (Acts 26:19). On the road to Damascus, God gave Saul a vision and a narrative of who he was to become. *"This man is my chosen instrument to carry my name before the Gentiles and their kings and before the people of Israel. I will show him how much he must suffer for my name"* (Acts 9:15-16, NIV). God released Saul into his destiny and Paul emerged with a kingdom purpose.

At this point, you begin to get a revelation of the charge Paul gave to Timothy concerning prophecies spoken over his life. *"This charge I commit unto thee, son Timothy, according to the prophecies which went before on thee, that thou by them mightiest war a good warfare; Holding faith and a good conscience"* (1 Tim. 1:18-19, KJV). How do you war a good warfare with your prophecies? You rehearse the sound, saying it over and over by faith until it is digested into your spirit. And as you progress in your faith and spiritual maturity, glimpses become sustained pictures etched in your spirit. You begin to rehearse the narrative of your life and destiny over and over until you possess the real you as the highly-esteemed prize God originally designed you to be. Therein lay your true value, your kingdom purpose.

But, you must be consistent. **In consistency lies the power**. Again, Paul admonishes Timothy to *"Cultivate these things. Immerse yourself in them. The **people will see you mature right before their eyes!** Keep a firm grasp on both your character and your teaching. Don't be diverted. Just keep at it. Both you and those who hear you will experience salvation"* (1 Tim. 4:15-16, MSG, author's emphasis). "And what I show you will come true. It may seem slow in coming, but wait for it; it will certainly take place, and it will not be delayed" (Hab. 2:3, GNB).

It is not God's will for you to **"de-gene"** or circumvent the original **gene** or **genius** that He planted in you. The pure seed contains everything it was intended by God to become. The complete knowledge and care of God is encoded within you. *"I planted you like a choice vine from the very best seed. But look what you have become! You are like a rotten, worthless vine"* (Jer. 2:21, GNB). Sadly, many Christians find themselves in this state. Not because they have to be, but because many continue to override the Creator's plan; they don't trust God enough to accept who they are and allow Him, over time, to unveil the progressive picture of who they really are.

Many have misunderstood or misinterpreted the word of God, and have allowed religion to put a leash on them, restraining them from "becoming." In that vein, they have relegated themselves to a façade – a false design, a false cover or mask of pretense which is not a kingdom purpose and has absolutely no kingdom value because it is a copy – fake. The result is that they become blinded to the reality of their kingdom identity, and what they were to become in alignment with the original design of God. In so doing, they forfeit their kingdom purpose for mere existence.

To be clear, every living person has a purpose. But, all believers have a kingdom purpose. Let's define what kingdom purpose is and compare it to the life of a saint who never discovers his kingdom purpose and simply exists in life. *"To everything there is a season, A time for every purpose under heaven"* (Eccl. 3:1). To be sure, on earth God has given everyone a purpose and time to fulfill it. Within time, we experience seasons, and seasons produce particular circumstances, features, growth and events – awakenings. However, if we simply exist, we forfeit what the seasons produce throughout life for us.

According to Merriam-Webster's Collegiate Dictionary, 11th Edition, the word **exist** means to have life or the functions of vitality; to live at an inferior level or under adverse circumstances. So, those believers who simply exist have the qualities of being alive, but they also live at an inferior level well beneath the level that the seasons of life produce for those who have discovered their kingdom purpose and progress toward their assignment and destiny. Believers can't advance God's kingdom if they are stagnant in life or simply existing. In order to advance God's kingdom, we must first advance ourselves, and provision for advancement lies within the assignment, the mission, the kingdom purpose.

The Greek word for **kingdom** is *basileia*, pronounced *bas-il-i-ah*, meaning royalty, rule, a realm; to reign; a foundation of power; a sovereign: king (Strong's). It also means sovereignty, royal power, and dominion (Vine's Expository of New Testament Words). In this sense, kingdom is used to denote the sphere of God's rule as acknowledged by the saints who declare His purpose to establish it in the earth. This is what is meant by kingdom purpose. The discovery of kingdom purpose does not come within the range of the natural powers of observation (see Luke 17:20); it must be spiritually discerned within your spirit where Holy Spirit resides. The eternal is internal, meaning that the kingdom is present in the person of its King, Jesus. That is why Jesus' teaching in Matthew chapters five through seven is all about living in alignment with the pattern, the government of the kingdom.

> *"For I say to you, that unless your righteousness exceeds the righteousness of the scribes and Pharisees, you will by no means enter the kingdom of heaven."* (Matt. 5:20)

> *"But seek first the kingdom of God and His righteousness, and all these things shall be added to you."* (Matt. 6:33)

> *"Not everyone who says to Me, "Lord, Lord," shall enter the kingdom of heaven, but he who does the will of My Father in heaven."* (Matt. 7:21)

The Amplified version of the Bible says, *"As a precious prize – a share in the heavenly kingdom is sought with most ardent zeal and intense exertion"* (Matt. 11:12b). Seeking a share in the heavenly kingdom begins with the discovery of your kingdom purpose.

Purpose is defined as something set up as an object or an end to be attained: Intentionally, determination; by design (Merriam-Webster). Now let's take a look at the Hebrew and Greek definitions. The Hebrew word for **purpose** is *chephets*, pronounced *khay- fets.* It means pleasure, a desire, a valuable thing; a matter (as something in mind): acceptable, delightsome, pleasant and willingly. It is taken from a primary root, *chaphets (khaw-fates)*, which means to be pleased with. Another Hebrew word for purpose is *machashebeth*, pronounced *makh-ash-eh-beth.* It means an important plan: cunning work, curious work, imagination, something invented, a thought (Strong's Hebrew).

The Greek word for **purpose** is *prosthesis*, pronounced *proth-es-is*, which means a setting forth; proposal, an intention. Prosthesis comes from the word *prothumia (proth-oo-mee-ah)*, meaning forwardness of mind; ready willing mind. This word is further taken from *prothumus (proth-oo-mos)*, meaning forward in spirit (Strong's Greek). So, now, let's get a Holy Spirit revelation of kingdom purpose.

Kingdom purpose is the predetermined assignment or mission for each person formed in the mind of God before the creation of the world. It is the forwardness of God's mind set forth through time to attain a predetermined end. It is God's intention, determination and design that He is pleased with; the cunning work invented in His imagination and set forth as His plan for those who would be heirs of salvation through Jesus Christ. It is God's delightsome and pleasant mandate to the saints to secure in the earth His sovereignty, royal power and dominion as it is in Heaven. It is the royal reign of His sons and daughters as ambassadors who reflect the eternal value of the pattern and government of the Kingdom of Heaven.

It is vitally important to the Body of Christ that you understand your value as the original design of God. You are of royal descent – a king and priest unto God (see Rev. 1:6). God did not make a mistake in assigning you your purpose and destination in life. Your purpose is wrapped with a kingdom mandate orchestrated by God, and is available upon discovery. Loving God and pursuing Him as your first priority opens the door to intimacy with Him. It is about relationship! Relationship with God is built upon the consistency of spending time in His presence and communicating with Him. This leads to trust and obedience to His commandments.

Jesus said, *"If you love Me, keep my commandments"* (John 14:15). This is the process that leads to discovery of your kingdom purpose. Your kingdom purpose is powerful because it was formed in the mind of God and it possesses the power of God's incorruptible Seed, the same spiritual DNA Jesus possessed as He fulfilled His kingdom purpose. And the result of fulfillment is conformity to the image of God's Son. Those who are called according to His purpose have been predestined to be conformed to the image of His Son.

*"We know that all things work together for the good of those who love God: those who are **called according to his purpose**. For those he*

*foreknew he also predestined to be **conformed to the image of His Son,** so that He would be the firstborn among many brothers. And those He predestined, he also called; and those He called, He also justified; and those He justified, He also glorified."* (Rom. 8:28-30, Passion, author's emphasis)

You have been called according to His purpose, which evolves around His kingdom. You must learn how to hold on to kingdom purpose and ride on it, because kingdom purpose stays anointed; kingdom purpose stays on fire; kingdom purpose stays in power. Kingdom power will never dry out. Latch onto it! Hold on to it! Pray for it! Fast for it! Seek God continuously for it! Non-discovery is dangerous because it relegates you to mere existence. It permits the possibility that you will live all of your life never knowing your true identity or why you lived. Thank God you have discovered your kingdom purpose or having read this far, you are now committed to the discovery of your kingdom purpose. But, be apprised of the fact that the discovery of your kingdom purpose requires a process of kingdom preparation.

Your kingdom purpose contains greatness – success and fulfillment– through obedience to God. And, if greatness lay within kingdom purpose, there must be great preparation to expose it. **Preparation involves process, and process involves time.** The world system teaches you that you don't have to go through the process of preparation in order to be great. That takes too long. You can have greatness now, without the hassles and hazards of preparation or character development. You simply use your personality and your gifts and talents. Granted, to a degree this may be true. But, by and large, it does not have longevity and probably doesn't include succession to the next generation.

People with this mindset choose personality over character. Many even quote Prov. 18:16 to boost their personality. *"My gifts will opens doors for me and usher me into the presence of great people."* But, as one saying goes, "a person's gifts can take him to places where his character can't keep him." The world's way to greatness is an immediate leap to fame and fortune – fast and furious. But, God tests His children for character prior to deploying them into their destiny. His way is slow and steady. It is deliberate, intricate, sure and pure. This is God's path to greatness, and it begins with preparation.

Merriam-Webster defines **preparation** as the action or process of making something ready for use or service or of getting ready for some occasion, test, or duty: READINESS. ***Kuwn***, pronounced ***koon***, is a Hebrew word meaning to be erect (i.e. to stand perpendicular); hence, to set up: establish, fix, prepare, apply; to appoint, render sure, proper or prosperous: confirm, direct, faithfulness, ordain, order, perfect, prepare self, be ready, set forth; be stable. Its Greek counterpart is ***paraskeue (par-ask-yoo-ay)***, meaning readiness: preparation.

This is what is written concerning John the Baptist relative to his kingdom purpose. Notice that his kingdom assignment includes greatness and four key components that make one ready or prepared to carry out his kingdom mandate, therefore pleasing God.

> *"For he will be **great** in the sight of the Lord, and shall drink neither wine nor strong drink. He will also be filled with the Holy Spirit, even from his mother's womb. And he will turn many of the children of Israel to the Lord their God." He will also go before Him in the spirit and power of Elijah, "to turn the hearts of the fathers to the children," and the disobedient to the wisdom of the just, to **make ready a people prepared for the Lord."** (Luke 1:15-17, author's emphasis)*

Let's take a look at four of the key components that lead to preparation or readiness to successfully fulfill your kingdom purpose. They are: 1) process, 2) development, 3) transformation, and 4) time.

Process is a series of actions or operations conducing to an end; gradual changes that lead toward a particular result; advance proceeding. **Development** means to set forth or make clear by degrees or in detail; to acquire gradually; the act, process, or result of developing. **Transformation** is a sequence of advancement that changes the outward form or appearances of; to change in character or condition: convert. And, **time** is defined as the measured or measurable period during which an action, process, or condition exists or continues (Merriam-Webster). It seems that God is very deliberate, intricate, and meticulous about preparing you for your kingdom purpose through discipleship so that as you carry out your divine assignment, you are strong, durable, sustainable, and spiritually mature.

Look back at the Scripture text concerning John the Baptist's kingdom purpose and let's identify each of these four components. **Process** – "For he will;" "And he will;" "He will also." **Development** – "He will be great;" "and shall drink neither wine nor strong drink." **Transformation** – "He will also be filled with the Holy Spirit;" "go before Him in the spirit and power of Elijah;" "turn many of the children of Israel to the Lord their God;" "turn the hearts of the fathers to the children, and the disobedient to the wisdom of the just." **Time** – "make ready a people prepared for the Lord."

Your kingdom purpose is all about possessing the character of Jesus Christ by allowing God to prepare you through His order and method of process, development, transformation and time. As you persevere in this order, you should fully acquire the character of Jesus through the Holy Spirit's fruit which is actively alive in your spirit. The Holy Spirit's fruit is indicative of **character**, which is an evaluation of a particular individual's stable moral qualities including the existence of virtues such as empathy, courage, fortitude, honesty, and loyalty, or of good behaviors or habits (Wikipedia).

> *"But the fruit of the Spirit is love, joy, peace, patience, kindness, goodness, faith, gentleness, self-control. Against such things there is no law."* (Gal. 5:22-23, Passion)

> *"But what happens when we live God's way? He brings gifts into our lives, much the same way that fruit appears in an orchard – things like affection for others, exuberance about life, serenity. We develop a willingness to stick with things, a sense of compassion in the heart, and a conviction that a basic holiness permeates things and people. We find ourselves involved in loyal commitments, not needing to force our way in life, able to marshal and direct our energies wisely."* (Gal. 5:22-23, MSG)

These verses hopefully will say to you that God is actually working in you the depth of character needed to sustain you in your kingdom assignment. Godly character is unshakeable. This is why God has set in motion His growth plan. You grow down before you grow up. Without going through the process God has set in motion, you will never fully mature in your kingdom purpose. Your experiences in life will most likely become polluted and short-lived because it will have conformed to the corruption of this world. *"Whereby are given unto us exceeding great and precious promises: that by these ye might be partakers of the divine nature, having escaped the corruption that is in the world through lust"* (2 Pet. 1:4, KJV).

God's order and method of preparation is to set in motion His plan of spiritual maturity which includes humility, sacrifice and the testing of your heart to know whether you will keep His commandments or not. For this very purpose, God allowed the children of Israel to wander in the wilderness for 40 years. Yet, He supplied all their needs and brought those who mixed His Word with their faith into the land that He promised them (see Deut. 8). In the same way, God's desire is to do you good once He releases you into your kingdom purpose.

So, learn to love God's method of preparation for your kingdom assignment, and be willing to avail yourself to Him even when the method becomes painful and takes you through seasons of suffering for Christ's sake; seasons of affliction and persecution; seasons of great sacrifice, disappointments and warfare; or seasons of testing or discipline. Know that the kingdom assignment of every hero of the Bible required preparation. Even Jesus prepared 30 years for a public ministry that lasted only three and a half years. Staying in your comfort zone will not inspire growth. But, at the point of being stretched beyond your comfort zone, you will also begin to grow.

Yes, suffering for the sake of Christ and for the gospel of the kingdom is a vital part of your development into a spiritually mature saint who can carry out your kingdom assignment. And, when it comes to suffering, you have Christ's example to guide you and comfort you as you press into your kingdom assignment.

"Though He was a Son, yet He learned obedience by the things which He suffered." (Heb. 5:8)

"That I may know Him and the power of His resurrection, and the fellowship of His sufferings, being conformed to His death." (Phil. 3:10)

"But when you do good and suffer, if you take it patiently, this is commendable before God. For to this you were called, because Christ also suffered for us, leaving us an example, that you should follow His steps." (1 Pet. 2:20-23)

Yes, God's order and methods of preparing you for your kingdom purpose were designed in His mind before the foundation of the world for your success and fulfillment – greatness! And, God's preparation is in accordance with the regulations of His kingdom. The greater the call, the greater will be the preparation. Discover your kingdom purpose and stay focused. Keep your eyes on the prize that God has set before you. Your victory will come through your ability to commit to the assignment, humble yourself before God, and be a faithful, loyal, dedicated and devoted student willing to sit in the classroom of God's kingdom order and fulfill the requirements for graduation. Now go for it. Your greatness is grafted into your kingdom assignment.

"Not that I have already attained, or am already perfected; but I press on, that I may lay hold of that for which Christ Jesus has also laid hold of me. Brethren, I do not count myself to have apprehended; but one thing I do, forgetting those things which are behind and reaching forward to those things which are ahead, I press toward the goal for the prize of the upward call of God in Christ Jesus." (Phil. 3:12-14)

CHAPTER THREE

"YOU ARE ETERNALLY ENGINEERED, SOVEREIGNLY SITUATED AND SUPERNATURALLY SUSTAINED"*

*"O yes, you shaped me first inside, then out; you formed me in my mother's womb. I thank you, High God — you're breathtaking! Body and soul, I am marvelously made! I worship in adoration — what a creation! You know me inside and out, you know every bone in my body; You know exactly how I was made, bit by bit, how I was sculpted from nothing into something. Like an open book, you watched me grow from conception to birth; all the stages of my life were spread out before you, The days of my life all **prepared before** I'd even lived one day."*

(PSA. 139:13-16, MSG, AUTHOR'S EMPHASIS)

I believe that as God sculpted us from nothing into something, before we had even lived one day, He could sense the excitement of watching us grow from conception to birth and all the stages of our life. If you can conceive this in your mind, then you will begin to get a revelation of what it means to be eternally engineered. God is eternal. His Word is eternal. As a child of God, you, too, must learn to think from an eternal perspective rather than from your natural mind. Because God is eternal, He sees the end from the beginning. In other words, if God were to go out the back door, He'd immediately be in the front door. Why? There is no time in eternity. *"I declare the end from the beginning, and from long ago what is not yet done, saying: My plan will take place, and I will do all My will"* (Isa. 46:10, Passion).

It is evident from the previous verse of Scripture that God wants to see those things that He has declared for your life manifest as He watches you grow. He has stated clearly that He will do all that He wills according to His plan. *"Declaring the end from the beginning, and from ancient times the things that are not yet done, saying, my counsel shall stand, And I will do all my pleasure"* (Isa. 46:10, KJV). It is obvious from this text that God's pleasure is to perform in you that which fulfills your unique purpose and maximizes the potential of your life – a life elevated in character, in accordance with the fruit of the Spirit. This is the lofty position you should enjoy as a son or daughter of God. And, in order to become a son or daughter of God, you must first learn to be led by Holy Spirit. *"For as many as are led by the Spirit of God, they are the sons of God"* (Rom. 8:14).

This is one reason why, as you grow in spiritual maturity and learn how to walk in your true identity as a son or daughter, you should have a spiritual father or mother or both to teach, train and mentor you into sonship. It is easier to follow in the footsteps of someone who has gone through the arduous task of climbing to the summit of a mountain than to embark upon a quest of climbing and traversing the rough terrain of unfamiliar territory.

God places spiritual mentors, apostolic fathers and mothers, in your path as you progress in your kingdom purpose to lead you into sonship or discipleship – the place of being forged into a person of accountability and reliability through relationship and mentoring. A true son or daughter, properly mentored, will be able to reflect the ministry or pattern of his spiritual father. The process of mentoring is also designed to produce sons and daughters who effectively reflect the Kingdom of Heaven as they carry out their kingdom assignment.

My spiritual father, Dr. Gordon E. Bradshaw, says this concerning mentors: "The power of the Kingdom of God can be received into the hearts of men and women who are in the divinely-appointed position of leadership and transferred to the lives of disciples. This is done through leaders who are known as mentors. A **mentor** is defined as: A trusted counselor or guide (Webster). Jesus' relationship with God and with his disciples is a demonstration of mentorship. It was a good example of the "transfer of power" and should serve as the template for our present-day kingdom growth patterns. Mentoring should be the transfer or impartation of one's skills, qualities and abilities to an understudy or follower." (*The Technology of Apostolic Succession*, Kingdom House Publishing, Lakebay, WA, 2010, p. 184)

Discipleship and sonship are imperative for spiritual growth. This is the pattern of Jesus. He knew that if He reflected His father's purpose, He would be exalted to a high place in due time. You, too, will need a spiritual father to counsel and guide you into the place of spiritual maturity where you, having imitated your spiritual father, will be able to reflect his ministry and advance the kingdom of God in the earth. *"For though you might have ten thousand instructors in Christ, yet you do not have many fathers; for in Christ Jesus I have begotten you through the gospel. Therefore I urge you, imitate me"* (1 Cor. 4:15-16). Every son should develop an established spiritual identity through their spiritual father as part of their maturation process in Christ and for fulfillment of their kingdom assignment. Apostle Paul said: *"For this reason I have sent **Timothy** to you, who is my **beloved and faithful son in the Lord**, who **will remind you of my ways in Christ"*** (vs. 17, author's emphasis).

I submit to you that one of Paul's apostolic duties as a spiritual father was to impart the gifts, skills and anointing that God had graced him with to his spiritual sons so that they would be established, set or strengthened in their kingdom assignment. *"For I long to see you, that I may impart to you some spiritual gift, so that you may be established"* (Rom. 1:11). This is exactly what transpired in the mind of God

35

when He assigned your kingdom purpose before the foundation of the world. He engineered you from eternity; He situated you in time and established your boundaries through His sovereignty; and He sustained you supernaturally in order *"that the purpose of God according to election might stand, not of works but of Him who calls"* (Rom. 9:11). Now, God eagerly and patiently desires to **see** what He has imparted to you manifest in your life as you discover your kingdom purpose and commit to God's program of growth and maturation through Holy Spirit.

You must realize that your life in God is lived on different levels and arrived at in stages. Any time you move from one stage to the next stage (faith to faith, glory to glory), process is involved. Whenever you move **from** something **to** something, process is involved. Concerning the Israelites' move from Egypt to Canaan, Moses said, *"Then He brought us out **from** there, that He might bring us in, **to** give us the land of which He swore to our fathers"* (Deut. 6:23, author's emphasis).

However, this advancement required the Israelites to move through a series of processes of development in order to secure the land of promise. In the same way, each progressive step advances you to a new level of knowledge, responsibility, authority, and calls for a further deepening of Holy Spirit character because God wants to move you from one thing and bring you in to another in order to advance you. At the height of your Christian walk, you should display the very apparent presence and glory of God, on ground level. In other words, you are created and designed to manifest heaven on earth. However, in order to reach this height where you display the splendor of God's glory, you must be willing to climb.

To **climb** means to go upward with gradual or continuous progress: RISE, ASCEND; to ascend in growth; to go upward on or along, to the top of, or over (Merriam-Webster). What you must understand is that the view from the top is different from what you are accustomed to seeing in your normal, comfortable, sea level position. That view is often blurred by limitations and with issues that tend to enslave. It can also lead to stagnation and may cause you to defer your dreams.

The view from the top is worth the climb because it displays a spectacular dimension of God's glory. From the top God shows you the brilliance of life that is within your kingdom purpose; He shows you the good things that are yet to come. From the top, you are entrenched or covered in your kingdom identity and you receive the impartations for permanent function in the kingdom of God. Nevertheless, if you opt for a life of ease or simply a life of existing in your comfort zone – the same climate you've been accustomed to – then stay where you are… Because on top of the mountain, the air is thinner, the climate is colder, and breathing can be quite difficult at times. But, if you choose to experience the magnificent glory of God– living a full, varied and abundant life that includes days of heaven on earth – as you advance His kingdom, you must be willing to climb. Spiritually, it means that you will devote yourself and commit to the process of ascension or elevation to God's standard, which is a royal or kingdom standard.

The mountain top is the place of revelation. It is the place of spiritual maturity that has been built on relationship. It is the place where God invites you to "come" when He knows that you have devoted yourself to His process of developing and preparing you for deployment into your kingdom assignment. The climb is not always easy. It can be an arduous task at times. It can seem monumental and too big to navigate. As you climb, you will be met with adversity. But, as you forge your way upward, completely trusting God's faithfulness to His own Word, you will endure the adversity and adjust to your new climate on top of the mountain.

This is where you will know that you have evolved and transformed. You will possess a kingdom mindset – a major change in form, nature, and function through the renewing of your mind. This is the position in Christ where you will get a revelation of what God has done in you before you were in your mother's womb. Here you will know what it means to be "eternally engineered, sovereignly situated and supernaturally sustained."

Every person that God raises and uses greatly, He generally grounds them to powder first; so, don't get discouraged. If you follow the vision, God will ensure your provision. What I mean is that prior to your elevation upon your mountain, God has to humble you as a son through His transformation process. On the mountaintop, transformation is complete and new revelations and visions take place. Jesus was transformed before His disciples on the mountain. His appearance changed. He was morphed right before their eyes. He was transformed. According to Merriam-Webster, **transform** means to change in composition or structure; to change the outward form or appearance of; to change in character or condition.

Let's take a look at God's process of transformation in the life of Abraham. God instructed Abraham to go to the land of Moriah and offer his son Isaac there for a burnt offering. Let us not forget that Isaac is the son of his old age, whom he loved dearly. Abraham had waited 25 years, according to God's promise, for the birth of his son Isaac. Wow! What an instruction. But, the key to acquiring the anointing that accompanies elevation is faith and obedience. It is complete trust in God and obeying His instructions.

Abraham trusted God and obeyed God. He faced the hard fact of sacrificing Isaac by his faith. Abraham was about to experience a different climate; a new reality. This new elevation would be a permanent display of the glory of God on his life, which was also promised to his seed, of whom we are by our faith in Jesus Christ (see Gal. 3:29). The God Abraham knew on ground level is a different God on the mountain top. On the mountain Abraham experienced Jehovah-Jireh, the God who provides abundantly in advance because his faith was secured in God's faithfulness to His own Word, "IN ISAAC SHALL THY SEED BE CALLED." Whenever you possess this level of faith, obedience is always easy. So, Abraham proceeded to offer his son as a sacrifice unto God. In doing so, he displayed what kingdom faith looks like.

As he was about to slay Isaac, God said, *"Don't lay a hand on that boy! Don't touch him!* ***Now I know*** *how fearlessly you fear God;* ***you didn't hesitate*** *to place your son, your dear son, on the altar* ***for me"*** (Gen. 22:12, MSG, author's emphasis). It is truly amazing what God will accomplish for us when we trust and obey him. Abraham trusted God to the degree that he knew that if he sacrificed Isaac, God would be faithful to His Word and raise him up from the dead. *"Because you have gone through with this, and have not refused to give me your son, your dear son, I'll make sure that your children flourish – like stars in the sky! Like sand on the beaches! And your descendants will defeat their enemies. All nations on Earth will find themselves blessed through your descendants* ***because you obeyed me"*** (vss. 16-18, author's emphasis).

*"By faith Abraham, when he was tested, offered up Isaac, and he who
had received the promises offered up his only begotten son, of whom it was
said, "In Isaac your seed shall be called," concluding that God was able to
raise him up, even from the dead, from which he also received him
in a figurative sense."* (Heb. 11:17-19)

It seems necessary, at this point, to make a definitive statement highlighting
the fact that you are eternally engineered, sovereignly situated and supernaturally sustained, based on revelation knowledge given to me by Holy Spirit. Let's
begin by defining each of the base words that make up our theme for this chapter from the Hebrew and Greek concordance and from the dictionary.

The Hebrew word for **eternal** is *olam*, pronounced *o-lawm*, which means
time out of mind (past or future), i.e. (practically eternity; always: ancient
(time), continuance, perpetual, (beginning of the) world (+ without end). The
Greek word is *aion (ahee-ohn)*. It means an age, perpetuity; the world; eternal,
for ever more, beginning of the world (began, without end) (Strong's Hebrew
& Greek). Merriam-Webster defines **eternal** as having infinite duration: EV-
ERLASTING; of or relating to eternity; characterized by abiding fellowship
with God; continued without intermission: PERPETUAL; valid or existing at
all times: TIMELESS.

Engineer means to contrive or plan out, construct, or manage usually with
more or less subtle skill and craft; to guide the course of; to plan and direct skillfully; superintend; guide (a measure, action, etc. *through*) (Merriam-Webster).

You are **eternally engineered** means that God, Who is Eternal, Everlasting,
Perpetual, and Timeless – from ancient times (eternity) – before He created the
world, has taken you out of His mind, and shaped your identity in Him. His
plan is to construct or build you up in stages and skillfully manage your development into a spiritually mature leader. He guides your course in life, bringing you through each level of growth for deployment and success within your
kingdom assignment. *"You created every part of me...When my bones were being
formed, carefully put together in my mother's womb, when I was growing there in
secret, you knew that I was there – you saw me before I was born. The days allot-*

ted to me had all been recorded in your book, before any of them ever began" (Psa. 139:13, 15-16, GNB).

Sovereign means superlative in quality: EXCELLENT; of the most exalted kind: SUPREME; having undisputed ascendancy: PARAMOUNT; possessed of supreme power; unlimited in extent: ABSOLUTE; FREE (Merriam-Webster).

Situate is a rare or archaic variation of situated. From the Hebrew concordance, *yashab (yaw.shab)* is translated **situate**. It means to dwell, to remain; to settle down, to marry: (make to) abide, continue, endure, establish, and remain (Strong's). **Situated** means, places as to site or position; location (Merriam-Webster).

You are **sovereignly situated** means that God, Who is Excellent, Supreme, Paramount, Absolute and Free has situated or placed you in a specific position in Him (your calling) and defined your physical location, where you will dwell and settle down; where you will abide continually and be established; where you will endure and remain. In that place you will be delightfully married to the Lord. *"And He has made from one blood every nation of men to dwell on all the face of the earth, and has determined their preappointed times and the boundaries of their dwellings...for in Him we live and move and have our being"* (Acts 17:26, 28).

Supernatural means: of or relating to an order of existence beyond the visible observable universe; a departing from what is usual or normal, especially so as to appear to transcend the laws of nature (Merriam-Webster).

Camak, pronounced *saw-mak*, is the Hebrew word translated as **sustained**. It means to lean upon: bear up, establish, uphold, rest self, stand fast, stay, sustain (Strong's). Sustain means to keep in existence; keep up; maintain or prolong; to provide for the support of ; to provide sustenance or nourishment for; to strengthen the spirit, courage, etc. of; comfort; buoy up; encourage; to bear up against; endure; withstand; to uphold the validity or justice of; to confirm; corroborate (Merriam-Webster).

You are **supernaturally sustained** means that God has ordered His best for you. His best is beyond what is usual or normal. The blessing of God transcends the laws of nature. By faith, you are borne up by God and established. God maintains and supports you, providing sustenance and nourishment that will strengthen, encourage, comfort, and bear you up against the attacks of wicked people driven by the demonic strategies of Satan. God has already upheld you in justice; He has confirmed you and validated your kingdom assignment. Rest yourself in what God has already done.

"Blessed be the God and Father of our Lord Jesus Christ, who has blessed us with every spiritual blessing in the heavenly places in Christ." (Eph. 1:3)

"By faith we understand that the worlds were framed by the word of God, so that the things which are seen were not made of things which are visible." (Heb. 11:3)

"Cast your burden on the Lord, And He shall sustain you; He shall never permit the righteous to be moved." (Psa. 55:22)

"Be sober, be vigilant; because your adversary the devil walks about like a roaring lion, seeking whom he may devour. Resist him, steadfast in the faith, knowing that the same sufferings are experienced by your brotherhood in the world." (1 Pet. 5:8-9)

"There remains therefore a rest for the people of God…Let us therefore be diligent to enter that rest, lest anyone fall according to the same example of disobedience." (Heb. 4:9, 11)

So, my Holy Spirit revelation of what it means to be eternally engineered, sovereignly situated and supernaturally sustained is this: **God, Who is Eternal, Everlasting, Perpetual, and Timeless – from ancient times (eternity) – before He created the world, has taken you out of His mind, and shaped your identity in Him.** He guides your course in life, bringing you through each level of growth for deployment and success within your kingdom assignment. God, Who is Excellent, Supreme, Paramount, Absolute and Free, has situated or placed you in a specific position in Him (your calling) and defined your physical location, where you will dwell and settle down; where you will abide continually and be established; where you will endure and remain.

His best is beyond what is usual or normal. The blessing of God transcends the laws of nature. By faith, you are borne up by God and established. God maintains and supports you, providing sustenance and nourishment that will strengthen, encourage, comfort, and bear you up against the attacks of wicked people driven by the demonic strategies of Satan. God has already upheld you in justice; He has confirmed you and validated your kingdom assignment. Rest yourself in what God has already done.

That is a rather lengthy revelation for defining our theme; however, it is imperative that you have a present-truth revelation of who God is, and what He has already done for you. *"…just as he chose us in Him before the foundation of the world, that we should be holy and without blame before Him in love, having predestined us to adoption as sons by Jesus Christ to Himself, according to the good pleasure of His will, to the praise of the glory of His grace, by which he made us accepted in the Beloved"* (Eph. 1:4-6). He chose us in His love, holy and blameless, before He created the world. This sounds to me like God created the world to conform to the purposes of His children rather than Him creating us to be conformed to the world. All you have to do is simply accept this by your faith in God's faithfulness to His own Word. *"And do not be conformed to this world, but be transformed by the renewing of your mind, that you may prove what is that good and acceptable and perfect will of God"* (Rom. 12:2).

When I was pursuing my masters degree in public management, the professor who taught me graduate statistics had a frequent saying that he would always interject when I would struggle trying to put together a formula or solve a problem. He would say, "Brewton! Don't make it hard!" It took me a while to finally get a revelation of what he was trying to convey to me: He was telling me to relax, trust and rely on all I'd learned to get me to that point. My success in all of my undergraduate courses had prepared me for success on the graduate level, or I wouldn't be there. He was telling me to be confident. The same spirit of excellence exhibited on the undergraduate level is working to excel on the graduate level!

I want to admonish you in that same vein: "Don't make it hard!" You are a God-original. And you've been eternally engineered, sovereignly situated and supernaturally sustained. But, you must understand and claim your supernatural identity. Claim your identity as the chosen of God, *"who has saved us and called us with a holy calling, not according to our works, but **according to His own purpose and grace**, which was **given to us in Christ Jesus before time began**"* (2 Tim. 1:9, Passion, author's emphasis).

Identity! Identity! Identity! **Your identity in God is by promise, and not by works.** The promise supersedes your natural genetic heritage. Apostle Paul teaches us so much about purpose, mercy, grace, and being called or chosen according to God's own purpose and not ours. Let's take a look at this process from the account written in Paul's epistle to the Romans. Paul talks about God's gracious election of Israel as His chosen, and Israel's rejection of Christ. Why did Israel not embrace the Messiah? Did God fail to live up to His promise? Absolutely not! God's Word cannot fail; and God's promises always hold true for the person who, by faith, will believe the report – the promise. Paul said, *"For not all who are descended from Israel are Israel"* (Rom. 9:6b, NIV). God's promises are made only to the true Israel, people of faith like their father Abraham. Likewise, your identity in God, and the promises that He has made concerning you, must be claimed with your faith, for there is no unrighteousness in God.

"Don't suppose for a moment, though, that God's Word has malfunctioned in some way or other. The problem goes back a long way. From the outset, not all Israelites of the flesh were Israelites of the spirit. It wasn't Abraham's sperm that gave their identity here, but God's promise. Remember how it was put: "Your family will be defined by Isaac"? That means that Israelite identity was never racially determined by sexual transmission, but it was God-determined by promise. Remember that promise, "When I come back next year at this time, Sarah will have a son"? And that's not the only time. To Rebecca, also, a promise was made that took priority over genetics." (Rom. 9:6-10, MSG)

"For the children not yet being born, nor having done any good or evil, that the purpose of God according to election might stand, not of works but of him who calls," (Rom. 9:11, NKJV, author's emphasis).

"God told Rebecca, "The firstborn of your twins will take second place." Later that was turned into a stark epigram: "I loved Jacob; I hated Esau." (Rom. 9: 12-13, MSG)

In the above Scripture passage, Paul used the Old Testament examples of Jacob and Esau to explain election. He lets us know that God sovereignly decided to set His love on Jacob. God deliberately showered Jacob with His mercy and grace. Jacob did not receive this amazing mercy from God because of something he did, because works were never included in God's choice of one over the other. Paul clearly states that before they had lived to do any work, good or evil, God had already chosen Jacob over Esau. What was the reason that God would do this? He did it so that the purpose or promise of God according to election would stand, not based on works of the flesh, but of His own choice. *"What God did in this case made it perfectly plain that his purpose is not a hit-or-miss thing dependent on what we do or don't do, but a sure thing determined by his decision, flowing steadily from his initiative"* (vs. 11, MSG).

"Is that grounds for complaining that God is unfair? Not so fast, please. God told Moses, "I'm in charge of mercy. I'm in charge of compassion." Compassion doesn't originate in our bleeding hearts or moral sweat, but in God's mercy. The same point was made when God said to Pharaoh, "I picked you as a bit player in this drama of my salvation power." All we're saying is that God has the first word, initiating the action in which we play our part for good or ill" (Vss. 14-18, MSG).

The above passage is a full revelation of the doctrine of God's free and sovereign grace. **"I'm in charge of mercy. I'm in charge of compassion,"** says God. God never said, "I will show mercy only to those who fulfill the conditions I set forth as the prerequisite of My plan for salvation." No! He literally says, **"I will mercy on whom I will have mercy, and I will compassion on whom I will have compassion."** Therefore, the source of mercy and compassion both find their ultimate ground only in the free choice of God, with their individual application, and not man. And so, this is the conclusion of the matter. Divine election is not decided through the will of man, nor of human effort, but of God. Mercy and compassion are His to freely give. Man strives through choice and effort, but God is the Architect of mercy. *"So then it is not of him who wills, nor of him who runs, but of God who shows mercy"* (vs. 16, NKJV).

Just as God chose Israel as an act of His sovereignty, so also He chose your identity in Him. He assigned you a kingdom purpose in the earth, and equipped you for the fulfillment of your assignment – before you were formed in your mother's womb. You have been eternally engineered, sovereignly situated and supernaturally sustained. But, in order to foster the reality of this marvelous grace gift, you must receive it by faith or take it with your faith.

Because Israel was chosen by God, His righteousness was theirs through His grace, mercy and compassion. They did not have to attain this grace through works of the law. *"But Israel, pursuing the law of righteousness, has not attained to the law of righteousness. Why? Because they did not seek it by faith, but as it were, by the works of the law"* (vss. 31-32). But, you are not living under the law; you are living under grace. Jesus, who came full of grace and truth (see John 1: 14), is the fulfillment of the law. So then, New Testament grace supersedes Old Testament law, because it is a better covenant established on better promises (see Rom. 8:6). By your faith in what God has already declared over your life from before the creation of the world, you can claim your identity.

God has chosen you and created you perfect in His heart and mind. But, your spiritual identity must be intact in order to successfully carry out your kingdom assignment. When you know your identity in Christ, it becomes easier to accept your kingdom purpose. Also, when you are secure in your identity, you will be able to extract your blessings and benefits from your assignment. God does not want you to accept anything less than what He created you to be. Yet, many believers never rise to the standard of the seed God planted them to be. *"Yet I had planted you a noble vine, a seed of highest quality. How then have you turned before Me into the degenerate plant of an alien vine?"* (Jer. 2:21).

Once you claim your identity in Christ as a person of nobility, created in the image and likeness of God, which is the highest quality, it releases the passion to become who God created you to be. This is the point at which you begin to seek God like never before. You begin to study the Word, spend time in the presence of God reflecting and rehearsing the Word; you begin to declare and decree the intent of God for your life, and you praise Him for your identity. Through your diligent pursuit of Him, God will bring you to the place where you will discover your kingdom purpose. Sadly, many saints never arise to this place. You've got to know who you are in God before you can discover your divine purpose. Those saints who never discover their divine assignment usually turn degenerate. They undergo a process of spiritual decline and defer to a life of existence within the church – a collection of saved folks with no spiritual authority, waiting for Jesus to come back and rapture the church.

God wants you to soar into your destiny, the predetermined course of events for your life on earth engineered by God in eternity. Don't violate your divine calling by turning into the degenerate plant of an alien vine. God said to Jeremiah, *"Before I formed you in the womb I knew you; Before you were born I sanctified you; I ordained you a prophet to the nations." Then said I: Ah, Lord God! Behold, I cannot speak, for I am a youth." But the Lord said to me: "Do not say, I am a youth"* (Jer. 1:5-7).

God does not change His mind concerning the plans and purposes He has predetermined for your life on earth. But, doubtless some of you, like Jeremiah, will question God's assignment for you. Like Moses, you will question God as if surely He has made a mistake. He couldn't possibly be talking about you. Jeremiah said to God, "Surely you've made a mistake. I am but a child. There's no way I could ever be a prophet to the nations." Moses questioned God, asking Him, "Who am I that I should go to Pharaoh and demand that he release the Hebrew slaves. Don't you know that he's the most powerful man in the world"?

In both instances, God reassured Moses and Jeremiah that He had not made a mistake, and that He would not change His mind relative to their assignment. You, too, can stand assured that whatever God has predetermined your kingdom purpose to be, He will not change His mind. His purposes, according to election, will stand, *"For the gifts and calling of God are without repentance"* (Rom. 11:29, KJV). Don't miss the discovery of your kingdom assignment because you were too busy seeking the temporary pleasures of life rather than seeking and pursuing God's righteousness, which releases you into His original plan for your life. Don't miss out on your kingdom assignment. If you do, you will get off track and begin to wander; eventually, you will lose hope and life will become a façade, a portraying of someone you were never meant to be; and, you will live in a reality you were not designed to live in. That is what a degenerate vine looks like.

Go to the Manufacturer of all life! *"For whom He foreknew, He also predestined to be conformed to the image of His Son, that He might be the firstborn among many brethren. Moreover whom He predestined, these He also called; whom He called, these He also justified; and whom He justified, these He also glorified"* (Rom. 8:29-30). David reflected upon the sovereignty of God pertaining to our predetermined lives, and made it clear that God has a book or manual about each person who was, is, or will be born; and each one, regardless of how or under what circumstances he got here, has a divine purpose and destiny. *"I will praise You, for I am fearfully and wonderfully made; Marvelous are Your works, And that my soul knows very well. My frame was not hidden from You, When I was made in secret, And skillfully wrought in the lowest parts of the earth. Your eyes saw my substance, being yet unformed. **And in Your book they all were written, The days fashioned for me, When as yet there were none of them**"* (Psa. 139:14-16, author's emphasis).

As you go to the Manufacturer of life and read the manual that pertains to your life and assignment, the surety of your calling, your kingdom assignment and destiny will be revealed to you. And, as you accept that assignment and allow God to cultivate and process you, spiritual growth for deployment will occur. You will indeed become an epistle of God, known and read of all men (see 2 Cor. 3:2). Your earthly life will reflect the kingdom pattern of heaven, because the original plan is always the property of the originator. Spend quality time seeking and pursuing the presence of God – the Manufacturer of the original plan for mankind. Don't run ahead of God's timing and development program, being swayed by the world system's desire to taste the grapes before they've been properly cultivated. Understand that the grapes (health, wealth, favor, peace, power, etc. – kingdom success) are not placed within your mouth; they are placed within your reach.

So, don't make it hard! It is not difficult. You simply have to discover and accept your divine assignment and allow God to cultivate you into the noble vine of the highest quality that He predetermined you to become – before He created the world. If you have gotten off track, repent and be transformed by the renewing of your mind toward your kingdom purpose. Begin to think differently about yourself, and see yourself as God sees you. Allow God to raise you as His child, and He will cause you to ride upon the high places of the earth so that you may eat the increase of the field (see Deut. 32:13). In this place, you will call the heavenly pattern of God's government to the earth, and reflect that you indeed carry your Father's Incorruptible Seed (His spiritual DNA). You will bring glory to God!

My dear fellow-saint, you have a choice. You can be passive concerning your kingdom purpose and never discover it, or you can seek God for your kingdom purpose, discover it, and allow God to mature you into a kingdom-level leader, commissioned to carry out and joyfully fulfill your kingdom assignment. By using your faith to maintain your devotion, loyalty and commitment to God, you will pass successfully through the many life-factors that God strategically places in your path to ensure your victorious kingdom life. In order to do this, God must elevate you and transition you from mere footmen to horsemen, as we will discuss in Chapter 10 and other places. You are eternally engineered, sovereignly situated and supernaturally sustained.

END NOTE: Chapter title used by permission from the teaching series entitled – *"Becoming Eternally Engineered, Sovereignly Situated and Supernaturally Sustained"* Part I, II & III, (March 13th, 16th, and 20th, 2016) by Dr. Gordon E. Bradshaw, President GEMS (Global Effect Movers & Shakers) Network, Chicago, Illinois. Copyright © 2016 by Dr. Gordon E. Bradshaw www.gemsnetwork.org

SECTION TWO:

MATURITY INVOLVES
A PROCESS OF SPIRITUAL GROWTH

You Must Not Remain a Baby Christian!

*"Therefore, laying aside all malice, all deceit, hypocrisy, envy,
and all evil speaking, as newborn babes, desire the pure milk
of the word, that you may grow thereby, if indeed you have tasted
that the Lord is gracious."*
(1 PET. 2:1-3)

*"For everyone who partakes only of milk is unskilled
in the word of righteousness, for he is a babe.
But solid food belongs to those who are of full age,
that is, those who by reason of use have their senses
exercised to discern both good and evil."*
(HEB. 5:13-14)

CHAPTER FOUR

BABY CHRISTIANS CAN NEVER BECOME WISE MASTER BUILDERS

"According to the grace of God which was given to me, as a wise
master builder I have laid the foundation, and another builds on it. But let each
one take heed how he builds on it. For no other foundation can anyone lay than that
which is laid, which is Jesus Christ."

(1 COR. 3:10-11)

I received Jesus as my Savior and Lord in 1972. Five years later, I was still a baby Christian. I had hardly grown spiritually, and what little growth I thought I could measure was drawn from my religious mindset based on Old Testament Law. I was trying to live right so I would go to heaven. Obviously, that wasn't working for me; and, as I mentioned in Chapter One, by the end of my junior year in high school, I had backslidden.

Soon after our family stopped attending the holiness church that we'd been members of since 1963, my parents established a nightly prayer time at 10:00

which none of the family was allowed to miss. Of course, this put a damper in my newfound freedom. Even if I were already out having fun, I had to be back at home before 10:00 to be present for prayer. This was in early 1977.

After prayer, which lasted anywhere from five to 30 minutes, my parents would always retire to their bedroom. And, I would be ready to hit the streets again. I knew that my parents would never give me permission to leave the house after prayer. So, I devised the ultimate plan for escape. Our two-story home made things quite easy. My brothers and I slept upstairs; my parents and my sisters slept downstairs. My plan was simple. My father was a carpenter, among other trades. He had several old ladders tossed behind his tool shed that he no longer used. So, whenever I wanted to slip out for the night, I would station a ladder next to the roof of our laundry room.

From my bedroom window, I could step onto the roof, scale down the ladder and I was out for most of the night. This method worked for me all during the summer of 1977 and throughout my senior year. I would hang out with my best friend Steve, riding in his new 1977 Monte Carlo. It was grey with red leather interior. We would drink beer and listen to the top R&B artists on his 8-track tape player.

During my junior year, I had decided to attend college just 22 miles away from home. Several of my friends had planned to do the same, including Steve. But, things were still escalating on the religious front at home. And, I wanted no part of that. With Georgia Southern College so close to home, I realized that my parents would still have more influence over me than I wanted them to have. So, early in my senior year, I applied to several colleges that were at least 150 miles away, one of them out of state.

Three weeks prior to graduation, I received a letter of acceptance to attend Florida A&M University in Tallahassee, Fla. I had applied there on the recommendation of a regional counselor, who had come to Claxton High School at the beginning of the school year to assist seniors with the college selection process. FAMU was his alma mater.

"I think that Florida A&M would be an excellent fit for you, James," I remember him telling me.

My mother wanted me to become a famous musician, so I applied to the university's College of Music because of its excellent staff and high standard of musicianship established by the late Dr. William P. Foster, who was a long-time director of the McDonald's All-American High School Band. So, the school's excellent music program reputation had preceded it.

I really didn't want to leave Georgia, and to be honest, I didn't think my parents would allow me to leave the state. But, I knew I couldn't attend Georgia Southern either, though I dreaded losing everyday contact with Steve. I wanted my college career to be an adventure, and Georgia Southern was too close to home for the fulfillment of this risky undertaking. My parents and my religious upbringing would clash with my plans to explore the worldly lusts I once feared. In Florida, there would be no one to monitor my behavior. I wanted to be free to experiment. Most of all, I wanted to be free of the guilt I still felt since my family had left the holiness church we once attended. To my surprise, my parents were jubilant, especially my mother, who encouraged me to go for it.

On the afternoon of my graduation from high school, I sat in my upstairs bedroom reminiscing about my high school years and how I had become a totally different person. I had gone through an ominous change in character as well as scruples. The person who I had known two years prior, sent chills racing across my body as I retraced my transition from a church-going, God-fearing teenager to a liberal, outgoing person, who couldn't wait to get my piece of the action.

In my sensitive nature, having just compared a long past with a very short present, I felt ashamed and embarrassed as if I were the worst person in the world. I felt like a hypocrite – a backslider. Two years prior, I would have repented for the slightest error; now, I could harden my heart and look the other way. I began to cry, but my tears were of mixed emotions. I was excited to be graduating with honors, after a supercharged high school career in which I did not miss one day of school. Also, I felt guilty — dirty even, because of the person I had become. Still, I couldn't resist my new attitude, which rejected my Christian upbringing. In my mind, I felt a force compelling me to taste the pleasures of the world.

"See what Satan has to offer," this force said.

There was lots of excitement around the breakfast table on the morning I was to leave for college, especially from my mother and Veronica, the oldest of the Brewton children, who had already graduated from Georgia Southern and was an elementary school teacher. My mother kept saying how excited she was that I was attending a university.

"I know you're going to do well and make the family proud of you, son."

She must have repeated that sentence a dozen and one times. But, I understood my mother's excitement. She had graduated from Claxton's "colored" high school in 1955 and never had the opportunity to go to college. However, she never stopped believing that her children would get the opportunity that she didn't have. She always encouraged us to value our education as a means of getting ahead in the world. She would tell me consistently that I could be great at whatever I chose to do because I was smart. My mother's faith in God, along with her ministry of helping the less fortunate, permeated my spirit. I had understood what she meant when she constantly encouraged her children to "look up and live."

My father didn't say much at all. Whenever he did speak, it was about how much money he would be spending for my college education.

"Don't go down to Florida to play son…you hear me? I want you to study hard and make good grades. Do all your school work the best you can do it; that way, you can be proud to sign your name to it. It's going to cost your mother and me too much money to send you all the way to Florida to flunk out of school," he'd said.

I remember chill bumps forming all over my arms when he said that. What he said put extra pressure on me, because until that very moment I felt confident that I could handle college. But, I understood my father's concern. He never got to graduate from high school. He had to quit when he was in eleventh grade to go to work, after his father died.

I admired my father's courage. He worked hard every day and most nights to provide for his huge family. I knew that I and my sisters and brothers were fortunate because our father could have been like many other men who walked away, leaving their wives to raise their children. So, I highly regarded the sensible man my father was. He transmitted to me the responsibility of doing my work with a spirit of excellence, and doing a thorough job the first time so I'd be proud to put my name to it.

That morning after breakfast, I loaded our van and everyone got situated. As I sat under the steering wheel, I felt sick. Funny thing, though, the further we got from home, the better I began to feel. By the time we reached Tallahassee, five hours later, I didn't feel sick at all. I was anxious to get settled into my room, meet new friends and be on my own.

Fifteen years later, on the morning of March 21, 1992, I remember tossing and turning from one side of the bed to the other for a full hour before realizing that I wasn't going to fall asleep again. My mind was racing from one thought to another, all of them vivid snapshots from my precarious past; each one climbing on top of the other, clinging to the one ahead of it, contending for first place in the race for what was then my present despair.

Suddenly, a chill seized me and I began to shiver. My heartbeat became sporadic. Fear gripped me. Flashes of death raced through my mind, as I tried desperately to make sense of what was happening to me. I felt like I needed to pray. But, I was not sure that I could, or if God would even hear my prayer. My shivers intensified. I wanted to pray. I needed to be delivered. *Delivered from what?* I thought. My mind went blank. I didn't know what to say, how to pray anymore. But, somehow words came out.

I said, "God, Lord, Jesus. I need help…I need help now. I don't know how much more I can take. I've tried to be a good person, but I've become an addict, a liar, a deceiver, and a thief; I can't help myself. I need to be free. And you are my last hope. Oh Lord, save me. Save me from this terrible disease. I don't know what to do anymore, but I know you do. I know I don't deserve your help. I haven't been faithful to you, Lord, for a long time. Please forgive me and help me to get my life back."

I finished my prayer and sat on the side of the bed trying to compose myself. But, all I could think of was the religious influence my parents had instilled in me…another thought about my last two years of high school…another thought about my risqué college years and the many destructive relationships that had led to my addiction. Glancing at each of the once white walls, I could relate them to my then-current dilemma. Faded pictures of two men hunting deer in the winter hung crooked, one on each of the four walls displaying a slightly different depiction. The room smelled of crisp toe jams and stale smoke and alcohol.

I remember getting up and walking into the bathroom, which was located off a small hallway that led to the door of this sleazy, outdated motel room. But, given my state at that time, I had to be satisfied with the accommodations at a cost of $20 per night. Besides the bed there was a nightstand and a dresser, all of which had probably given at least 20 years of loyal service. The color television fared somewhat better having dedicated, I'd guessed, close to 10 years. The dark brown carpet, dampened over the years with alcohol spills and draft seeping through the cracks around the window and air conditioning unit, was filthy; and the phone was a rotary style. All of these hotel amenities had to be vintage 1970's but there they were in 1992.

Leaving the bathroom, I sat down at the foot of the bed and thought, *'Maybe I should call home and tell my mother that I changed my mind about moving back home. No. No. I can't stay in Tallahassee any longer. I need to go back home for my own good.'* At the same time, I knew that I could cause great pain and hardship on my parents by moving my demons into their home. Plus, I was embarrassed to move back in with my parents, supposedly after I had made it in life.

I remembered that my mother had once told me, "It's during the valley experiences of life that you grow into the person God wants you to be. It's your steadfastness in faith and prayer to God when you're at your lowest point that pleases Him and releases his mercy."

For over 15 years, I had ignored her advice. Now, my older brother was on his way to Tallahassee to pick me up and drive me back to Georgia. My car had been repossessed several months earlier, and I did not have a dollar to my name. The few clothes that I had were stuffed into two grocery-sized, brown paper bags. A sudden barrage of knocks on my room door startled me, snapping me out of the subdued state in which I'd been reliving episodes from my past most crucial to creating the drug-addicted derelict I had become.

I had a lot to think about while driving back to Claxton. Mostly, I thought about yet another period of adjustment, something I had become accustomed to throughout my backslidden years. However, this one would be different. I would be living under my parents' roof again — not as a child, but as an adult. And, because of my respect for them, I would submit to their rules. This meant going to church regularly again. But, actually, that was the least of my worries. I didn't want to hurt them by my inability to control my demons.

Once I was home, my parents welcomed me with their love. They gave me the upstairs guest bedroom. Yes, I was ashamed to be living with my parents again. After all, I had left 15 years earlier, earned two degrees, and had come back flat broke. I avoided going out in public, but didn't fight going to church. My mother consistently affirmed that God still loved me, and that He would forgive me no matter what I had done.

After I'd been home for almost two months, I drove my father to a church in Anderson, S. C. one Sunday morning where he was to preach. However, it was the pastor of that church who saw my pain as I sat among the congregation. Something was happening to me. As I praised God in that service, I could feel the Holy Spirit moving all over me. I could hardly contain myself.

"Come here, son." He beckoned to me from the pulpit. "You've been sitting there with the Spirit of God all over you. I see your past and I'm going to pray that your relationship with Christ be restored."

I stood before him in tears. I trembled as if I was afraid, but there was no fear. For me, it was simply an acknowledgement that I was tired of being sick and I needed to get well.

"There is no sin too big for God to forgive," the minister said. "If you ask Him, He will forgive you right now. First John, chapter one, verse nine says, 'If we confess our sins, he is faithful and just to forgive us our sins, and to cleanse us from all unrighteousness.' All you have to do is confess your sins with a sincere heart, and God will restore you. This is your opportunity for a new beginning. Let God give it to you."

As I stood in front of the pastor, I remember taking a deep breath and exhaling.

I simply released the pressure, as if I were releasing the air from an over-inflated balloon. I envisioned my sinful past being poured out and covered over by a huge blanket. I knew that this was my time to repent, to turn and go the opposite way of my ruin. I needed to repent. I wanted to repent. I might not have this opportunity again. I was sincere and my mind was focused on the only One who could forgive me.

I stood broken. I acknowledged that I could not help myself. From a heart of contrition, I confessed my sins and asked God to forgive me and restore my relationship with Him. And, I proceeded to forgive myself. I could feel a cleansing taking place throughout my body. I didn't know how to respond. All I knew was that I felt clean, and I knew that I was remitted. I no longer felt guilty. I was a new man.

*****

I shared that part of my life with you because I know that this is what can happen if you are not properly discipled, growing in your relationship with God to the place of discovering your kingdom assignment. I had no one to disciple me once I got saved and I did not understand that God had ordained my purpose in the earth. And, because I was a spiritual baby in Christ, Satan took that opportunity to try to steal, kill and destroy my destiny. But, I realized after becoming spiritually mature, that what I'd experienced over that 15-year period, in reality, served only to strengthen me for my kingdom purpose in life. I can now comfort those baby Christians who may be experiencing a similar pattern in their lives that I experienced, with the same comfort that God used to comfort me in all of my tribulations (see 2 Cor. 1:5).

After my restoration, God put me on the road to becoming a wise master builder. And, I quickly learned that this road is not paved with milk. It is paved through discipleship, which is a process of spiritual growth. I had to be weaned from milk and taught how to digest strong meat. This required me to go through the process of being fathered and mentored, which required development and transformation over time. *"Who is he trying to teach? Who is he trying to instruct? Infants [just] weaned from milk? Babies removed from the breast? For [he says]: 'Law after law, law after law, line after line, line after line, a little here, a little there'"* (Isa. 28:9-10, Passion).

Spiritual growth is a process that begins with discipleship. Jesus illustrated this when He called 12 men from among those who followed Him. And, they became His leaders, whom He ordained as apostles. However, Jesus understood that these men required development and they would have to endure the process of transformation over time, a period of three years, in order to effectively build the kingdom once He was gone.

> *"And He went up on the mountain and called to Him those He Himself wanted. And they came to Him. Then He appointed twelve, that they might be with Him and that He might send them out to preach, and to have power to heal sicknesses and to cast out demons"* (Mark 3: 13-15).

This is a process that demands spiritual growth. And, spiritual growth is from the inside out. The nature of discipleship is to mature you to the place where you are conformed to the image of God's Son, Jesus. True discipleship deals with your entire make-up – spirit, soul and body. It is the process by which you become mature, fully functioning as a commissioned, kingdom-level leader. As you allow Holy Spirit to release His fruit into your spirit, it transforms your soul, which transforms your body. This is the point where you begin to see things from having matured in your understanding of God's kingdom assignment for your life. *"Now may the God of peace Himself sanctify you completely; and may your whole spirit, soul, and body be preserved blameless at the coming of our Lord Jesus Christ. He who calls you is faithful, who also will do it"* (1 Thess. 5:23-24).

As I stated earlier, spiritual maturity is about relationship with God, growing to know Him as Father. Baby Christians know God as God. In other words, they love God and they thank Him for saving them. But, they don't know God as Father. There is no intimate relationship. God is still "up there" and they are "down here." They've never learned to walk in a sustained faith in the Word of

God they say they believe. Jesus never prayed to God; He prayed to His Father. There is no Father separate from Jesus. There is no Jesus separate from Holy Spirit. And, if you be in Christ, there is no separation between you and the Father, you and the Son, or you and Holy Spirit. *"But he who is joined to the Lord is one spirit with Him"* (1 Cor. 6:17). How does one become joined to the Lord, becoming one spirit with Him?

> *"Sanctify them by Your truth. Your word is truth."*
> *"...that they all may be one, as You, Father, are in Me, and I am in You; that they also may be one in Us, that the world may believe that You sent Me."* (John 17:17, 21)

God has provided a process to transformation – from a spiritual babe in Christ to a spiritual giant, someone who carries out his kingdom assignment as a king and priest unto God, and an ambassador for Christ – which involves intimacy with Him through Holy Spirit empowerment.

As you abide in Christ, intimacy is maintained and the process to transformation is forged. In this process, God reveals His will to your mind. Abiding in Christ as His Word abides in you transports you into a spiritual dimension of prioritizing Scripture. You give God your mind and He sanctifies it by His truth. His Word is truth. This truth governs your thoughts and illuminates your mind, bringing you into the place of expectation for manifestation of your kingdom assignment. *"For as he thinks in his heart, so is he"* (Prov. 23:7). Whatever you focus on in your mind is what you will become. So, if you are acting spiritually mature as a wise master builder, it is because you established a consistent pattern over time of thinking like a spiritually mature, wise master builder.

Throughout the New Testament, growth and spiritual maturity of every Believer is emphasized. And, the key elements of this growth involve a revelation of Scripture, Holy Spirit empowerment, trials and tests to reveal your strengths and weaknesses, and spiritual fathers who mentor you to keep you on track toward discipleship, which is conformity to the image of Christ. Through discipleship, you develop the ability to conceive and understand God's divine plan for your life so that you are thoroughly equipped to complete your kingdom assignment, *"that the man of God may be complete, thoroughly equipped for every good work"* (2 Tim. 3:17).

You become spiritually mature, reflecting and demonstrating the fruit of the Spirit. In this standard, your spiritual eyes are always open to see the movement and works of God; your spiritual ears are always open to hear divine rhema from God; and, the eyes of your mind are constantly illuminated with the spirit of wisdom and revelation in the knowledge of Him: *"That the God of our Lord Jesus Christ, the Father of glory, may give unto you the spirit of wisdom and revelation in the knowledge of him:* ***The eyes of your understanding being enlightened that ye may know what is the hope of his calling,*** *and what the riches of the glory of his inheritance (in the saints)"* (Eph. 1:17-19, KJV, author's emphasis).

Let's take a look at what can occur in the life of a believer who never matures in Christ after their initial salvation. One very obvious result is that he never discovers what the hope of God's calling is for his life. Why? The eyes of his understanding were never enlightened with the spirit of wisdom and revelation in the knowledge of God, which leads to never acquiring the riches of the glory made available for him as a saint of God. He never got on the discipleship track through studying the Word of God; he never allowed Holy Spirit to empower him in the form of developing godly character; he never sought the Lord for a mentor or spiritual parent who could guide him through the discipleship process; and, he became unwilling to endure trials that would have revealed his strengths and weaknesses, not knowing that God would use his trials to make him better.

The lack of spiritual maturity most often results in dullness of hearing. In other words, baby Christians do not hear God clearly. They cannot distinguish the still small voice of the Lord because they have failed to make use of the above stated resources that would have trained their spiritual senses to discern both good and evil. Making reference to Melchizedek's kingly and priestly order, the author of the epistle to the Hebrews makes it clear that the Jewish Christians were slow and lacked the ability to spiritually comprehend the depth of revelation relative to this kingly and priestly order as it related to their current standard through New Testament grace. The writer of the epistle to the Hebrews could not interpret into their spirit the wisdom and revelation of the

Order of Melchizedek in the knowledge of Jesus. Why? The eyes of their under-standing had never been enlightened to receive the gift of grace as opposed to strict adherence to the law. This made it difficult to teach them.

> *"I have a lot more to say about this, but it is hard to get it across to you since you've picked up this bad habit of not listening. By this time you ought to be teachers yourselves, yet here I find you need someone to sit down with you and go over the basics on God again, starting from square one – baby's milk, when you should have been on solid food long ago!* **Milk is for beginners, inexperienced in God's ways;** *solid food is for the mature, who have some practice in telling right from wrong.*

> *"So come on, let's leave the preschool fingerpainting exercises on Christ and get on with the grand work of art.* **Grow up in Christ.** *The basic foundational truths are in place: turning your back on "salvation by self-help" and turning in trust toward God; baptismal instructions; laying on of hands; resurrection of the dead, eternal judgment. God helping us, we'll stay true to all that. But* **there's so much more. Let's get on with it!"** (Heb. 5:11-14; 6:1-3, MSG, author's emphasis)

I love this translation from The Message Bible. It speaks in contemporary language. It basically points to the fact that these Christians had been saved long enough to have matured in the Word and their understanding enlightened to receive revelation knowledge of present truth. When there is no revelation of present truth, people tend to get stuck in their Old Testament mindset. This means that they have to be trained or taught again, referring to stagnation rather than advancement. This ultimately led to their lack of maturity. Obviously, they had been saved for a substantial period of time and should have matured in the Word of grace. But, lack of spiritual maturity resulted in the fact that they were unskillful in the Word, not understanding the benefits of the Cross. This is the status of a spiritual baby.

However, as it is explained in the text, if you are going to mature in the Lord, you must learn to walk after the Spirit by placing your faith in the finished work of the Lord Jesus on the Cross and not walking according to your flesh (see Rom. 8:1-2). Consistency in this process will prepare you to digest "strong meat." You will mature and receive deeper revelations of wisdom and knowledge of Christ because you will have had your spiritual senses exercised to go forward into completion of your kingdom assignment; rather than being just a Christian who heard the gospel of salvation, got saved, and never advanced into the gospel of the kingdom as a mature believer where saints get commissioned as kingdom leaders equipped to carry out their kingdom assignment, similar to the commissioning of military officers. Spiritual commissioning was practiced both in the Old and New Testaments (Num. 23; Matt. 10; Mark 3).

Discipleship requires discipline. You must learn to discipline yourself for your kingdom assignment. Obviously, if you don't consistently exercise yourself spiritually, you will take on more carnality and not be in very good spiritual shape. The carnal state is the result of Christians who never exercise their spiritual muscles to lift heavy objects or endure hardship as a good soldier of Jesus Christ (see 2 Tim. 2:3). Baby Christians allow little things to keep them from advancing and becoming wise master builders through spiritual maturity. They pile one excuse on top of another. "I really did try it, but it didn't work for me." "I just can't read the Bible for long periods of time. It makes me sleepy." "Well, I'm not a very disciplined person to begin with. It's just the way I am." "Child, God knows my heart." Have you ever heard any of these lame excuses?

If you are currently saying any of these things, you have not yet submitted yourself to the empowerment available to you through Holy Spirit. His presence within your spirit is a provision of power from which you may draw from to discipline yourself. God already knows your weaknesses and has already taken them into account. That's why He supplies you with His grace. God does for us what we could never do for ourselves. So, you can find self-discipline in the grace of God as you seek God and His kingdom pattern first (see Matt. 6:33). This is the kind of intimate relationship God requires of you. It builds within your spirit the power of His presence and strengthens you to meet the demands of your kingdom assignment.

Discipline is a requirement of sonship, of spirituality, of excellence, of covenant, and of intimate family relationship. Richard Foster, for example, is a prolific Christian teacher and author widely-known for his books on Christian living, including a best-seller, *Celebration of Discipline*. Paul the Apostle said, *"So I run with purpose in every step. I am not just shadowboxing. I discipline my body like an athlete, training it to do what it should. Otherwise, I fear that after preaching to others I myself might be disqualified."* (1 Cor. 9:26-27, NLT).

The writer of Hebrews adds this poignant passage about the necessity and benefit of discipline:

> *"**Endure hardship as discipline; God is treating you as his children.** For what children are not disciplined by their father? If you are not disciplined—and everyone undergoes discipline—then you are not legitimate, not true sons and daughters at all. Moreover, we have all had human fathers who disciplined us and we respected them for it. How much more should we submit to the Father of spirits and live! They disciplined us for a little while as they thought best; but **God disciplines us for our good, in order that we may share in his holiness.** No discipline seems pleasant at the time, but painful. Later on, however, it produces a harvest of righteousness and peace for those who have been trained by it."* (Heb. 12:7-11, NIV, author's emphasis)

Baby Christians never get that far, choosing ultimately to remain in their baby or carnal state where they are still fed on spiritual milk, although they have been saved for many years. It is very difficult to speak spiritual things to a Christian locked in a carnal mindset for lack of growth, even though he has the mind of Christ (see 1 Cor. 2:16). Rom. 12:2 says, *"Do not conform any longer to the pattern of this world, but be transformed by the renewing of your mind."* Renewal is an ongoing process, not a one-time event, and requires effort, obedience, and discipline.

The problem for baby Christians is in letting or allowing the mind of Christ to possess them rather than trusting in their sense knowledge. *"Let this mind be in you which was also in Christ Jesus"* (Phil. 2:5). When you "let" something happen, it is capable of operating under its own power. Just don't interfere! However, the carnal mind, the undisciplined spirit, cannot restrict itself from interfering with the process that God has already put in place. As a result, he struggles to receive revelation knowledge that is beyond what he has learned through the gospel of salvation and generally rejects the more spiritually mature route that leads to the gospel of the kingdom.

> *"And I, brethren, could not speak to you as to spiritual people but as to carnal, as to babes in Christ. I fed you with milk and not with solid food; for until now you are still notable to receive it, and even now you are still not able; for you are still carnal. For where there are envy, strife, and divisions among you, are you not carnal and behaving like mere men?"*
> (1 Cor. 3:1-3)

Baby Christians possess this same mindset today. They are spiritually immature, not having disciplined themselves to allow the process of development and spiritual maturity to take place through their intimate relationship with God, their Father. They are carnal Christians still functioning in spiritual immaturity. They act and speak like worldly men. They never develop beyond just being saved.

So, then, baby Christians can never become wise master builders. As a believer, you *"are God's field, you are God's building"* (1 Cor. 3:9). This means that you are God's property, His possession. And, since God formed you in His mind before He created the earth, He has a special assignment for you that fits within the earth He created and the time period in which you were born. Remember, God did not create man for the earth. He created the earth for man. As a Wise Master Builder, God used His skill, His established standard, principles and predominance as a chief constructor and thoroughly equipped you for the successful completion of your kingdom assignment. You, too, are a wise master builder in the mind of God. This is how God sees you!

Dr. Gordon E. Bradshaw says, "Christ, who is our creative "**Master Builder**," has a definite design and structure for His body. Being the "**Head**," He gives the Body of Christ the motivation and movements that are necessary for the development of the Kingdom of God in the earth." (*The Technology of Apostolic Succession*, 2010, p. 270)

The Greek word *architekton*, pronounced *ar-khee-tek-tone*, is translated as **master builder**. It is taken from *arche* which means chief in order, time, place or rank; and, *tekton*, an artificer; a chief constructor: Architect. **Wise** is the Greek word *sophia* taken from *sophos*, meaning clear spiritual wisdom (Strong's). I would submit to you that a **wise master builder** is a spiritually mature saint who has discovered his kingdom assignment through intimate relationship and trust in Holy Spirit to empower him to endure the process of development – transformation [over time] to the image of Christ. He is a kingdom-level leader filled with the spirit of wisdom and revelation in the knowledge of Christ. He is God's workmanship – a spiritual architect who knows how to build upon the foundation of Jesus Christ with superior materials – who God has commissioned to complete his divine assignment in the earth by advancing the kingdom of God and bringing glory to His Name.

You are a spiritual architect whom God has placed in the earth to build His kingdom. *"According to the grace of God which was given to me, as a wise master builder I have laid the foundation, and another builds on it. But let each one take heed how he builds on it. For no other foundation can anyone lay than that which is laid, which is Jesus Christ"* (1 Cor. 3:10-11). God has equipped you with His nature, power and glory to build upon the foundation of His dear Son. Take heed how you build. Jesus was not a weak, immature saint. He was strong, mature and learned obedience through the things that He suffered. *"And **having been perfected,** He became the author of eternal salvation to all who obey Him"* (Heb. 5:8-9, author's emphasis).

You too, must be perfected or fitted for completion of your kingdom assignment through things that will definitely require suffering for Christ's sake. But, in the process, you are transformed to become the author of your kingdom purpose. Being perfected for your kingdom assignment requires a process of being built into a spiritually mature, kingdom-level leader, commissioned to carry out your assignment and build other faithful men and women along the way. Your sincere desire should reflect your loyalty, devotion and faithful commitment to your Wise Master Builder, Jesus Christ. But, be assured, baby Christians can never become wise master builders!

CHAPTER FIVE

TRANSFORMATION OF THE MIND FOR KINGDOM USE

""So here's what I want you to do, God helping you: Take your everyday, ordinary life – your sleeping, eating, going-to-work, and walking around life – and place it before God as an offering. Embracing what God does for you is the best thing you can do for him. **Don't become so well-adjusted to your culture that you fit into it without even thinking. Instead, fix your attention on God. You'll be changed from the inside out,** *Readily recognize what he wants from you, and quickly respond to it.* **Unlike the culture around you, always dragging you down to its level of immaturity, God brings the best out of you, develops well-formed maturity in you."**
(ROM. 12:1-2, MSG, AUTHOR'S EMPHASIS)

Keenness is a component of God's nature. God wants you to be spiritually sharp at all times. He wants you to be able to discern between good and evil, knowing that your spiritual senses have been exercised or trained through **use** – the act or practice of employing something: APPLICATION; habitual or customary usage;

to carry out a purpose or action by means of (Merriam-Webster). God wants to share with you His secrets and mysteries that have been hidden for you from before the foundation of the world, which will show others His glory operating in your life (see 1 Cor. 2:7). The author of the epistle to the Hebrews says that some of these mysteries may be *"hard to be uttered"* to the spiritually immature because they are *"dull of hearing"* (Heb. 5:11).

I'll say it again: Baby Christians can never become wise master builders! As His child, God desires you to be wise in building upon the foundation laid by His Son, Jesus. And in doing so, you are a co-laborer together with Him. God has the blueprint, and He only gives it to His sons. You only become a son as you are led by Holy Spirit (see Rom. 8:14). We can see this clearly in the life of David, as he exhorts his son Solomon to build the Temple. David gave Solomon the pattern by which the Temple was to be constructed. *"Then David gave to Solomon his son the pattern...the pattern of all that he had by the Spirit"* (1 Chron. 28:11, 12; KJV). David also gave Solomon the materials needed to complete the construction of the Temple.

In the same way, God gave Jesus, His Son, the pattern or blueprint of the Kingdom of Heaven by the Holy Spirit. Jesus has given this kingdom pattern to those who believe on Him, having laid the foundation for us through His Word. As we become spiritually mature sons, we, too, are supplied with the superior materials required to build the kingdom of God in the earth. TAKE HEED HOW YOU BUILD!

"If anyone builds on the foundation with gold, silver, costly stones, wood, hay, or straw, each one's work will become obvious, for the day will disclose it, because it will be revealed by fire; the fire will test the quality of each one's work. If anyone's work that he has built survives, he will receive a reward. If anyone's work is burned up, it will be lost, but he will be saved; yet it will be like an escape through fire. Don't you know that you are God's sanctuary and that the Spirit of God lives in you? If anyone ruins God's sanctuary, God will ruin him; for God's sanctuary is holy, and that is what you are." (1 Cor. 3:12-17, Passion)

The Spirit of God lives in you. You are a co-laborer with God. You work with God, and God works through you. You can never perform any work to advance God's kingdom apart from God. You are God's instrument, His vessel. You are His mouthpiece in the earth, but the words belong to Him. You make the decree for healing, but the power to perform is God's. You do the natural; He does the supernatural. You teach and preach the gospel of the kingdom, and God confirms it with signs. As God works through you, you receive His grace to perform. *"We then, as workers together with Him, also plead with you not to receive the grace of God in vain"* (1 Cor. 6:1).

Your heavenly Father wants you to work smarter, not harder. *"Remember: The duller the ax the harder the work; Use your head: The more brains, the less muscle"* (Eccl. 10:10, MSG). The King James Version of the Bible states it like this: *"If the iron be blunt, and he do not whet the edge, then must he put to more strength: but wisdom is profitable to direct."* A blunt iron or ax, in this context, can be symbolic of one's dullness of hearing revelation knowledge of the Word for lack of use.

Let's revisit the phrase "dull of hearing." When you are dull of hearing, you have not yet ascended to the spiritual height that God intends for you. Spiritual maturity is a reflection of time spent in the Word; the empowerment of Holy Spirit; the trials, tests and sacrifices made during the process of development; and the mentorship of a spiritual father or mother to guide you through the transformation of your mind for kingdom use. God cannot give you the kingdom pattern and resources for proper construction of and completion of your kingdom assignment if you are dull of hearing, which means you are spiritually dull – a baby Christian who needs milk and whose mind is yet carnal.

"For to be carnally minded is death, but to be spiritually minded is life and peace. Because the carnal mind is enmity against God; for it is not subject to the law of God, nor indeed can it be. So then, those who are in the flesh cannot please God" (Rom. 8:6-8). Did you get that? The carnal mind does not subject itself to God's will, but chooses to follow the natural process through sense knowledge. Therefore, it opposes God and can never please Him.

Working with a blunt iron is dangerous. The blunt iron is symbolic of anyone who is a believer and has not allowed himself to grow spiritually, within an allotted time period, into a mature believer who discovers his kingdom purpose and is processed, developed and transformed for deployment. The Hebrew word for **blunt** is *qahah (kaw.haw)*. It is a primary word meaning to be dull, be set on edge; be blunt (Strong's O. T.). The Greek word for **dull** is *nothros (nothros)*. It means to be sluggish, lazy, slothful and stupid. It is a derivative of the word *nothos*, meaning illegitimate – bastard (Strong's N. T.). *"But for right now, friends, I'm completely frustrated by your unspiritual dealings with each other and with God. **You're acting like infants in relation to Christ, capable of nothing much more than nursing at the breast.** Well, then, I'll nurse **you since you don't seem capable of anything more.** As long as you grab for what makes you feel good or makes you look important, are you really much different than a babe at the breast, content only when everything's going your way?"* (1 Cor. 3:1-3, MSG, author's emphasis)

Spiritually-mature believers are skilled craftsmen in how to use the Word – better yet, how to wield the sword of the Spirit. Using the Word of God requires skill, because the sword of the Spirit is not only the logos Word, but also a Holy Spirit rhema word. Your mouth has to become a sharp two-edged sword that releases the living Word which carries the power to pierce, divide, and discern. When you properly understand your kingdom purpose as a spiritually mature believer who has obtained his commission as a kingdom leader, you can use the sword to execute the mission. *"For the word of God is quick, and powerful, and sharper than any two-edged sword piercing even to the dividing asunder of soul and spirit, and of the joints and marrow, and is a discerner of the thoughts and intents of the heart"* (Heb. 4:12, KJV). The thoughts and intents of the heart must flow from a mind that has been renewed – transformed and converted.

On the day of Pentecost, suddenly there came a sound from heaven like the sound of a rushing mighty wind. He made His entrance into the upper room where the disciples were assembled. He occupied the whole building, like a wildfire spreading through the ranks of the disciples, filling each one and prompting all of them to speak in other languages. Soon afterward, confusion arose relative to the different languages being spoken, for those devout Jews who were living in Jerusalem from every nation on earth heard their own native tongues being spoken by Galileans expressing the wonderful works of God. Apostle Peter took this opportunity to explain that what these men were witnessing was what the prophet Joel said, 800 years prior to this event, would happen. God was pouring out His Spirit upon all flesh to renew, transform and convert the minds of the people from law to grace.

Peter had been discipled by Jesus for three and a half years. Now he was filled with the Holy Spirit and began to teach the Word of God with boldness and spiritual authority, leading others into the kingdom. Peter became a spiritual mentor who could teach and train others and lead them into their kingdom assignment.

"Then Peter said to them, "Repent, and let every one of you be baptized in the name of Jesus Christ for the remission of sins; and you shall receive the gift of the Holy Spirit. For the promise is to you and to your children, and to all who are afar off, as many as the Lord our God will call." (Acts 2:38-39)

"And with many other words did he testify and exhort, saying, Save yourselves from this untoward generation. Then they that gladly received his word were baptized: and the same day there were added unto them about three thousand souls." (Acts 2:40-41, KJV)

In the process of leading 3000 people to Christ, Peter issued a stark warning to the multitude he was preaching to: *"Save yourselves from this untoward generation."* The word **untoward** means difficult to guide, manage, or work with: Unruly, adverse, and improper (Merriam-Webster). It is the Greek word *skolios*, which means morally crooked, perverse, and forward as these relate to a particular generation (Vines Expository).

In order to have your mind transformed for kingdom use, you will have to make a conscious decision for or against spiritual maturity. God offered salvation through Jesus Christ, but you had to believe in your heart and confess with your mouth that Jesus is the resurrected Son of God who died for the sins of the entire world, past, present and future. In the same way, and with the same faith, you have to make a conscious decision to become a disciple of Jesus Christ. Contrary to what some people believe, you can be saved and never become a disciple of Christ.

> *"If anyone comes to me and does not hate his father and mother, wife and children, brothers and sisters, yes, and his own life also, he cannot be My disciple. And whoever does not bear his cross and come after Me cannot be My disciple. So likewise, whoever of you does not forsake all that he has cannot be My disciple."* (Luke 14:26-27, 33)

The Greek word for **disciple** is ***Mathetes (math-ay-tes)***, meaning a learner, a pupil; to disciple, instruct, teach; enroll as scholar (Strong's). This indicates thought accompanied by endeavor to imitate the teacher (Vine's). Jesus told those Jews who believed on Him that if they would continue in His word, then they would be His disciples indeed (see John 8:31).

There is a sad dilemma being played out by the modern Church in that it has not generationally trained disciples who can witness, reflect, and imitate their teachers and grow into the place of discovery of their kingdom assignment. Over the years, the Church became complacent, barricaded itself within its four-walled structures, and for the most part stopped training and guiding members of the Body through the process that develops and transforms ordinary humans into disciples – stewards who are spiritually mature and are able to disciple others.

The Church has lacked spiritual fathers, who demand discipline from their sons and daughters. As a spiritual father, Apostle Paul had to place righteous demands on his sons and daughters. He said: *"I do not write these things to shame you, but as my beloved children I warn you. For though you might have ten thousand instructors in Christ, yet you do not have many fathers: for in Christ Jesus I have begotten you through the gospel. Therefore I urge you, **imitate me**"* (1 Cor.

4:14-16, author's emphasis). **There must be a return of apostolic fathering and mothering if the church is to maintain a generational succession of disciples commissioned for kingdom-level leadership.**

Let's take some time to discuss the process of discipleship transformation and what is required to commit to its development. Spiritual parents (fathers and mothers) play a vital role in the success of transforming a saint into a disciple. Remember, **transformation** is a sequence of advancements that changes the outward form or appearance of; to change in character, nature or condition: convert. Spiritual conversion takes place from the inside-out. So then, **discipleship transformation** is the process of changing the nature and character of a believer through a sequence of advancements through which the believer is converted through the instruction and mentoring of a spiritual parent into a pupil, a learner who endeavors to imitate his teacher. The truth of his discipleship is that he has committed to give up his life to follow Christ, bear his own cross, forsake all that he has, and continue in the Word of God.

As you can clearly see, God is very deliberate, intricate, and meticulous about building through discipleship, so that you will be strong, durable, and sustainable – fully equipped to carry out and complete your kingdom assignment as a commissioned, kingdom-level leader who understands God's process of developing spiritual maturity through transformation, which is the renewal of the mind for kingdom use.

Oswald Sanders said, "True disciples are not manufactured wholesale. They are produced one by one because someone has taken the pains to discipline; to instruct and enlighten; to nurture and train one that is younger." This, I believe, is the job of the apostolic parent.

Dr. Gordon E. Bradshaw, a chief apostle and spiritual father, puts it this way: "In the past, many leaders have only been "**instructors**" in Christ rather than "**fathers**." This is easy to do, considering that little relational contact is necessary to fulfill that responsibility. In fact, the word "**Instructors**" is taken from the Greek term "**Paidagogos,**" meaning: **A boy leader or one who takes children to school.** If being an instructor is restricted to dealing with "**boys**" or children, this would imply that only a rudimentary or basic curriculum is being taught. It also implies that the "**instructor**" only has a limited contact with the students for as long as the "**instructional period**" requires.

Like natural schools, after the instructional period is over, the school sends the children back home to their "*parents*" who have a "*full time*" job of raising the children. Spiritual "*fathers*" and "*mothers*" need more than just a "school day" experience with spiritual sons and daughters. They must provide the type of consistent spiritual parenting that ensures proper growth and development. Now leaders must become full-fledged parents in Christ – a position which requires a completely different technology than that of being an "*instructor.*"" (*The Technology of Apostolic Succession*, 2010, pp. 67-68)

Too many leaders, who should have become spiritual parents leading sons and daughters into discipleship, have viewed the above mandate as overbearing, too difficult, or beyond what they were willing to do. Spiritual mentoring that leads to discipleship requires a spiritually mature parent who is willing to give himself wholeheartedly to the process of transforming the pupil's mind for kingdom use.

What if Jesus had not humbled Himself and become a disciple, a learner of His Father? *"Though He was a Son, yet **He learned** obedience by the things which He suffered" (Heb. 5:8, author's emphasis).* *"Who, being in the form of God, did not consider it robbery to be equal with God, but made Himself of no reputation, taking the form of a bondservant, and coming in the likeness of men. And being found in appearance as a man, **He humbled Himself and became obedient to the point of death**, even the death of the cross"* (Phil. 2:6-8, author's emphasis).

Jesus remained steadfast in the will of His Father. He showed genuine commitment as He endured the process that led Him to be crucified. Even Jesus' mind was transformed for kingdom use – the transformation that was to take place at Calvary where Jesus was made sin for us, so that we might be made the righteousness of God through Him (see 2 Cor. 5:21). That was His kingdom assignment, and He was prepared to fulfill it. But, fulfillment didn't come without a challenge. During the process of discipleship, as your mind is being transformed for kingdom use, there will be many opportunities to give up. However, there can be no fulfillment of purpose where there is no commitment. And where there is no commitment, there will be no transformation. Jesus shows us what commitment to the Father's will, His kingdom assignment, looks like.

"My soul is exceedingly sorrowful, even to death...O My Father, if it is possible, let this cup pass from Me; nevertheless, not as I will, but as You will...O My Father, if this cup cannot pass away from Me unless I drink it, Your will be done." (Matt. 26:38, 39, 42)

"Then I said, 'Behold, I have come – in the volume of the book it is written of Me – To do Your will, O God.'" (Heb. 10:7)

"Jesus said to them, "My food is to do the will of Him who sent Me, and to finish His work." (John 4:34)

Jesus endured the process that led Him to the Cross, even as He discipled 12 men. He endured Gethsemane, the betrayal of Judas Iscariot, His arrest and arraignment, Peter's denial, judgment before Pontius Pilate, being stripped naked, a crown of thorns thrust onto his head, spat on by Roman soldiers, slapped, mocked, beaten with a whip of thorns that literally tore and pulled His flesh apart, nails that weighed two pounds each driven into His hands and feet, and nailed on a cross between two criminals.

Yet, Jesus, in His great love and humility, had the presence of mind to save one of the criminals who repented, forgive those who crucified Him, and commit the care of His mother to Apostle John. What a transformation! Jesus' passion empowered Him to endure the shame – to look beyond it – and see the glory of a Father who was well-pleased. That is what true commitment to a kingdom assignment looks like!

Some might say, "That was Jesus. There's no way a 'normal' man could ever go through what He went through." To that, I'd say, let's take a look at some of the qualities of Apostle Paul that made him a true disciple of Jesus Christ and a successful spiritual father and mentor.

"But what things were gain to me, those I counted loss for Christ." (Phil. 3:7)

"For to me to live is Christ, and to die is gain." (Phil. 1:21)

"I bear in my body the marks of the Lord Jesus." (Gal. 6:17)

"I am crucified with Christ." (Gal. 2:20)

"Are they ministers of Christ? ...I am more; in labours more abundant, in stripes above measure, in prisons more frequent, in deaths oft." (2 Cor. 11:23)

"We are fools for Christ's sake." (1 Cor. 4:10)

"For I am ready not to be bound only, but also to die at Jerusalem for the name of Christ." (Acts 21:13)

"But I trust in the LORD Jesus to send Timotheus shortly unto you, that I also may be of good comfort, when I know your state. For I have no man likeminded, who will naturally care for your state. For all seek their own, not the things which are Jesus Christ's. But ye know the proof of him, that, as a son with the father, he hath served with me in the gospel." (Phil. 2:19-22, author's emphasis)

"For this cause have I sent unto you Timotheus, who is my beloved son, and faithful in the LORD, who shall bring you into remembrance of my ways which be in Christ." (1 Cor. 4:17, author's emphasis)
(All scriptures quoted from King James Version of the Bible)

As you can see, Paul modeled Jesus' life as a disciple and spiritual father. And, if you model Paul's life, I'd say you will do well. However, Jesus' life is the permanent model of discipleship and spiritual maturity. His life on earth was an example of what transformation of the mind for kingdom use looks like and the commitment that powers it. Spiritual maturity does not form in a vacuum. It grows over time through your personal relationship with God, and allowing Holy Spirit to empower you. It requires a personal commitment formed out of a foundation of love, humility, faithfulness, obedience and patience. It forms as you willfully confront and overcome every challenge, difficulty, struggle, hardship, and pain.

Jesus' life on earth exemplifies this process, and you are encouraged to follow Jesus' model of discipleship and spiritual maturity, which will lead you also to the place where your mind will be transformed for kingdom use. "***Keep your eyes on Jesus, who both began and finished this race we're in. Study how he did it***. *Because he never lost sight of where he was headed – that exhilarating finish line in and with God – he could put up with anything along the way: Cross, shame, whatever. And now he's there, in the place of honor, right alongside God. When you find yourselves flagging in your faith, go over that story again, item by item, that long litany of hostility he plowed through. That will shoot adrenaline into your souls*" (Heb. 12:2-3, MSG, author's emphasis).

Paul teaches that the "old man" has to be put off, and the "new man" has to be put on. That sounds a lot like changing clothes or changing appearance. He talks about renewing the mind, putting on the new man which was created in the mind of God and founded on His holiness. The old man is your flesh nature which had dominion over you until the moment you were born again. Paul testifies that the newborn believer should no longer live a lifestyle of sin like those who are unsaved, for they live in the futility of their mind and they are alienated from God. But, once you were taught the good news about Jesus Christ and believed, you got saved.

Paul basically says that you should have learned specific things about Christ as you were being taught the good news. The main thing you should have learned is that your former conduct, the old man which supports deceitful lusts of the flesh, must be brought under subjection of your regenerated spirit. And, the only way this happens successfully is to be renewed in the spirit of your mind. Delete the old mindset, which is ungodly, and replace it with the new mindset which was created in God's mind according to righteousness and holiness (see Eph. 4:17-24). *"And have* **put on the new man,** *who is being* **renewed in knowledge according to the image of his Creator***"* (Col. 3:10, Passion, author's emphasis).

At this point, it is imperative that you get a Holy Spirit revelation of what it means to put on the new man who is being renewed in knowledge according to the image of his Creator. Apostle Paul teaches that God's foreknowledge of you included your being predestined to be conformed to the image of His Son, Jesus (see Rom. 8:29). However, before you can be conformed to the image of Jesus, your mind must be renewed in knowledge according to God's knowledge. There are many saints who have a zeal for God, but not according to knowledge (see Rom. 10:2). Your mind is where you store knowledge. *"For this reason also, since the day we heard this, we haven't stopped praying for you. We are asking that you may be filled with the knowledge of his will in all wisdom and spiritual understanding, so that you may walk worthy of the Lord, fully pleasing [to Him], bearing fruit in every good work and growing in the knowledge of God"* (Col. 1:9-10, Passion, author's emphasis).

Being renewed in knowledge according to the image of your Creator requires that your mind is consistently filled with knowledge of His will, through His wisdom, which supplies you with spiritual understanding. Possessing spiritual understanding allows you to walk worthy of the Lord, fully pleasing Him. The result is that you will bear fruit in every good work, which will empower your continuous growth in the knowledge of God. *"For we are His creation – created in Christ Jesus for good works, which God prepared ahead of time so that we should walk in them"* (Eph. 2:10, Passion).

The word **knowledge**, as used in the context above, is the Greek word ***epignosis (ep-ig-no-sis)*** which comes from ***epignosko (ep-ig-in-oce-ko)***, which means to become fully acquainted with, to acknowledge, to perceive; recognition, full discernment (Strong's). But, what does it mean to be renewed in knowledge? According to Merriam-Webster, **renew** implies a restoration of what had become faded or disintegrated so that it seems like new. In our context, it applies in a spiritual sense. In other words, to make new spiritually: REGENERATE; to restore to original existence: REVIVE; to make extensive changes in, according to the blueprint: REBUILD; and, to do again as it was done in the mind of God: REPEAT.

From the Greek text, the word *anakainoo (an-ak-ahee-no-o)* is translated renewed. It means to renovate, renew, reform, and restore. The prefix *ana (an-ah)* means repetition, intensity, and reversal (Strong's). As a new person (new man) in Christ, your spiritual life will become stronger, being consistently regenerated, revived, and rebuilt by repeating the original intent of God for your life according to His knowledge. This happens when your mind is constantly renewed in knowledge as you have become fully acquainted with God's original intent for your life on earth. *"Therefore we do not lose heart. Even though our outward man is perishing, **yet the inward man is being renewed day by day**"* (2 Cor. 4:16, author's emphasis).

Man or woman of God, when your mind is consistently renewed in knowledge, you are being transformed from within. A powerful conversion takes place. The Greek word translated conversion is the word *epistrepho (ep-ee-stref-o)*. It means to revert, come (go) again, return. It is a combination of *epi (ep-ee)*, superimposition of time, place, order, etc, as a relation of distribution and *strepho (stref-o)*, to turn quite around or reverse; turn self about (Strong's). Conversion is a method God uses to strengthen you, not only for fulfillment of your kingdom assignment, but also to strengthen others for their destiny.

God's desire is to superimpose Himself on you for your specific time, place and order here on earth, so that you become a distributor of His knowledge. The devil hates knowledge. And, as he tried with Peter, he'll do his best to sift you of it. *"And the Lord said, 'Simon, Simon! Indeed, Satan has asked for you, that he may sift you as wheat. 'But I have prayed for you, that your faith should not fail; and when you are **returned to Me**, strengthen your brethren'"* (Luke 22:31-32, author's emphasis). The King James Version uses the word "converted" rather than "returned to Me."

One of the most profound revelations I've ever received came from Apostle Dr. Gordon E. Bradshaw in 1998. I was stunned when I heard it. The eyes of my mind were illumined. He said, **"The only anointing that is a lasting anointing is the anointing that activates the mind."** Believe me, that was an illumination point for me. Anointing refers to diversities of gifts given by Holy Spirit for the profit of all (see 1 Cor. 12:6-7). Your anointing should be perpetual in nature, so that you're not on fire for God in one season, lukewarm in another season, and cold as ice in yet another season. The lasting anointing or the anointing that continually renews your mind in knowledge changes your behavior and brings it into alignment with godly character.

In this place of spiritual maturity, you will have a godly influence on people, leading them to behavior modification and a lifestyle that is the result of true conversion through the renewing of their minds in the knowledge of God. You have the spiritual authority to strengthen and confirm other believers as true disciples. This is what transforming the mind for kingdom use looks like. **Transformation of the mind, in this context, deals with the saints' commitment to exchange their mindset of religiosity to one built on spiritual maturity for kingdom use.**

God desires that you renew your mind constantly with knowledge of His original plans and purposes for your life. A mind built for kingdom use carries the anointing of prevailing grace and governmental authority of Jesus Christ to change atmospheres and environments, and transform mindsets from unbelief and religion to the kingdom of God's government. It is the life of a mature believer who lives by his faith as he is empowered by Holy Spirit to carry out his kingdom purpose of transforming lives and building spiritually mature saints who understand their role within the church to reclaim the Seven Mountains of Culture for the Kingdom of God, bringing in the greatest harvest of souls ever, and paving the way for the conversion of earthly kingdoms to become the kingdoms of our Lord and His Christ (see Rev. 11:15). In this place, the saints are empowered for kingdom conversion. Their minds have been transformed for kingdom use.

"Now salvation, and strength, and the kingdom of our God, and the power of His Christ have come, for the accuser of our brethren...has been cast down. And they overcame him by the blood of the Lamb and

the words of their testimony. For the devil has come down to you, having great wrath, because he knows that he has a short time." (Rev. 12:10-12)

"And the God of peace will crush Satan under your feet shortly. The grace of our Lord Jesus Christ be with you. Amen." (Rom. 16:20)

CHAPTER SIX

ACCEPTING YOUR KINGDOM ASSIGNMENT

"Therefore, brethren, be even more diligent to make your call and election sure, for if you do these things you will never stumble; for so an entrance will be supplied to you abundantly into the everlasting kingdom of our Lord and Savior Jesus Christ."
(2 PET. 1:10-11)

In Chapter Four I shared my story of how God brought me back to the place of recognition, where I came to the end of myself, in my backslidden state of being separated from God for over 15 years. I had to become broken before Him and repent so that I would be restored in relationship with Him. What I didn't know is that I had been running from God's purpose for my life which was conceived in His mind before He created the world. God's purpose for your life is etched in eternity. You just have to discover it or, as my case was, rediscover it.

From a child I have always been drawn to helping people. And there was a certain level of leadership that I possessed and displayed, mostly among my sisters and younger brother and also in church. I was the leader of a group I formed comprised of three of my sisters and my younger brother. Our mission was one of adventure. The purpose of our group was to explore and capture insects, especially bees, various species of ants, grasshoppers, dragon flies, and butterflies. We were amazed by the social complexity of insects. Our bid to capture them usually involved risks and unknown dangers. I was once stung all over my body from a swarm of bees. But, even that couldn't deter me. I was the fearless leader of the Beekay group. We were beekeepers in our own right.

In church, after Sunday school, I was the one who wanted to represent my class and give a summary of what was taught and what I had learned. By the time I was 12, I was teaching the Card Class in Sunday school, likely named for the illustrated cards we taught from. I loved to learn and I loved to teach. When I went to college, this love led me to major in education. After I graduated, my first job was working with high school students who were above average in their academics but came from low-income homes where no one had ever gone to college, making it unlikely that they would ever go as well. My job was to assist them with making application to college, acquiring financial aid, and preparing them for academic success by building their self-concept, self-esteem and confidence so that once they were in college, they would have a better than average chance to succeed.

The following is an essay written by a college freshman in his English Composition class, whom I worked with while he was in high school. The topic is: "The Person Who Has Influenced My Life the Most and Why."

"Mr. James Brewton who is very young but prosperous in his career, is a trustworthy man who excels in his job. Not only has he laid down for me several facts about life and what is expected in it, but he is also a true friend indeed. In fact, James is ambitious, sociable, and helpful to himself and to me.

"Although it takes time, Mr. Brewton is striving to make his life useful. Not only does he have degrees from college, but also he is shooting for higher education. James holds a nice counseling job and is involved with the Upward Bound program as well. Furthermore, he is becoming a prominent figure at Florida A&M University.

"Mr. Brewton can be very friendly and sociable as well as being serious in the classroom and during counseling when necessary. Moreover, he tries to be kind and he associates with just about everyone at any place. He does not feel that he is better than any other person and he proves this by attending dances and other activities wherever students attend.

"While doing the things that he has to do, Mr. Brewton takes time out to help me with any problem that occurs. Because he is older and has been through the things that I'm going through, he always lets me know what to expect. Since he is not much older than I am, and we are both males, he relates personal aspects of life to me and we can talk and get along fine.

"In short, Mr. James Brewton is just like a brother to me, and I enjoy being around him and talking with him. He makes me look at the finer things in life and lets me know that I have to strive and work for them. Whenever I need help or get in trouble with any matter, I know that he will be there for me to turn to."

You may be asking yourself this question. "If his life was so prosperous, how did he ever manage to screw it up?" Well, life has a way of manifesting what we consistently think and say, eventually attracting them into our lives. *"For as he thinks in his heart, so is he"* (Prov. 23:7). After I left the Holiness church, I'd said, "I can't wait to get away to college then I'll make my own damn decisions and see what Satan has to offer." Those thoughts and words were consistently played out in my mind and spoken out of my mouth, which means they proceeded from my heart. And believe me, Satan took every opportunity to oblige me by making available what he had to offer.

Fast forward 15 years. After I was restored in relationship with God in 1992, I couldn't seem to find my way. I couldn't find a job, and I really missed life on campus. But, I had begun reading and studying Scripture and felt that I was called to preach, something my mother had told me time and time again – before I left home for college, while I was attending college, and after I graduated from college. Of course, I wasn't hearing any of that then. But now, there I was with a Bible in my hand telling her I felt like I should be ordained for ministry. I had been speaking regularly at the church where my father was pastor and people seemed to be impressed and attentive whenever I spoke. So, in July of 1992, I was ordained as a Minister.

I still could not find a job. I had applied to every college and some high schools within a 60-mile radius. Not one of them hired me. I began to question God as to why I couldn't find a job. On top of that, I was bored all the time. I had gotten used to a much faster pace of life filled with people who were more sophisticated than those of this little town where I had grown up. Add to that the fact that I was living with my parents at age 32 with no social life at all. And in November of that year, I packed my bags and moved back to Tallahassee, Fla.

I had gotten a letter from a young lady I had been dating prior to leaving Tallahassee for home eight months earlier in March. She informed me that the position I'd held as a radio voice for the university's basketball program for the past six seasons was never filled. So, I got on the phone and called my one time partner, who was the Sports Information Director, and found out that I could return to the job. That is what propelled me to go back, against the advice and counsel of my parents. But, I assured them and my brother in law, who was also a minister and a prophet that I was spiritually mature enough to handle returning to Florida. After all, I was restored; and the things that I once did, I didn't do anymore.

My return to Tallahassee lasted only five months. By the end of the basketball season, I was once again down and out in Tallahassee. First of all, I had made plans to live with my friend Dan. We had been roommates off and on for several years. But, we both liked to party. It wasn't long before we were in the club or hanging out drinking. I allowed the devil to trick me like he usually does to spiritually immature believers.

"You are at the club drinking alcohol. You already have backslidden. You might as well go all the way now."

I took the bait. At the time, I did not have a revelation of grace. I didn't know that I could confess my sin according to 1 John 1:9, repent and move forward. Rather, I was eaten up with guilt, feeling low and unworthy to be called a minister of the gospel. The devil used that guilt to open the door once again to my addiction to cocaine.

I went to one of my friend's apartment who sold cocaine and he was happy to see me again. He was unusually gracious in giving me extra beyond the amount that I paid for. That night, I got a motel room and snorted cocaine all night. When I had finished, I lay across the bed crying and feeling all the guilt the devil could muster. And suddenly, deep in my spirit I heard the Holy Spirit say, **"I'm still with you."**

The next day, back at Dan's apartment, I began to read my Bible and pray. This I did for several days and had not drank or snorted cocaine. Then, I got the news from Dan. He was being evicted from his apartment. He would be moving in with one of his friends at the end of the week. I was shocked. I had nowhere to go, nor the monetary means to sustain myself. I had signed a five-month contract with the university and had not gotten my first stipend. I had to honor the contract at all costs.

I called my one time girlfriend who had written me, informing me of the job opening. She was excited and readily offered me the downstairs bedroom in the two-story flat she lived in on her parent's property. I had informed her that I was a minister prior to my return to Florida, so I reiterated that fact to her. I also told her that as soon as I received my stipend, I would pay for the room. It was supposed to be a landlord/tenant agreement. It lasted less than a week! She was in my room every night, dressed as the seductress she intended to be as soon as I moved in.

And there I was – Mr. Spiritually Mature, who could handle the things that once ruined my relationship with the Lord. I found out quickly that God hadn't given Solomon wisdom just to pass the time of day. It was very prevalent in my situation. *"For by means of a harlot A man is reduced to a crust of bread; And an adulteress will prey upon his precious life. Can a man take fire to his bosom, And his clothes not be burned…Whoever commits adultery with a woman lacks understanding; He who does so destroys his own soul"* (Prov. 6:25, 27, 32). Verse 32 from The

Message says, *"Adultery is a brainless act, soul-destroying, self-destructive."*

I had gotten myself in yet another bind. And within two weeks, I had moved upstairs with her. And, that's when my real troubles began. I was completely dependent upon this woman, and she took every opportunity to exploit that fact. I could not function without her. I drove her car, stayed in her house, and ate her food. This was completely nerve-racking for me, but I endured it because I'd signed a five-month contract and my pride wouldn't let me return to my parent's home.

This woman was so conniving that she successfully maneuvered a self-imposed engagement on Christmas morning by announcing to her family that she and I were going to be married. Much to my delight, I was out of town on road trips with the basketball team for several days at a time. Even being away from this woman didn't ease the pain I was experiencing due to the guilt and condemnation of having backslidden again. The devil had me thinking that I could not break the current state of sin that I lived in and be restored to God. I felt like I was on a slippery slope to hell.

My contract with the university was about to end in early March, 1993. And, for an entire week prior to its end, this woman plotted one scheme after another, even pretending to be pregnant. She used this false pregnancy to convince me to marry her. And, it almost worked, until we got rear-ended one evening after I picked her up from work. At the hospital, I informed the emergency room physician that she was pregnant. When the test came back negative, I knew that I had no choice but to leave her as soon as possible. However, getting away would not be as easy as it sounded; I had nowhere to go.

I had been jobless since basketball season ended. And, I had not mustered the courage to move back to Georgia. So, I started looking for a job. That meant taking the 30-minute ride into Tallahassee with this woman and staying there all day until she got off from work at five. Part of the day I spent researching and applying for jobs at the unemployment office. The other part of the day was spent at my friend's apartment snorting cocaine. I was sliding further and further down the slippery slope, and I couldn't stop. I had come to the end of my strength. I cried out, "Lord, save me!"

Suddenly, I heard these words in my spirit, **"Put God first in your life and**

everything else will fall into place." I had heard my mother say that often. It was her paraphrase of Matt. 6:33. Then, I heard my mother say something that she'd said to me after I'd moved back home the first time.

"It's during the valley experiences of your life that you grow into the kind of person God wants you to be. It's your steadfastness in faith and prayer to God when you're at your lowest point that pleases Him and releases His mercy."

Once again, I was back at my parent's home, but I didn't stay. My father and mother felt that my return would be an embarrassment to them and offensive to their ministry family. I understood. They had heaped high praises upon my head and ordained me as a minister of the gospel. My sister, Stephanie, had agreed to take me into her home in Augusta, Ga.

My battle with cocaine continued for eight more months. I was receiving an unemployment check every two weeks from Florida, and every dime of it went towards my addiction. Once I depleted my unemployment money, in early November, I was in dire straits. I was thinking of committing a crime to get money. Then, one day my older sister Veronica, who also lived in Augusta at that time, began inviting me to church. One night we drove to a little church in Sylvania, Ga. called Refuge: Church of God in Christ. The prophet who was ministering there prophesied over my life and decreed that I would be restored and be elevated in ministry. He told me to memorize Psalm 91 and recite it over and over until it was in my spirit, telling me that God was going to break addiction off of my life.

I did exactly as he told me. I memorized the entire Psalm, and I'd recite it often – even while I was getting high on cocaine. By the end of December, I was praying sincerely to God for deliverance. And, I vowed that if God would deliver me, I'd serve Him with all my heart. I told God that I didn't want to pretend or be a charlatan. I wanted be the person that He'd ordained me to be and fulfill His purpose for my life.

I had heard Veronica say that her church family was going on a three-day fast beginning January 1, 1994. It seemed as if I could sense in my spirit that God was telling me to go on this fast, too and, I would receive my breakthrough. So, I made up my mind that I was going to fast and receive my deliverance. I had never fasted for three days before, and the devil kept telling me that I'd mess that up, too. But, I ignored his bullying tactics. I was determined to complete the fast.

The grace of God was upon me and I didn't even get hungry for the entire fast. As I prayed and read from the Bible, I sensed that I was being refreshed. At the end of the fast, I knew without a doubt that I had been completely delivered from cocaine. And, I've never had a taste for it to this day.

This was a new beginning for me, and I began reading and memorizing large portions of Scripture. During that time, Holy Spirit began teaching me from the book of Romans. It was as if the words on the pages leaped off and into my spirit. For the first time since I'd gotten saved in 1972, I was receiving a revelation of faith and grace. As I read and reread Romans, I heard the Lord say, **"I want you to teach My people faith."** Each day, I would read from morning until evening. Before going to bed, I would memorize at least one new verse, sometimes more.

All of a sudden, resources began pouring in pertaining to faith and grace from men of God such as Fred Price, Charles Stanley, John Osteen, Kenneth Hagin, and Norman Vincent Peale. I was being flooded with their materials. And, I submerged myself in them all day, every day. By June of that year, I was ready for the pulpit again. I conducted a five-night youth revival in my home town, Claxton. And, I hosted Vacation Bible School at the largest Baptist church there. I taught at several local churches, crossing several denominations. One thing stood out very clear. The people who attended these churches were not accustomed to being taught. And, soon the demand for my ministry waned.

I soon learned that some pastors were reluctant to invite me to speak at their church because I taught on grace, faith, and sanctification as a life-long process of Holy Spirit empowerment and not by religious laws and legalism. As you can well imagine, I was not liked very much. That religious mindset was one of control, self-righteousness, poverty mentality and unbelief. Pastors were very defensive and did not want their congregation of believers to get a revelation of grace, since this meant that possibly they could no longer control them and use them to advance their own lifestyles and agendas. Saints who get trapped in this scenario can't even make basic decisions on their own without getting permission from their pastor.

I hate religion! In its basic form, it is simply tradition without obedience. Jesus constantly condemned this spirit during His earthly ministry. He knew that the tradition of the Elders was no more than man-made laws handed down by the rabbis, to ensure that the people kept the law. Jesus showed that their tradition actually opened the door for them to disobey God. However, these church leaders were less concerned about disobeying God and more concerned about ensuring that the people obeyed the tradition of the Elders. They asked Jesus, *"Why do Your disciples transgress the tradition of the elders? ...He answered and said to them, "Why do you also transgress the commandment of God because of your tradition?* **For God commanded, saying...But you say... Thus you have made the commandment of God of no effect by your tradition. Hypocrites! ...** *"* (Matt. 15:2, 3, 4, 6, author's emphasis)

After my move back to Claxton from Augusta, I moved in with my sister Twila and her husband, Scott, who was a prophet. They had just established an independent ministry and his prophetic ministry was in demand. I still hadn't found a job, so I was available to travel with them as his armor-bearer. This allowed me access to what goes on behind the scene in the pastor's office. It also allowed me to meet and connect with prominent pastors within the region. I was privy to private conversations and private actions, some good and some bad. I quickly found out that many of these pastors were not living by their faith, as much as they were preaching faith messages to the people. This stirred something in me. It was just as hypocritical as the Pharisees who held the people accountable to keep the law that they themselves could not keep.

By the end of 1994, I had not found a job, and I was beginning to get restless again. I had applied to every institution of higher education for some position that I qualified for, but to no avail. Then, one night after a church service, my mother called me to her and said that God was giving me a new beginning. She told me to humble myself before God and trust Him to raise me up.

"What God has planned for you, son, will require a genuine commitment on your part and complete trust in Him," she said.

Then, she told me that I should move to Statesboro with yet another sister, Cynthia, and take the first job offered to me. She said that God was preparing a wife for me who would be able to stand with me as I was being prepared for the level of ministry God had ordained for my life. Well, that didn't sound like God to me. First of all, take any job? I couldn't fathom that. I'd worked hard for my bachelors and master's degrees. I couldn't possibly condescend myself to that level. My dignity would be shattered. On top of that, I didn't want to be married, especially to some unsophisticated, plain Jane, holier than thou woman steeped in religion. These were a dime a dozen. But, God reminded me what He had brought me out of, and gave me a glimpse of the glory that was in my future. This got my attention and I asked, "What do I have to do?"

He said, **"If you humble yourself before Me, I'll raise you up far beyond what you ever could have accomplished through natural means."**

In January of 1995, I moved to Statesboro and began looking for common employment. To my surprise, I couldn't even land a job on that level. I mean, how hard could it be to make sandwiches and subs? After a week of job hunting with no success, I stopped at a convenience store for a snack. On the door was a sign that read: "Now Hiring." So, I applied. It so happened that the district manager was there, and he interviewed me on the spot. I got the job.

"I like to hire preachers," he said.

I started out as a clerk. And, it didn't take long for the manager to notice that my work ethic was beyond that job level. I was soon moved to another store within that chain that stayed open 24 hours and placed on the night shift. I did not want to work at night, but I knew it would afford me 40 hours a week. And, I needed a steady paycheck, such as it was. So, each night I went to work prepared to work hard and study hard. There was very little customer flow between 1:00 a.m. and 6:00 a.m. I used the first three hours to empty the trash, stock the beverage coolers, clean the restrooms, mop the floor, and make sure that the products on the shelves were orderly and in their proper place. After that, I would go outside and wash down the windows and wipe them down with a squeegee. Next, I would use the industrial push broom to sweep the parking lot clean of the day's debris. Finally, I would wipe down the gas pumps and refill the towel dispenser and window cleanser containers. All of this work was accomplished while talking to the Lord and praying in the Spirit.

The next two hours were spent reading, studying, meditating and memorizing the Word of God. Oh, how I grew in revelation knowledge of the Word. My environment was clean and quiet. My mind was clear, and I could hear the Holy Spirit talk to me as He opened my understanding to the Scriptures. My mind was being renewed in knowledge according to the image of my Creator. I would leave work at 7:00 a.m. and drive 30 miles to Sylvania where I was the assistant coordinator of a six-week summer camp for children – from kindergarten to high school – from 8:00 a.m. until 12:30 p.m. This was held at St. Andrews Methodist Church. God would always refresh me and I would have loads of energy as I interacted with the children. I led the morning devotions, taught the high school kids Bible stories, literature from the Harlem Renaissance Period, and read to them biographies of famous people. I played with the participants at break time, and assisted the staff with preparing their lunch. I was on a pathway to discovery. I would soon discover the kingdom assignment my Father had already written in my heart before He created the world.

After a few months working the night shift, I was promoted to assistant manager. In this capacity I took on more administrative duties and one of my jobs was to place the weekly order for the products sold in the store. A few months later, I was promoted to manager. My store had a problem with thefts and hadn't received an employee bonus for years. Within two months of managing that store, I earned that bonus for me and my employees. I had turned that store around and it was making such great profits that the owner of the franchise drove from Savannah to meet me. The district manager had plans to move me to the highest grossing store in the area. But, God intervened first.

My mother had made it her mission to see to it that the woman that God had prepared to be my wife would actually become my wife. I believe that she, along with all of the praying women in our church family, held consistent prayer vigils to that effect. And by September, I was engaged. Margie and I were married on April 27, 1996.

In December, as I was working in my store, a man walked up to the counter with a beer in his hand. I knew that he was the guy who, along with his wife, owned and operated the antique furniture refinishing business across the street adjacent to the store. His wife was a regular. I could tell that she was not much older than me, maybe in her early forties. He, on the other hand, was slightly older, early to mid fifties, I supposed. She would come in several times a day to use the restroom, since they did not have a restroom on the premises. Her name was Vicki and she was a petite blonde, always smiling, and she moved with such enthusiasm and vigor. She was extremely graceful.

He said to me, "My name is Jim. My wife, Vicki, and I own the antique furniture refinishing business across the street. My wife just thinks the world of you. And we've both watched you turn this store completely around. We like what we see. My wife seems to think that you can bring the same enthusiasm to work for us at the shop. I'm sure you know you're worth much more than these people are paying you. What do you think? Is this something you'd be interested in?"

"Thank you, sir. I'm honored that you've taken notice of my accomplishment here at the store. But, I know absolutely nothing about antique furniture refinishing."

"We don't want you just for the sake of refinishing furniture. Hell, we can train a monkey to do that. We want your enthusiasm, your keen sense of order, your affable personality, and that sociable smile of yours. Whatever you're getting paid per week here, we'll double it."

"Wow! I'm interested. But, I would never quit without giving a two-week notice to the district manager."

"That's fine. We would expect that. Meanwhile, why don't you come over for a couple of hours after your shift each day and get some hands on experience. You can get a feel for the environment. You'll find that, like yourself, we excel in what we do. You can start tomorrow."

The next day, after my shift, I went over to their establishment, which consisted of a show room, a small area for crafting furniture and making repairs, and three small warehouses in back. One of the warehouses was used to store furniture that had been refinished and hadn't made it to the show room. A second warehouse was used to store furniture waiting to be refinished, and the third was the warehouse where the refinishing process actually took place. That was my place.

Almost immediately, I began to see the spiritual value of this craft. It was almost as if God was using it to draw a parallel to how He takes someone who is a sinner, justifies him by grace through his faith in Jesus Christ, regenerates his spirit, renews his mind, and brings him to the place of discovering his true purpose and value. It was a process – from what some people would call worthless junk to a work of art crafted by an artisan who labored meticulously and endured the process of transformation, development and time to produce something that possessed quality and longevity.

I thought I had found the field that possessed the pearl of great price (see Matt. 13:45-46). Two weeks later, in January 1997, I was working full-time as an antique furniture refinisher apprentice. I loved being able to see the finished product – the end from the beginning. That's how God sees you. *"Declaring the end from the beginning, And from ancient times things that are not yet done, Saying, 'My counsel shall stand, And I will do all My pleasure'"* (Isa. 46:10, KJV). Each day on the job was one filled with anticipation of what I would discover next. I was full of energy and I worked steadily all day, as I listened to men and women teaching the gospel of the kingdom on the radio.

At home, I continued to study the Bible. I felt I was growing closer to God and stronger in my spiritual walk. At work, I learned the refinishing craft very well. I also learned different qualities of wood and how to magnify the beauty of its grain. I studied different styles of furniture, the artisan who crafted the design, and how to date them. It wasn't long before the owners entrusted me to take a valuable piece of furniture and refinish it from beginning to end. I could actually see in my mind the end beauty and value of that product from what its current state and value was. God said to me:

"This is how I desire for you to see My people. All of them are valuable to Me. Some have lost their way and become old and decrepit. But, My Spirit is within them. I want you to restore people. I want you to see their

Creator in them regardless of their current state. The process involved to refinish and bring restoration and value to antique furniture, is a parallel process to renewing the mind of a saint, developing and transforming him to the image of My Son, and equipping him for kingdom use. I want you to empower people through revelation knowledge of My Word, restoring them to the value that I've ascribed to their lives."

After about six months on the job, God really begin talking to me. The eyes of my mind were being enlightened with the revelation of my kingdom assignment, and I began to see glimpses of what it looked like. I had grown a lot spiritually mainly through my personal commitment to study, meditate, memorize Scripture and listen to teaching tapes. This had become my daily routine at home and at work. The grace of God followed me on this job. Jim was Catholic and Vicki was what I would call "a good Baptist." They allowed me to listen to Christian radio as I worked.

They knew that I was a minister; and also, it provided a peaceful and serene environment for work. Our productivity was outstanding and their profits increased. They even gave me a raise and an occasional bonus, whenever they had a really great sales week. Some days, they would even kiss the ground of their business. They purchased insurance for my family and co-signed for my new truck. They taught me that you can never go backward. Everything that is good is always in front of you. That principle had led to their success in business, they said.

As I worked, I had access to hearing the word of God taught throughout my workday. I was receiving revelation of the Scriptures that no one in my area seemed to be teaching or preaching. And, whenever I had an opportunity, I taught revelation knowledge of the word of God. I would always emphasize as I taught that every word means something; and, that saints should stop reading past words they didn't understand, but stop and reflect on each word as it relates to the context. That didn't go over very well. The saints simply did not possess the spiritual stamina required to be taught. My invites and opportunities to teach continued to be few and far between. I felt isolated. I wanted to know why people of God would not want to know as much as they possibly could about the God they called "Father?"

On the job God continued, day by day as it seemed, to reveal to me His kingdom purpose for my life. I would have visions of ministry – tent crusades – where I would be empowering people with revelation knowledge of the Word of God. I saw myself teaching and ministering to multitudes in large venues. I saw healings and miracles taking place. I saw myself prophesying, laying hands on people, stirring up their gifts and unlocking their destinies. I saw myself writing books that would motivate people to discover their divine purpose. I saw community resource centers and places of refuge and safe haven for saints to recover and be restored into their identities as sons and daughters of the Most High God. I remember God speaking to me and saying:

"What I have ordained for your life is a kingdom assignment that cannot be fulfilled if you remain on a secular job. Your assignment is greater than what you know about it now, and it will require your full attention. I am preparing you to leave the secular job market and enter ministry on a full-time basis. This will be a faith move. It is imperative that you walk this out in faith, for the just shall live by his faith. And know this: I will never leave you nor forsake you. I will open doors that will elevate you consistently from one level to the next until you are deployed into your kingdom assignment."

I was awestruck. "How am I going to leave a job which offers so much security and profit for me and my family and step into full-time ministry?" I asked myself. As much as I wanted ministry over my secular job, I still had doubts. I knew this would be a huge step into uncertain territory, and I could never do this in my own strength. So, I began asking God to increase my faith and give me the courage to step away from my secular job and into ministry full-time, for His glory.

I remember asking God, like Solomon, to give me wisdom on how to lead His people, even if it was only one third of the wisdom He'd given Solomon. I

FROM FOOTMEN TO HORSEMEN

would pray, *"Father, give Your servant, **James Brewton**, an understanding heart to judge your people and to discern between good and bad. Give me "now wisdom" – a renewed mind of wisdom, knowledge and understanding each day – that I may go out and come in before Your people; for I cannot do this in my own strength, in Jesus' Name."* [Based on 1 Kings 3:9 & 2 Chron. 1:10, KJV]

On November 8, 1997, my mother graduated from this earthly life to be with the Lord. Jim and Vicki were very instrumental in helping me through this ordeal of life. But, soon after, I noticed a shift in how I felt about my job. I was no longer eager to get to work. My enthusiasm had waned, and all I could do was think about ministry. However, the more I thought about ministry, the more Jim and Vicki would talk to me about expanding their business and turning over the refinishing and upholstery component of the business to me and Margie. By now, Margie had joined us as an upholstery apprentice. Although we had both learned our craft well, neither of our hearts was really into making a career out of it.

In January of 1998, Jim and Vicki began their expansion project. They had purchased a large property east of Statesboro and borrowed $750,000 to build their new facility. On several occasions, as the project was being constructed, Jim and Vicki had made plans to take me to their bank to sign some paperwork pertaining to my proprietorship over the refinishing component of the business. This would have allowed me to purchase furniture, purchase all refinishing products, hire additional workers, and draw a percentage from each piece of furniture after it was refinished and sold. Also, they were going to purchase a new home and transition their current two-story home to Margie and me. Sounds like a really good deal, right?

Each time we were scheduled to meet with bankers, something would suddenly come up and Jim and Vicki would have to cancel the meeting. By May, the pressure was mounting for me to leave. Construction was almost complete and Jim and Vicki had made plans to have their grand opening in June. They had to get me to the bank to complete their plans and everything would be in order prior to the move. So, they scheduled a meeting for the first week in June. As I was driving in to work on Monday May 25, I heard the Lord say:

"This will be your last week working on this job. I've prepared you for this time and your faith will not fail. Make sure that you have all of your affairs relative to this job in order. Friday will be your last day."

Friday, May 29, 1998 was filled with excitement and fear. I was excited for ministry because I thought that God would immediately usher me into full-time ministry in the form of meetings and tent crusades, just as He'd shown me in the visions. On the other hand, I was still experiencing fear. I kept asking myself, "Are you really going to do this?" Each time, I'd answer, "Yes. This is it. If I don't do it now, I'll get locked into a career I know God did not call me to. Plus, I will be out of the will of God. Father, I trust You."

Before I left that evening, all of my affairs were in order and I left my work warehouse immaculately clean. I hadn't told Jim and Vicki that I would not be returning. I wasn't ready to hear or put up with Jim's infamous tirades that he would have from time to time, when things didn't go his way. And, this would definitely be one of those times, but of monumental proportions. Jim could certainly be belligerent and vindictive. Simply put, I did not have the courage to confront them with my plans to resign, effectve immediately.

Over the weekend, I played out over and over, in my head, my decision to walk away from my job, and how I'd not confronted Jim and Vicki with my decision. There was no two-week notice and no reason for them to believe that I had been contemplating leaving for nearly six months. I didn't miss any work days, and my work was always thorough and complete. I remember becoming fearful, thinking that since I had not said anything to them about leaving, I should just go back to work on Monday as if nothing had happened. But, each time I'd entertain that thought, Holy Spirit would remind me of God's word to me. God had prepared me to leave the job, and my faith was imperative because this was a faith move. And, for six months I had prayed for faith and courage to leave the job. It occurred to me that I had not prayed for courage to confront my employers, which would have been the proper thing to do, in spite of what might have transpired.

I asked God, "Father, I know what You've shown me and told me concerning Your assignment for my life. I know it was Your voice that said 'You cannot accomplish your divine purpose and work on a secular job at the same time.' I know that You have increased my faith for such a time as this. Please Father, give me a sign that I have made the right decision according to Your will and timing. If this is Your will, provide for me additional finances so that I can take my family to Florida for a fun-filled week. Then, after we return, I will officially begin ministry full-time.

Sunday night came and I was seriously contemplating going to work Monday morning. But, our phone rang around 8:30 and it was my brother-in-law Scott, a prophet of God. He wanted Margie and me to drive to his home and pick up some clothes that were given to us by one of the church mothers. Once we were there, I shared with him about what God had been showing me and how He'd prepared me to leave my job for full-time ministry. I don't think that he was convinced that I'd made the right decision. Nevertheless, he prayed that if this was God's will for us, the provision would follow. As we were about to leave, He went into his bedroom and emerged with a white envelope in his hand.

He said, "Here, this is for you. God told me to give you this."

He handed me the envelope, I thanked him, and Margie and I were on our way home. Once we got back home, I went into our bedroom and put the clothes given to us on the bed to be sorted. I really didn't think that much about the envelope, except that it was thin and probably contained a few dollars. But, when I opened it, I saw several hundred dollar bills. I took them from the envelope and there were seven of them, the number for completion and perfection. God had answered my prayer, and I knew I would not be going back to my secular job.

Monday morning, June 1 at 6:00 a.m., I phoned Jim and Vicki and told them that I would not be returning. When they asked me why, I told them that the Lord had called me into full-time ministry. Jim was obviously agitated, but he tried to remain calm as he voiced his disapproval and hung up. Vicki was her usually calm self. She remained on the phone and attempted to communicate that she understood, but I could detect hurt and betrayal in her voice. Within five minutes, we'd finished our conversation and what was to be a happy and profitable relationship was destroyed.

My family and I had packed our bags as an act of faith prior to receiving the money from Prophet Johnson, and so we headed to Florida. After a fun-filled week, we returned home and I set up my ministry office in the RV that I was housing for my father. Monday morning, June 8, I begin my full-time ministry at 8:00, as if I were going to work. I surmised that if it was full-time, it required a full 8-5 work day. Later the same day, I received two separate letters – one from Jim and the other from Vicki. I will share each with you it its entirety.

From Jim: "Dear Mr. Brewton, This letter is in reference to your telephone call this a.m. As you indicated to Mrs. Winters, it is my understanding that you have, effective June 1, 1998, terminated your refinishing business and have decided to pursue your ministry on a full-time basis.

"While the news came as quite a surprise to us, we completely understand the difficulties which you were encountering and your reasons for no longer wishing to refinish furniture. In that vein, we can only hope that your decision will be one in the best interest of your family and yourself. We have notified the group insurance carrier and the bank that we no longer have either a business or personal relationship with you. Best to you in your future endeavors." -- Jim

From Vicki: "James, I'm returning the last tape you gave me to listen to – actually I can't listen to it anyway because the words are meaningless to me. It's amazing what a 5 minute phone conversation at 6:15 a.m. on a Monday morning can do!

"You have really disappointed me. First, from a lack of professionalism in giving us notice. Need I remind you that two weeks is expected, but one week would have been nice. You even gave Time Saver two weeks notice. Second, from a lack of personal integrity to even tell us face to face. In that instant, I understood what we truly meant to you. Nothing. Nothing at all.

"That hurt deeply, James. Jim, my mom, and I cared about you and your family. We tried to show that in all the little things we did. You were part of our family – people who meant a lot to us. People who were in our prayers and our hearts on a daily basis. Obviously, that was not a reciprocal feeling.

"But most of all, I will never forget the reason you gave – You're going into the ministry full time – the Lord has called you. Even if the Lord had called you, he would not have wanted you to treat us the way you did. As my nephew, Randy, said upon hearing the news, "Aunt Vicki, Christians don't treat people that way."

"You may talk a good talk, James, but you must learn to walk a good walk. Remember me telling you that ministers should hold themselves to a higher standard. A true minister of the Lord would not abruptly turn his back on people who were always there for him. A true minister of the Lord does the "right thing."

"When you needed help over the last year whom did you turn to? It wasn't your own Mother or Father. It was us, and we cared enough to help. When Margie needed work, or you couldn't pay for car repairs, and most especially when you needed a vehicle – we came through for you. We could have turned our backs on you, but we didn't.

"That's what Christianity is all about, James. It's not about sitting in church on Sundays, or teaching nice lessons on the radio, or telling people I'm an elder, I know what I'm talking about. It's how you live life each day. It's about making donations to somebody's Bible School. It's about giving someone a kind gesture and meaning it. It's about trust.

"We trusted you, James. And you destroyed that trust in five minutes. If you found other employment, or if you just couldn't handle things anymore, we deserved to be told the truth. We also deserved notice. You walked out on us, and you had always said you would never leave us like that. Lies. Lies. Lies.

"This brings me to the end. About the truck – before you think about letting the truck fall into disrepair or not making the payment, please return it to me. You can just leave it at the store – when we're not there. Also, please return my study materials. You can just mail them. I think that says it all. **I feel very sorry for you. You have much growing to do – spiritually, personally, and professionally."**

- Vicki (author's emphasis).

I'm sure there are some of you who would agree with what was said to me by Jim, and especially from Vicki. And, my response would be that I understand. However, just because you are a Christian doesn't mean that you won't make mistakes, never handle anything improperly, or even display ill-tempered mannerisms at times. Nevertheless, after I read Vicki's letter for the first time, I agreed with her. I did have much growing to do – spiritually, personally and professionally. And believe me: I have kept these letters over the years as reminders of that fact. Each year on June 8th, for the past 18 years, I have read these letters and used them to measure the standard of my spiritual, personal, and professional growth.

Yes, I was still spiritually immature. But, I was indeed growing. Had I measured up spiritually, personally and professionally? No. But, I had discovered my kingdom assignment and accepted it by faith and I had obeyed God. God was not shocked or appalled by the way I mishandled that situation. It was like taking a baby step of faith, from crawling to walking. I simply had not learned how to run. He had my attention, and He was about to take me on a journey of spiritual growth that I never could have fathomed. I was about to learn what it really means to live by my faith and endure the persecutions, afflictions, lies, sacrifices and godly sufferings of a disciple indeed.

"The servant is not greater than his Lord," Jesus said. *"If they have persecuted Me, they will also persecute you"* (John 15:20, KJV). Apostle Paul understood persecution, and he endured it as a good soldier of Jesus. The fulfillment of his kingdom assignment required it. That is why Paul was assured of his heavenly crown prior to his earthly departure. One of Paul's assignments as a spiritual father was to confirm the souls of disciples and exhort them *"to continue in the faith, and that we must through much tribulation enter into the kingdom of God"* (Acts 14:22, KJV).

Once you accept your kingdom assignment, you must devote yourself to it in loyalty, commitment and faithfulness, allowing no man or woman to trouble you. Like Paul, as you carry out your kingdom assignment you will bear in your body the marks of the Lord Jesus (Gal. 6:17). What are you willing to give up or endure in order to accept your kingdom assignment? Whatever you must give up or endure as you accept and carry out your kingdom assignment, your testimony should be in alignment with Paul's: *"God will deliver you out of them all... Endure afflictions, do the work of an evangelist, make full proof of your ministry"* (2 Tim. 3:11, 4:15). *"Keep your eyes on Jesus, who both began and finished this race we're in. Study how he did it. Because he never lost sight of where he was headed"* (Heb. 12:2).

SECTION THREE:

GETTING EQUIPPED FOR KINGDOM DEPLOYMENT

You Must Be Equipped For Your Kingdom Assignment!

"He sent a man before them – Joseph – who was sold as a slave.
They hurt his feet with fetters, He was laid in irons.
Until the time that his word came to pass, The word of the LORD tested
him. *The king sent and released him, The ruler of the people let him go free.*
He made him lord of his house, And ruler of all his possessions,
To bind his princes at his pleasure, And teach his elders wisdom."
(PSA. 105: 17-22, AUTHOR'S EMPHASIS)

"And He Himself gave some to be apostles, some prophets, some evangelists, and
some pastors and teachers, for **the equipping of the saints for the work of**
ministry, *for the edifying of the body of Christ, till we all come to the unity of the*
faith and of the knowledge of the Son of God, to a perfect man, to the measure of
the stature of the fullness of Christ; that **we should no longer be children,** *tossed*
to and fro and carried about with every wind of doctrine, by the trickery of men,
in the cunning craftiness of deceitful plotting, but, speaking the truth in love, may
grow up in all things into Him who is the head – Christ –"
(EPH. 4:11-15, AUTHOR'S EMPHASIS)

CHAPTER SEVEN

EQUIPPING REQUIRES PREPARATION

"And that servant who knew his master's will,
and did not prepare himself
or do according to his will,
shall be beaten with many stripes."
(LUKE 12:47)

After you discover your kingdom assignment and accept it as the call of God upon your life, you must then be equipped before you can be deployed in the field. Equipping requires preparation through training. You must be prepared to live supernaturally in a natural world because you are being equipped for kingdom deployment. God's kingdom originates from the eternal realm, which is spiritual. God's kingdom is from above, not from the earth. His kingdom consists of His rule, His plans and purposes, along with His assignments to men which govern the relationship between God and man. God's desire is that you discover, accept and embrace your kingdom assignment and fulfill it with excellence. The way you commit to your assignment is to submit to God's way of manifesting His kingdom in the earth. *"Thy kingdom come. Thy will be done, as in heaven, so in earth"* (Luke 11:2, KJV).

Equipping, in a spiritual context, is a process of training, growth, development, and transformation – preparation. **Equipping** means to furnish for service or action by appropriate provisioning; to make ready: PREPARE (Merriam-Webster). Paul said that the ministry offices of the Lord Jesus were for equipping the saints for the work of ministry. The King James Version uses the word perfecting, which is translated from the Greek word **katartizo (kat-ar-tid-zo)**. It means to complete thoroughly; make perfectly; thorough equipment (**katartisis**); perfecting through complete furnishing (**katartismos**) (Strong's).

Preparation is defined as the action or process of making something ready for use or service or of getting ready for some occasion, test, or duty; a state of being prepared (Merriam-Webster). The Greek word **Hetoimasia (het-oy-mas-ee-ah)** is translated preparation, and denotes readiness and firm footing [foundation] (Vine's). Being properly equipped and prepared establishes a firm foundation from which to launch your kingdom assignment once you have been deployed.

During the preparation process, the word of God will test you to ensure that you are no longer a child, but that you've grown up in all things into Christ. God desires you to be a perfect man (one who is a completer), which is the measure of the stature of the fullness of Christ. If you stand steadfast in your calling to make your election sure, the Word that God spoke concerning your life before He created the world will come to pass. Apostle Peter said that you should give diligence to make your calling and election sure (1 Pet. 1:10). Apostle Paul said that you should abide in the same calling wherein you were called (1 Cor. 7:20).

The word of God will test you to find out if you are indeed abiding in your calling or your kingdom assignment. *"Until the time of his word came to pass, The word of the Lord tested him"* (Psalm 105:19). God's tests during preparation are to make sure that you are proceeding according to the word He's spoken over your life. He wants to bring it to pass so that you can advance His kingdom in the earth. Satan has a kingdom, too. So, you must understand that, during preparation for deployment into your kingdom assignment, God will test you to find out where your loyalty lies. You, then, must understand the contrast between the two kingdoms.

From Genesis to Revelation, the Scriptures make it clear that there are two kingdoms at work, and they oppose one another. The very nature of a kingdom is to conquer. In this case, however, God's kingdom is "The Kingdom of kingdoms." God is the originator of kingdoms, and His kingdom is an everlasting kingdom which cannot be subdued or destroyed.

> *"How great are His signs, And how mighty His wonders!* **His kingdom is an everlasting kingdom,** *And His dominion is from generation to generation."* (Dan. 4:3, author's emphasis)

> *"Then the kingdom and dominion, And the greatness of the kingdoms under the whole heaven, Shall be given to the people, the saints of the Most High.* **His kingdom is an everlasting kingdom,** *And all dominions shall serve and obey Him."* (Dan. 7:27, author's emphasis)

> *"The kingdoms of this world have become the kingdoms of our Lord and of His Christ, and* **He shall reign forever and ever!** *"* (Rev. 11:15, author's emphasis)

The Hebrew word translated as **everlasting** is *alam (aw-lam)*, which means remote in time, i.e. the future or past indefinitely; forever. It corresponds to *olam (o-lawm)*, which means concealed, i.e. the vanishing point; generally, time out of mind (past or future), eternity; always: ancient time, perpetual, beginning of the world [+ without end] (Strong's). God does not proceed from eternity; eternity proceeds from God – out of His mind! And God set eternity, which proceeded out of His mind, into the hearts of men. Why? You might ask? Because God wants you to seek Him through relationship and discover what He's thought, imagined and spoken concerning your life on earth which includes your kingdom assignment. God requires that you draw, from eternity that is within your heart, the original blueprint and intent for your life that is imprinted upon eternity in His mind. God requires it for you to successfully fulfill your kingdom assignment. This is the pattern for your life. It is your guarantee of God's intentions for you.

> "He has made everything beautiful in its time. **He has also set eternity in the hearts of men**; yet they cannot fathom what God has done from beginning to end...I know that everything God does will endure forever; nothing can be added to it and nothing taken from it. God does it so that men will revere him. Whatever is has already been, and what will be has been before, and God will call the past to account." (Eccl. 3: 11, 14-15, NIV, author's emphasis)

Satan also has a kingdom. He is referred to as the prince of this world (John 12:31) and the prince of the power of the air (Eph. 2:2). However, unlike the Kingdom of God which is powered by Holy Spirit in righteousness and peace and joy, Satan's kingdom is driven by evil, wickedness, fear and terror. It is marked by aggression, and is a kingdom of darkness in which you once lived, but not anymore. Having received salvation through your faith in Jesus and His finished work on the Cross, you were translated from Satan's kingdom into God's kingdom. This means that you are no longer a stranger, but a fellow-citizen with the saints, and of the household of God (see Eph. 2:19). You became a citizen of the kingdom of God. *"He has delivered us from the power of darkness and conveyed us into the kingdom of the Son of His love, in whom we have redemption through His blood, the forgiveness of sins"* (Col. 1:13-14).

Still, you must make a conscious decision to live in God's kingdom of light and righteousness as a citizen. Make no mistake about it; there are many believers who have not made a conscious decision to live within God's kingdom. One reason for this is because living within the kingdom of God is by invitation. God does not force Himself upon you to the breaching of your independent will. Saints who do not honor their citizenship within the Kingdom of Heaven are generally spiritually immature saints who straddle the fence, so to speak.

And, because they are too immature to make a definitive decision to live within the kingdom of God, as opposed to living according to the kingdoms of this world, Satan the aggressor makes the decision for them. They then become lukewarm Christians who run the risk of being vomited out of God's mouth (see Rev. 3:16).

As a believer, you must not straddle the fence or vacillate between the Kingdom of God and the kingdoms of this world. God, your Father, has fully equipped you to live physically within a kingdom that is governed according to the standards of the world – Satan's kingdom. For what purpose has He done this? To turn the hearts of men back to Him. That's why Jesus, in John chapter 17, prayed the specific prayer that He did to His Father relative to your ability to live in the world, and not be of the world. Remember, spiritually speaking, you are seated in heavenly places in Christ Jesus (Eph. 2:6). Jesus prayed, *"... they are not of the world any more than I am of the world. My prayer is not that you take them out of the world but that you protect them from the evil one. **They are not of the world, even as I am not of it. Sanctify them by the truth; your word is truth.** As you sent me into the world, I have sent them into the world. For them I sanctify myself, that they too may be truly sanctified. My prayer is not for them alone. I pray also for those who will believe in me through their message."* (John 17:14-20, NIV)

Having made a definitive decision to live as a citizen within the kingdom of God, you can continue the preparation process, being equipped for your kingdom assignment. During this process, you will be transformed from faith to faith and glory to glory. And, you are responsible for recognizing your identity as the image of Christ. *"But we all, with unveiled face, beholding as in a mirror the glory of the Lord, are being transformed into the same image from glory to glory, just as by the Spirit of the Lord"* (2 Cor. 3:18).

*****

I didn't know it at the time, but I was about to embark upon a process of spiritual growth and transformation that I hadn't anticipated. After I got back home from Florida with my family, I was poised to begin ministry full-time. Receiving and reading those letters I shared in Chapter Six wasn't how I expected the first day on my God-assigned job to be. But, after I acknowledged Jim and Vicki's perspective of how things transpired, I did realize that I had a lot of growing to do. So, I shook off any offense concerning the letters and began my ministry by going on a five-day fast.

I shut myself off from my family in the RV I'd transformed into my ministry office and began reading my Bible and praying in my Holy Spirit language. When evening came, I would spend several hours in meditation and thinking on the goodness of God. I wrote out faith Scriptures and posted them throughout the ministry area so that they were easily visible to me. On the third day, God began to show me the vision, and I wrote and made illustrations of what I was seeing. I was intently focused on what I was hearing and seeing. Each of the next two days was equally intense. Holy Spirit showed me an illustration of a new ministry campus inclusive of an auditorium that would seat 2,500 people, and I drew it according to the pattern I was shown. He even gave me the name of the ministry, along with its mission and five distinct components of the ministry.

I emerged from that fast victorious and with a blueprint from which to build – Community Empowerment Ministries, Inc. "Empowering Communities Through Revelation Knowledge of the Word of God." It was given to me in five phases or stages of growth, spanning 35 years. I felt on top of the world. I had just written the vision plainly for my kingdom assignment. And, I assumed that God would immediately send people to read it, who would then hasten to help me establish it. People would be banging at my door and my phone would be ringing off the hook with invitations for me to minister in churches, tent crusades, auditoriums, etc. In a short time, I would be known throughout the Southeast and I would have a huge following. But, I was in for a big surprise.

First, no one seemed to be excited about this grand vision except me. And the few saints that I did share the vision with thought that I was out of my mind. Some even said that I was possessed by demons. After all, how else could I have left a good-paying job that held so much potential for economic growth and security for me and my family if I didn't have a demon. Some saints said that I needed to get my head out of the sky. Others said that I was high-minded and conceited. Still others said that I should repent and ask for my job back. One story had it that I hadn't heard God and my family and I would starve if I didn't go back to work. Several of my wife's family even honed in with a Bible verse that described how they felt about my leaving the secular job market to enter ministry full-time; however, in this case, the Scripture was taken out of context, as Scripture often is when it comes from the mouth of immature Christians. *"God said, 'If any would not work, neither should he eat'"* (2 Thess. 3:10).

Paul was referring to those saints who were loafers, busybodies and idle. That didn't describe me. Like Jesus, I was about my Father's business. But, they could only perceive work as going to some job and working for a paycheck. My ministry was my work. Work, in the mind of God, is being diligent to do or carry out your divine assignment for kingdom advancement and success in life – all things richly to enjoy. Solomon said that this is the gift of God. A job, on the other hand, is more about trying to earn enough money to make ends meet. You can even hate your job. But, I have yet to find many people who can sincerely say that they hate their work – their God-ordained assignment.

So there I was, vision in hand, ready for ministry doors to open. After all, how else was I going to pay my bills and feed my family? I prayed earnestly for someone to invite me to minister. Then, at the end of the month, I received an invitation to minister for five nights at a church in Savannah, Ga. I was both thrilled and excited, as this was to be my entrance into the ministry spotlight through evangelism. So, I decided to journal my experiences in ministry, highlighting all of the healings, miracles, signs and wonders that I'd seen in numerous visions I'd had when I was still working for Jim and Vicki. I entitled it, "Journal of My Ministry," dated June 29, 1998. It is so short that I can share it with you here in its entirety.

"After working at Hodges Antiques in Statesboro, GA, for a period of about one and a half years, God promoted me to full time ministry, according to my steadfast faith – speaking consistently and fervently that May 29, would be my last work day.

By faith, I stepped out of the natural into the supernatural, believing in the Word of God, the name of Jesus, and the Blood of Jesus.

"Over the past four and a half years, God has consistently prepared me for full time ministry, having provided me with many necessary resources through which the Holy Spirit taught me about Jesus, opening my understanding and revealing to my inner man the mysteries of the gospel of Christ.

"I thank God that I purposed in my heart at the onset of 1994 that I would pre-pare myself by walking in love, being faithful, obedient, humble, and serving others. I purposed in my heart that God would exalt me in His time.

"The road to now has not been an easy one. But along the way, I've always re-mained faithful, obedient, humble, and a servant. I've seen God raise me up from drug addiction to an anointed, bold and confident Bible teacher. The anointing to teach has been on my life from my childhood, when I taught the "Card Class" in Sunday school, to my teaching jobs on the college level.

"Now God has elevated me and anointed me in the office of the teacher in min-istry so that His people may better understand His Word to the degree it draws them to His Word and they too, begin to walk and live out the principles of the gospel, for every believer is an heir of God, a joint-heir of Jesus Christ, a co-laborer with God, and a partaker of God's divine nature, power and glory. "And if we be Christ's, then are we Abraham's seed and heirs of the promise."

"Now Father, I have received Your call and have been sent by You with the power of Your burden-removing, yoke-destroying kingly anointing. I minister Your Word to Your people, being full of faith, full of wisdom, and full of power. I minister and the gifts of the Holy Spirit are in full operation, as the Spirit wills. I do it all totally dependent upon You. "You must increase, but we must decrease." I desire to do noth-ing by my own might or power, "but by My Spirit, saith the Lord of hosts." I trust You totally, Lord, in Jesus' name.

"Tonight begins the first full week of my ministry, June 29 – July 3. God has opened the door for me to minister at Power Pack Ministry, Evangelist Linda Rob-erts, pastor. My journal begins with the blessings (teaching, healings, prophecies, miracles, wisdom, etc.) of this meeting."

Monday, June 29, 1998.

That is as far as I got in my journal. I thought that the church would be filled with people ready for revival and healings and such. As it turned out, my wife and I drove the three-hour round trip each night and each night there were no more than five people in each service. On top of that, my wife and I gave in the offering each night to inspire the others to give, and you can imagine that by the end of the week, we did not have any money left. The "love offering" we received was enough for us to eat at a Chinese restaurant and purchase gas to drive home. Nevertheless, I had preached all week as if I were preaching to multitudes. Although I was disappointed that there were only a few people in attendance, it did not deter me from my duty to minister the word of the Lord to them, pray for them, and prophesy to them.

After that week, I put my "journal" away. I needed to regroup, re-plan and refocus. I needed a steady flow of ministry in order to survive. Our bills were beginning to pile up, and there was no money to pay them. But, God is faithful! Over the next few months, other ministry opportunities were made available to me, much with the same result. Many of the saints were not accustomed to being taught from the word of God; they were accustomed to preaching. Plus, many of them did not understand how to give according to the word of God. It seemed that God was giving me and my family barely enough to get by; yet, He kept challenging my faith to continue in my divine assignment.

On June 8, 1999, I celebrated one year in full-time ministry. Margie and I were still behind in our bills, my truck had been repossessed, and our mortgage was several months behind. The bank was threatening to foreclose on our home. These were times when I really had to press in and trust God. I knew what God had said to me about ministry. I knew what God had shown me in visions concerning ministry. And, I knew that provision comes with the vision. The problem was that I could see the vision very clearly, but I did not see the provision, at least in the terms I thought or expected it to be. My family was struggling, and church people persecuted us. Our situation became their testimony that God had not called me into the ministry full time.

In August of the same year, I was at a church service in Statesboro where Margie was speaking. There, I met an apostle from Augusta who invited me to minister for five nights at his church in September. I felt peace in my spirit and so I accepted his invitation. I really needed somewhere to minister, and I heard in my spirit, "**Go.**"

As I stated earlier, my truck had been repossessed. At this point, our car had broken and was beyond repair. My brother, Victor, let us drive one of his vehicles during this time but stated that the tag and insurance would expire at the end of August, and we would need to purchase both in order to keep driving the car. At the end of August his tag expired and there was no insurance on the vehicle. On top of that, our ministry appointment was the first week in September, which included Labor Day. We could not chance driving a car all the way to Augusta with no tag or insurance. In my RV ministry office, I began to cry out to the Lord.

"Father, You said that You would provide all my need according to Your riches in Christ Jesus. You know all things, and there is nothing hidden from You. I obeyed the Holy Spirit and accepted this invitation to minister in Augusta. I have not called Apostle Williams to cancel because I trust that since You assigned me to this ministry detail, You will make a way for me to honor my word, for my integrity stands in question if I do not follow through with my word. Thank You that You have already made the way, for tomorrow we must leave for Augusta."

As I finished praying, I looked out of the window to see my brother pulling into my driveway. I watched as he got out of his truck and placed a current sticker on the tag of the car he'd loaned us. Then he went inside our home. I left my office and walked the 50 feet or so to our house and went inside. There, Victor was explaining to Margie how God had blessed him and that he wanted to be a blessing to us. He pulled out an envelope containing five one hundred dollar bills and placed it into my hands and blessed us. Look at God! During that meeting with Apostle Williams and his wife, he prophesied that I would one day be ordained as an apostle.

After we returned home from that meeting, we were faced with the possibility of losing our home. We were several months behind and the bank was threatening foreclosure. This was an extremely difficult time for Margie and me.

The bank had informed our relatives, whose names were listed on our loan as close relatives, of our situation. We began getting phone calls telling us what we should do. I needed to get a real job ASAP, and we needed to file for bankruptcy. I was told that I needed to find somewhere else to live because the local sheriff would be serving us an eviction notice soon.

This was a time of real challenge to our faith. Would we bend and bow to the world's system or would we stand our ground rooted in the word of God by our faith? We began to make decrees in alignment with the word of God pertaining to victory, knowing that God is a righteous God who takes care of His children who stand in faith on the word of His promises. *"For God is not unjust to forget your work and labor of love which you have shown toward His name, in that you have ministered to the saints, and do minister"* (Heb. 6:10, KJV). *"But thanks be to God, who gives us the victory through our Lord Jesus Christ"* (1 Cor. 15:57, KJV). *"For the promises of God in Him are Yes, and in Him Amen, to the glory of God through us"* (2 Cor. 1:20, KJV).

We made up our minds in agreement that we would stand still and see the glory of God. We planted ourselves in the word of faith, and like a tree we declared that we would not be moved. We began saying what the three Hebrew boys said as they were being threatened by King Nebuchadnezzar to be thrown into the fiery furnace, *"If it be so, our God whom we serve is able to deliver us from the burning fiery furnace, and he will deliver us out of thine hand, O king. But if not, be it known unto thee, O king, that we will not serve thy gods, nor worship the golden image which thou hast set up"* (Dan. 3:17-18, KJV).

On the day that we were to be served with the eviction order, Margie and I were agitated. We could find no peace at home. Plus, we were not looking forward to receiving an eviction notice from the sheriff's department. So, we decided to drive into town just to get out of the house and relieve some of the tension. We could not drive very far because we had very little gas and no money to buy any. Soon, we had to make our way back to our home. I stopped at our mailbox to check the mail prior to turning onto our driveway. The box contained several pieces of mail. I surmised that they were all bills, and I did not want to look at any of them.

As I parked the car, I heard the Holy Spirit say, "Check your mail." So I began flipping through each one. "Bill!" "Bill!" "Bill!" "Bill!" Then, as I looked at the next one, I was about to say, "Bill!" But, my eyes were seeing something else. "Pay to the order of James Brewton." It was a check. I hurried to open it, and as I looked at the amount, Margie and I began to praise the Lord. It was for $16,000. And, I heard the Holy Spirit say, as clearly as I've ever heard Him speak, "Because of your faith."

After tithing to our local church, I caught up our mortgage, purchased our own car, and started my own refinishing business. I can't tell you how many times something similar to this scenario has played out in our lives as we were being equipped through preparation for ministry.

Shortly after that, I was given a cassette tape which contained a message by Apostle G. E. Bradshaw and told to listen to the level of revelation knowledge he was releasing. As I did so, I was totally blown away. My spirit was ignited, for I had never heard a word of God on that level before. He provided a Holy Spirit revelation to many of the Scriptures I'd wanted deeper revelation of. His message called "Doors of Destiny," July 19, 1997, was so powerful and full of revelation pertaining to destiny that I played it over and over and over again. Somehow, I had to meet this man.

On December 31, 1999, my brother-in-law, Prophet Scottie Johnson, who had given me the cassette tape, invited me to ride with him to a church in Columbia, S. C. where Apostle Bradshaw was to give the New Year's Eve message. Apostle Bradshaw had become his spiritual father and "covering." As we made our way through the assembly of what looked to be about five or six hundred people, I became more and more excited to see this man in person. I had formed a certain visual picture in my head based on how he sounded on the tape.

When the pastors of the church led the procession of ministers into the auditorium, Prophet Johnson pointed out Apostle Bradshaw. He looked nothing like I had imagined he would. As a matter of fact, he didn't look to me like he possessed the level of Holy Spirit "boom" that I had become accustomed to hearing on the tapes. But, when he took the microphone and opened his mouth...!

January 1, 2000. The meeting was over, and Apostle Bradshaw was gracious to stay in the auditorium and greet certain people who had been chosen to meet him, inclusive of Prophet Johnson, who introduced me to Apostle Bradshaw. I did not know it at the time, but Apostle Bradshaw was already scheduled to be in Jesup, Ga. in February for a series of teaching and training sessions which included day services and evening services. I could not wait to be a part of what I perceived would be a rise in the level and standard of my ministry under this man's tutelage.

Apostle Bradshaw's training seminar began on February 17th. In each of the sessions, I listened and took notes. I participated in the training sessions and sowed financial seed into this man's anointing, as I was praying diligently for wisdom and for Holy Spirit to infuse me with this level of revelation knowledge of the Scriptures. Margie and I drove the 45 miles back and forth to Jesup for the day service and the evening service. We sowed every dollar we had, not knowing how we would make it home and back the next day. But, God kept making a way. People would hand us a few dollars here and there. Others paid money that they owed me for services rendered in my refinishing business. Still others, who had no church home, would give me their tithe. That same week, after a morning session, Prophet Johnson asked Apostle Bradshaw if I could accompany them to lunch. His response was, "Absolutely."

Between February and July, Apostle Bradshaw had visited Jesup three times. During this time, I was privileged to be taught and trained in apostolic and prophetic ministry, and to be in his presence during his stay — at lunch and dinner, or in the pastor's office, even traveling with Prophet Johnson when he would take Apostle Bradshaw to the airport for his flight back to Chicago. This afforded me face time with Apostle Bradshaw. I would learn a lot by listening to his and Prophet Johnson's conversation, speaking only when I was spoken to.

God knows how to keep you in the "go forward" mode if you commit to pursuing your kingdom assignment. One way He does this is that He sends men and women to prophesy your future. Apostle Bradshaw was one of the first to prophesy my kingdom assignment. I will take the space here to share with you two of the prophecies spoken over my life and ministry during the five month period that I attended Apostle Bradshaw's teaching and training sessions, because **prophecy plays a major role in keeping you charged and focused for your assignment.** These two prophecies are lengthy but powerful.

The revelation of your purpose through prophecy will ignite the flame which burns within and motivate you to press into your destiny. Also, you will grasp a new level of understanding of what it means to war a good warfare with your prophecies. *"This charge I commit to you, son Timothy according to the prophecies previously made concerning you, that by them you may wage the good warfare, having faith and a good conscience, which some having rejected, concerning the faith have suffered shipwreck"* (1 Tim. 1:18-19).

February 17, 2000: *"The enemy has tried to keep you in a lower order. When you talk about life forms, you talk about a higher order of life form – like a human being, and you talk about a lower form of life – like a worm. I see the enemy attacking circumstances around you to lower your life value. He wants you to be an individual that just exists until Jesus comes – but that isn't working. God's saying some things to you that are powerful. He's saying things to you that are anointed, and it's a threat to the enemy that you are receiving the word of the Lord.*

"God's saying something to me in regard to your ministry. God says that you're going to have to deal with this worm situation – not that you're a worm – but I'm seeing clearly now. You're going to be sent to people with a worm mentality; people who are singing the song, 'Alas and did my Savior bleed and did my Sovereign die; would He devote that sacred Head to such a worm as I?' I'm hearing that in the realm of the Spirit. The enemy wants to attach that stigma to you – that you be a worm; but I'm seeing God saying, 'No! I'm going to take that and I'm going to send you to people whose esteem level is that of a worm – a people who have been preached to that they're nothing but worms, and that life only begins after they die.'

"God said that there is an assignment pending. I'm seeing the Lord begin to establish a net around you – a net. Are you pastoring yet? (No, I am an assistant pastor) I'm seeing a net around you. And the purpose of this net is that if you fall off of your platform, you don't hit the pavement. This net catches you. God said there's going to be a net. Everybody say net – 'Net.' That works – 'That works.' Say: We don't need

a hole in the net — 'We don't need a hole in the net.' We need a net — 'We need a net.' That works — 'that works.' Somebody say network — 'Network.'" Okay, now the network is a group of people around you that can catch you. It's a group of people with you that can hold you up.

"I'm not telling you to leave where you are right now — I'm not doing that. That's up to you and God. But I'm saying that God is going to establish a network of your own — a network. This will be a group of people that you will have brought from rock bottom — people who are crawling under rocks, brother; worms — crawling under rocks; ready to give it up; no self-esteem, low self-esteem — unable to arise. The Holy Ghost is saying there's a word being put in your mouth that is going to reach them right where they are.

"I'm looking at the activation today of six of the nine gifts of the Spirit — an activation of six of the nine gifts. God said you're going to be one that operates in the power gifts fluently. There's going to be open manifestations. I see a man with a blind right eye. I see you prophesying, laying hands on him and his eye pops open and it's clear. The eye was blood-shot, red and almost shut. He couldn't see; the pupil was dilated and very cloudy. I see you speaking to that brother, and his eye comes open and there's healing.

"I'm looking at a person with a foot disorder, a person whose heel bone deteriorated — some kind of calcium deficiency or something. You prayed and the heel bone grew back in place over a period of like three weeks. The person came back and the heel bone was there. I'm looking at creative miracles that God's going to begin to establish in your life. The best is yet to come, my brother. And God is saying that He's putting you in a divine position to begin to cultivate and to begin to activate those deep seated anointing and powers that are within you. God said get ready for an awakening; get ready for an awakening.

"Now the Word has been stirring you; you've been very stirred; but God said that's only a scratch, a scratch…God said layer by layer the old skin is coming off and He's reapplying a new skin to you. God said there's going to be a new scent; there's going to be a new grace; there's going to be a new anointing. Now don't go home and try to figure out how you're going to do this. It has nothing to do with your natural mind. You're not even in that process. That process is based on grace and time. But God said that He wants you to know it's coming, and He wants you to prepare yourself to be made aware. God said keep your esteem high; begin to do things to bring your esteem up for yourself. God said bless you. That means the blessing is for you. God told me to tell you – Bless you.

"Lift your hands. I'm getting ready to loose this thing: Six of the gifts stirred up; all nine in activation in eventuality – a stir, a new power, a new grace; a new release. 'For I the Lord would say unto thee son, that thou shall bring change unto many. And thou has become a generator of My presence and My power to the multitudes. There shall be young men from the age of 20 to 35 that I shall send thee to – that shall come to thee. And I shall build a network with thee, and an established group of faith warriors. And thou shall be tested heavily by the enemy and tried. The enemy shall seek to bring a scourging up against you. But I the Lord shall give you a new skin. And that skin shall resist and repel the scourging of the enemy, for your claim shall be, 'With His stripes I am healed. And I don't have to take the stripes that Jesus already took for me.' But, God is saying that you're going to wear the skin that Jesus wore when they whipped Him. You're going to wear the skin that Jesus wore when they pierced his flesh. God said invincible; a warrior of the latter days. This is the call and the cry of God's heart upon your life, in Jesus' Name!"

July 20, 2000: "Elder Brewton, the word of the Lord said this: God said, "Son, the many differences of things I'm about to show you – some things that you've perceived as the same here and the same there." God said, "I'm about to reveal to you the distinctive differences."

"God said, "I'm giving you a sword that is going to be able to finely divide things – things that look as if they are the same but they are really different; a masquerade of an enemy posing as the righteousness of God; and issue that looks like it's going to fail, but really it's going to succeed. But the only way to see two situations there is to have something sharp enough to divide between the two." The Word of God is quick and powerful and sharper than any two-edged sword, piercing even to the dividing asunder of soul and spirit. Both soul and spirit are invisible. Both soul and spirit is inside of a person. But the only thing in existence sharp enough to divide something that closely related is the Word of the Lord. The Word of the Lord has the power to di-

vide soul and spirit. Nobody can even see how, with the nature eye, you can separate soul and spirit. Then the Scripture goes on to say, 'and is a discerner of the thought and intents of the heart.'"

"The Lord says to you that he's about to give you a new intense sharpness in the use of the Word of the Lord. Whenever a situation looks like it's only one way, God is going to give you the Word to divide it, and you're going to see the good and the bad separated; you're going to see the light and the dark separated; you're going to see the blessing and the cursing separated. God said, "I'm about to separate areas of your life. I'm about to cause you to see that it's not just one big pile of dough." But God says "I'm going to separate what the enemy wants and what I want." God said, "I'm about to show you the difference between what the adversary would decree over your life and what God would decree over your life. But God said, "The only way that you can divide or separate the two is by the use of the Word." Because the Word is the only thing sharp enough to divide – it's like trying to split a human hair in half with a knife; you can't do it because the knife is not sharp enough.

"This is supernatural. This is not a natural intelligence; this is not a natural understanding. But you are nigh unto the time and place, the Lord says, in which you must divide between what you want to do and what you actually do. They can't be the same anymore. There has got to be a difference between intention and performance.

"God says, now you had a will; and the Scripture says, now there must be a performing of that thing. Now, it is the time and season for you to reap a position of change. And the Lord said everything is on hold until you are established in that place – until you step over into another standard. God said, "I cannot send the graces upon your life that I've ordained for you." Yes! It's going to be labor. Yes! It's going to be difficult at times. Yes! It's going to make you sweat. Yes! You're going to lose some time of leisure. But the Lord said, "You're making this My assignment for your life." And also, you're going to witness some of the greatest releases, and the pleasure of pleasing your God that's going to cause Him to reap your blessings for you from your enemy's hands – to literally snatch and pull from the hand of the enemy things that you thought you would have to fight for, God will do it for you.

"Make no mistake – light speed, good speed, God speed. So as I lay my hands upon you, I make a decree that now you will have sensitivity. Now you will have the

ability to discern the voice of God. Now you will listen to God speak to you. Now you will have a focus that is centered on what God wants, not what Elder Brewton wants; what God wants; what God requires; what God demands; what God commands. You will hear Him; you will listen for Him; you will understand His plan and you will be a recipient of His mercies.

"This is a very serious hour for you, my brother - a very serious moment of contemplation; a very serious time and season in your life. I'm loosing to you a great level of power. God says that you are to stand as a standard. God said that when the enemy comes in, like a flood the spirit of the Lord will lift up a standard against him. God said that you've been chosen as a standard, as a flag to portray the position, the territory, the land that God is taking for Himself. God said that you are one of the young lions that He's raising up in this hour; but God says that the place that you do it in is just as important as the fact that you are called to do it. God said that the territory is not the same. You cannot just say, "I can do this anywhere." No! God said that the destiny is ordained for a certain place for you to do it.

"One size does not fit all. Jesus would not have become the Deliverer of mankind if He had gone to Ethiopia to die on the Cross; that was not His assigned place. So the Lord said it's important that you understand timing and position. And I loose special grace on you to get it, in Jesus' Name."

*****

Your true prophecies will put you on the path that will lead you through the process that is required for your spiritual development. As you war a good warfare with the prophecies spoken over your life and destiny, they will play a major role in preparing and equipping you for deployment into your particular field. Again, you must be totally committed to your kingdom assignment and allow the process to take place. This will require grace and time.

Being equipped to carry out your divine purpose requires spiritual growth, which often involves great struggle. However, if you are willing to pay the price, you will discover new dimensions of God's blessing. But, you will have to "launch out into the deep" in order to get a huge catch. You will have to contend for your specific equipping because struggle is a fact of life and a part of any success you experience. Nothing ventured, nothing gained.

Margie and I have had to surrender to God's plan for our lives and struggle with the word of God spoken over our lives concerning our kingdom assignment. We were willing to **surrender** our lives to God and endure the **struggles** that led to growth in our faith in order to see some of the blessing manifested. We were willing to **suffer** for the sake of Christ, the Author of our kingdom assignment and for the Gospel. *"For this reason I also suffer these things; nevertheless I am not ashamed, for I know whom I have believed and am persuaded that He is able to keep what I have committed to him until that Day"* (2 Tim. 1:12).

Surrender is the action of yielding one's person or giving up the possession of something especially into the power of another (Merriam-Webster). In Christendom, it generally means to yield yourself and your plans to the will of God for your life. **Struggle** means to make strenuous or violent efforts in the face of difficulties or opposition; a violent effort or exertion: an act of strongly motivated striving (Merriam-Webster). This word is first mentioned in the Bible in association with the twins that were in Isaac's wife, Rebekah's womb. *"And the children struggled together within her…and the one people shall be stronger than the other people"* (Gen. 25:22-23, KJV). ***Ratsats (raw-tsats)*** is the Hebrew word translated **struggled**. It means to crack in pieces, break, bruise, crush, discourage, oppress, struggle together (Strong's). The Greek word translated as **suffer** is ***pascho (pas-kho)***, which means to experience a sensation or impression (usually painful): feel, passion, suffer, vex (Strong's).

Many of our churches today have embraced the "user friendly" approach and have formatted their services to this style of worship. In this model everything is presented as easy, agreeable, appealing, and timely. Usually, you will not find that "surrender," "struggle," and "suffering" are taught and embraced as components of spiritual maturity. On the contrary, the Bible is filled with stories about men and women who surrendered or yielded themselves to God for His use; they encountered many struggles as they endured the process that led them to victory, even suffering because of their obedience to God or for the sake of Christ and the Gospel. Referring to Apostle Paul's kingdom assignment, Jesus said, *"...he is a chosen vessel of Mine to bear My name before Gentiles, kings, and the children of Israel. For I will show him how many things he must **suffer** for My name's sake"* (Acts 9:15-16, author's emphasis).

Getting equipped for your kingdom assignment through the process of spiritual growth can sometimes be a lonely experience. And, the experiences encountered by each person are different. Personally, I believe that the greater your kingdom assignment is, the longer it takes to equip you for it. Plus, the level of surrender, struggle and suffering may be more intense. But, you will always grow from your experiences as you yield to the process of spiritual growth. Whenever you struggle with the Word that God has spoken over your life, you fall into the same type of scenario as Jacob. You have to wrestle or contend with God for your victory. But, the struggle leads to the strengthening that is necessary to sustain you in your kingdom assignment. Let's take a look at Jacob's struggle with God.

Jacob discovered his divine assignment during a dream in which he saw a ladder reaching from earth to Heaven. God laid out for Jacob what He would give him and all that he would become. And, God promised not to leave Jacob until he had accomplished what God had promised (see Gen. 28:12-15). However, Jacob did not receive the promises of God overnight. As a matter of fact, Jacob wrestled with God for the blessing. The Hebrew word for **wrestled** is ***abaq (aw-bak)***. It means to bedust, i.e. grapple; to float away as vapor, dust (Strong's). **Grapple** is defined as a hand-to-hand struggle; a contest for superiority or mastery (Merriam-Webster). So, we see that Jacob struggled or grappled with God for mastery of his divine assignment. God removed all of the "dust" (deceit) from Jacob's life and caused it to float away as vapor.

Jacob struggled for the benefits that came with the pursuit of his purpose. In his struggle, he had to surrender his plan for God's plan. God had to exchange Jacob's intent to remain a manipulator or deceiver for His original intent for Jacob's life. God changed Jacob's name to Israel, signifying that as a prince Jacob had striven with God and with man and prevailed. Jacob was actively seeking growth. During his experience with God, Jacob became a new person. He was both purified and transformed. Jacob suffered during, and as a result of, his experience with God. God dislocated Jacob's hip. Even though this was painful, Jacob held on. He said, *"I will not let You go unless You bless me"* (Gen. 32:26). You see, struggle was a component of Jacob's life.

Jacob struggled with Esau for Isaac's blessing; he struggled with his uncle Laban for proper wages and for Rachel, his wife; he struggled with Laban's jealous sons; he struggled with the barrenness of Rachel; he struggled to make peace with Esau; and, he struggled with himself, with his tendency to manipulate and the constant fear of being caught in his deceits. Jacob struggled with God and risked everything in his pursuit for his divine purpose. As a result, God transformed Jacob and moved him toward spiritual maturity, equipping him for his destiny – but not without cost to Jacob. He had to endure the process which involved surrender, struggle and suffering.

Jacob's dislocated hip was his constant reminder of his transformation from a schemer, relying on his ability to deceive and manipulate, to a simple trust in God's promises. God brought Jacob to the end of himself and made him realize that only by relying on God would he receive the blessing. Instead of acquiring the Promised Land through deception, Jacob learned that he had to receive it as a gift from God. Your purpose, your kingdom assignment, is a gift from God and must be accepted as a gift.

When God changes your name, it is an indication that your relationship with God has changed. Your new status means greater anointed power, which comes when you surrender to God and your strength fails and you learn how to cling to and trust Him. It may be painful. But, if you "wrestle with God" for your life's purpose, you will never be the same. You will experience great spiritual victories because you will be equipped to carry out your kingdom assignment.

Embrace fully the process that leads to your equipping. Equipping requires preparation. Allow God to prepare you in the process through your experiences as you surrender, struggle and suffer. Understand each season you enter and expect to glean from each season whatever God has scheduled. Extract every possible benefit. *"In this you greatly rejoice, though now for a little while, if need be, you have been grieved by various trials, that the genuineness of your faith, being much more precious than gold that perishes, though it is tested by fire, may be found to praise, honor, and glory at the revelation of Jesus Christ"* (1 Pet. 1:6-7). You will survive the fires of the furnace – surrender, struggle and suffering, where God perfects you and through preparation equips you for your kingdom assignment. The Lord will perfect that which concerns you (Psa. 138:8), and that is the original intent from the mind of God for your life.

CHAPTER EIGHT

BECOME A STEWARD OF YOUR KINGDOM ASSIGNMENT

"Let a man so consider us, as servants of Christ
and stewards of the mysteries of God.
Moreover it is required in stewards
that one be found faithful."
(1 COR. 4:1-2)

I am convinced that stewardship begins with humility. It is the foundation that will sustain the building of an excellent spirit without boasting about "me, myself, and I." It is the act of humbling yourself before God in total submission, in total dependence. Your desire should be for God to raise you up in His strength, not yours. Also, if you want to experience more and more of God's grace, you must learn to walk in humility. Apostle Peter urges believers to be clothed with humility. *"And be clothed with humility, for 'God resists the proud, But gives grace to the humble'"* (1 Pet. 5:5).

Obviously, God highly esteems humility. This is why He tells us to wear humility as if it were our clothing. When people look at you, they also see what you are wearing – what you have on. I believe that this is what God is saying here. Whenever anyone sees a saint of God, he should also see humility because as he looks at you he sees what you have on. Humility is that powerful. It can and should be seen at all times on a born-again believer. And, apparently, grace is always present where there is humility. There also seems to be an addition or an extension of God's grace to the believer who wears humility to the degree that it simply can be looked upon as clothing. *"But he gives us more grace. That is why Scripture says: 'God opposes the proud but gives grace to the humble'"* (James 4:6, NIV).

It is God's desire to raise sons and daughters unto Him. However, this, too, is a process. God stresses that He desires to exalt you in due time. *"Therefore humble yourselves under the mighty hand of God, that He may exalt you in due time, casting all your care upon Him, for He cares for you"* (1 Pet. 5:6-7). God's care for you also includes that He will not leave or forsake you as you walk in humility and learn how to faithfully steward your kingdom assignment.

Apostle Paul wore humility as a cloak upon his shoulders. It was a mantle that was representative of the powerful anointing that was on his life. As Paul was traveling by ship to Jerusalem to celebrate Pentecost, he said to the elders of the church from Ephesus, *"You know, from the first day that I came to Asia, in what manner I always have lived among you, **serving the Lord with all humility,** with many tears and trials which happened to me by the plotting of the Jews; how I kept back nothing that was helpful, but proclaimed it to you, and taught you publicly and from house to house, testifying to Jews, and also to Greeks, repentance toward God and faith toward our Lord Jesus Christ"* (Acts 20:18-21, author's emphasis).

Some of you may be asking, "What does it mean to serve the Lord with all humility?" To ensure clarity, let's define humility as it is being used in this context, because there is a true humility by the leading of Holy Spirit and there is a false humility which is exhibited through self-exaltation and pride. The Hebrew word translated **humility** is *anayv (aw-nawv)*, which means depressed in mind (gentle) or circumstances (needy, especially saintly): humble, lowly. **Anavah (an-aw-vaw)** is taken from this same Hebrew translation and is the divine and objective approach to life which means clemency: gentleness, humility, meekness as opposed to the human and subjective approach which means condescension (modesty) (Strong's Hebrew).

The Greek word translated **humility** is ***tapeinophrosune (tap-i-nor-ros-oo-nay)***. It means humiliation of mind, i.e. modesty: humbleness of mind, humility of mind, humility in condition or heart: abase self, bring self low (Strong's Greek). Merriam-Webster defines **humility** as the quality or state of being **humble** – not proud or haughty; not arrogant or assertive; reflecting, expressing, or offered in a spirit of deference or submission; humble in spirit or manner; and, to destroy the power, independence, or prestige of.

Saints of God are to live in true or righteous humility, being led by Holy Spirit who releases in our spirits the gentleness, meekness, and humbleness of mind – humility in condition or heart, where we abase or bring low ourselves in total trust and dependence upon God. We are not to express a false humility based on our human self-effort. To do so reflects a spirit of pride, haughtiness, and arrogance – a life independent of God. *"And whosoever shall exalt himself shall be abased; and he that shall humble himself shall be exalted"* (Matt. 23:12, KJV).

A righteous humility begins with reverence toward God. Solomon teaches us that this is where instruction in wisdom begins (Prov. 15:33). He teaches us that humility comes before honor (18:22). Solomon then combines humility with the reverence of the Lord and tells us that this is how we are to acquire riches and honor and life (22:4). False humility is deceptive, and it proceeds from a spirit of pride – a haughty spirit which Solomon warns leads to destruction (16:18).

Apostle Paul teaches us about false humility, which usually is displayed through religion. A false humility will seek to enslave you with enticing words; a false humility will seek to enslave you through vain philosophy; a false humility will seek to enslave you through the judgment of men; a false humility will seek to enslave you through improper worship; a false humility will seek to destroy the freedom that you have in Christ Jesus by enslaving you to the doctrine of men.

Paul said that these things truly appear to sound like wisdom, but they are really self-imposed through religion and false humility which have no value against the indulgence of the flesh (Col. 2:23). Like Paul, you should say, *"But none of these things move me…so that I may finish my race with joy, and the ministry which I received from the Lord Jesus, to testify to the gospel of the grace of God"* (Acts 20:24). God desires that you steward well your kingdom assignment. Humility is foundational to stewardship.

The Greek word translated **steward** is ***oikonomos (oy-kon-om-os)***, which means administrator of a household or estate; a house distributor – specifically a religious economy; a manager or overseer; a fiscal agent – treasurer in the handling and distribution of money; a governor; a preacher of the Gospel (Strong's). So, then, if you are to become a steward of your kingdom assignment, you must first invest in the Word of God and become a steward of the mysteries of God, which He reveals to those who love Him and are faithful to obey His Word. Jesus, your Commander-In-Chief, has given you a direct order: *"Occupy 'till I come"* (KJV).

I like The Message Bible translation: *"Operate with this until I return"* (Luke 19:13). The result of becoming a steward of your kingdom assignment is abundant life – a life of Kingdom benefits and advantages – as you advance God's Kingdom in the earth. *"Master, I doubled your money…Good servant! Great work! Because you've been trustworthy in this small job, I'm making you **governor** of ten towns"* (Luke 19:16-17, MSG, author's emphasis).

*****

This is the place that I found myself in August of 2000. God was about to teach me how to walk in humility. He had taught me how to become a steward of His Word. Now, He was about to teach me how to become a faithful steward of my kingdom assignment by teaching me first how to be faithful "in that which is another man's." *"And if you have not been faithful in what is another man's, who will give you what is your own?"* (Luke 16:12).

Around mid-August, Margie and I were about to enter a new chapter of our lives and ministry. It would be a new season of growth that would lead to the establishment of our own ministry. But, God is a God of order – first things first. I knew that God was speaking to me through the prophetic words that were spoken over my life and ministry by Apostle Bradshaw earlier on July 20th. Margie and

I agreed that we had absorbed all that we could in our current roles in the church we were attending. We were no longer growing or advancing spiritually.

At the time, I was the assistant pastor, church administrator, Sunday school teacher, Bible study teacher, and teacher of the radio ministry. Add to that, the fact that my father was my pastor. The decision to leave would be a difficult one, and it would open the door for further persecution. This is the time, as you progress from one level of glory or spiritual maturity into your next level of growth, you must reassure yourself and know what your kingdom assignment is and commit to it. As Apostle Peter said, *"We ought to obey God rather than men"* (Acts 5:29).

Dedication is the foundation of commitment. Without it you are unable to offer God anything else. You must be committed to your kingdom assignment in order to leap over these kinds of challenges that can easily hold you back. I took hold of Paul's charge that saints should war a good warfare with the prophecies spoken over their lives, being steadfast in faith and with a clear conscience. In this case, my conscience was clear and my faith was online. So, Margie and I prayed for courage to go to my father and ask him to release us from his ministry in order that we might pursue ours.

This was not going to be an easy task. But, I had grown and learned from Vicki. She had said that I had much growing to do spiritually, personally, and professionally. It was time for me to measure my growth. Margie and I had to follow righteous protocol in honor and out of respect for my father, for all that we had learned and for all of the opportunities we had been afforded which had led to my position as leader in that ministry.

As I said, this was not an easy thing to do. But, God graced us with courage, and we visited my father and his wife in their home. I remember that there were so many questions that my father had because he didn't understand or see why I would even want to leave. His perception was that I was leaving him. I explained as best as I could that I was not leaving him, as much as I was being obedient to my heavenly calling which required me to move beyond my current stage of growth. In the end, Margie and I were reluctantly released from the ministry.

On my father's face I could see the expression of abandonment. It was difficult to see him hurting. You may face a similar challenge as you move from glory to glory and from faith to faith. And it may cost you a diminished relationship with those closest to you. But, we could move forward with our heads held high because we had been faithful members, supporting that ministry and giving ourselves to it, and we were adherent to the protocol of righteousness in our departure.

My family and I joined the ministry led by my sister and brother-in-law in Jesup, Ga. At the time, Prophet Scottie Johnson was a spiritual son being mentored by Apostle Bradshaw. This was a good fit for me and Margie because it linked us directly to both the apostolic and prophetic ministries, which is the foundation of the New Testament church, Jesus Christ Himself being the chief cornerstone (see Eph. 2:20). So, I began to be trained by these men of God in both ministries.

What God had shown me in visions while I had been working for Jim and Vicki was about to manifest. Prophet Johnson conducted tent crusades as part of his ministry. Being in full time ministry, I could accompany him from town to town and assist with the erection of the tent and minister to the people, teaching them from the Bible and preparing them for prophetic ministry. Prophet Johnson would have me stand with him as he ministered prophetically to the people. Many of these sessions were teaching moments where he would share with me what God was speaking to his spirit. He would teach me the language, the vocabulary of the prophets. From time to time he would allow me to prophesy, standing behind me with his hand on my right shoulder.

We drove to Chicago in October and attended Apostle Bradshaw's prophetic training sessions, which were deeper wells in which to draw from. This level of training was intense and demanding. In 2001, Apostle Bradshaw would travel to Jesup quarterly to teach and train us. In the meanwhile, I was busy with Prophet Johnson conducting tent crusades. In the South, tent crusades usually begin in March and can be conducted throughout the fall because of the warm climate. I had grown and Prophet Johnson entrusted me to conduct the crusade while he was away conducting crusades with other prophets in other cities. God was teaching me how to be a steward of that which is another man's because He was about to give me that of my own.

Although I was growing in the apostolic and prophet ministries, things were still not good relative to our finances. We were in jeopardy of being foreclosed upon again. God was talking to me about the ministry He'd called me to, and I could see the handwriting on the wall. In order to succeed, I would have to establish the ministry that God had given me in a vision in 1998 as I was fasting for five days. But, certain things beyond my control had to take place and God had to push me and pull me into position to establish my ministry.

Meanwhile, God kept using Apostle Bradshaw to prophesy into my future and destiny. Had it not been for the prophecies God used him to speak into my life and ministry, I might not have had the foresight or the inner strength to keep pressing forward. But, God knew how to refresh me, and through prophecy He would stir the flames of my spirit and pour more coals on the fire. This would enable me to continue to war a good warfare with the prophecies that were being spoken over my life, a sampling of which I have included below.

April 24, 2001: *"You will lose nothing, said the Spirit of the Lord. For looks at a time like I see Prophet Johnson riding in a boat, and he's pulling you on a rope through the water; and you're all wet; you don't have on any water ski's, but you're just being dragged through the water on a rope. And at times it just seems like you're following him – he's in the boat but you're all wet.*

"But the Lord said, son, you're going to see a boat rise out of the water beneath your feet to take you and make you afloat. He said, but the Pastor, the man of God, is driving toward the place where there is a sunken treasure ship under the water that's going to rise up underneath you and bring you up out of the water son. For the Lord said, son, I've got treasures ordained and established for you. But stay tied to this man's boat; stay tied to it. I know he's running through some rough waters in the boat. I know he's going over some reefs and over some branches; but he's heading towards the place of the sunken treasure ship.

"I'm looking at a realm where there is an anointing that another man was supposed to have gotten, that had some relationship with him and it sank. But God said now it's going to be your treasure boat that's going to come up out of the low place, out of the water, and he's leading you directly to that spot in the river where the boat is sunken. And as soon as you get over that spot, the anointing is going to raise your

ship under you. And then you're no longer going to be wet. But God said you're going to find on that ship that comes up some young men that you're going to have to hand them a rope and push them over the side, and drag them through the water and lead them to their treasure ship as well, said the Lord.

"So son, I'm giving you endurance; I'm giving you the ability to see the vision. I'm giving you the ability to say, "Lord, whatever it is and whatever it's going to take, we're going to do it; we're going to stay focused; we're going to look through the smallest hole in the wall if we have to. But we'll keep our eyes pinned down to this thing."

"I hear the Lord saying, son, I'm going to establish you with great grace. And yes, there will be a home built for you, says the Lord. I'm looking at a ground-up facility – a house! Don't try to figure out how it's going to be. But God said, "I'm going to do this thing for you, son of faithfulness," says the Spirit of the Lord.

The tent crusades, led by Prophet Johnson, were going very well. The mantle of the office of the prophet on his life was keen and specific. Holy Spirit's gift of a word of knowledge was prevalent in his ministry. He would prophesy names, addresses, times and dates, looking by the Spirit into people's homes and describing exactly the different rooms and furnishings. By the Spirit, he would look into people's bodies and accurately describe what was going on as per their doctor's reports. Many healings took place in his ministry.

In 2001, we first erected the tent in Jesup, the home of Prophet Johnson's ministry. That crusade ran for three weeks and I was given more opportunities to minister and prophesy to the people. Honoring Jesus' ascension gift of teacher on my life, Prophet Johnson had begun to allow me to teach the people faith and prepare them prior to his prophetic ministry. This combination of faith teaching and prophetic ministry resonated with the people who attended his crusades, and sowed financially into it.

After Jesup, we traveled to Hinesville, Ga. for a crusade that lasted one month. There were mighty moves of God in that crusade and I was blessed to be a part of teaching people how to live by faith – how to believe in and trust God so that their lives would be established in the faith. Prophet Johnson would then teach them how to prosper through the ministry of the prophetic. *"...Believe in the*

Lord your God, and you shall be established; believe His prophets, and you shall prosper" (2 Chron. 20:20). Through Prophet Johnson, I learned more and more about prophetic ministry, and the anointing to prophesy began to increase on my life more and more.

Next we erected the tent in Pembroke, Ga. What a powerful crusade this turned out to be. For nearly two months people flocked into the tent night after night. Some nights there was standing room only. My responsibilities continued to increase to meet the demands of the ministry, and I found myself ministering more and more. There was one full week where Prophet Johnson was away ministering at another crusade out of the state. This gave me opportunity to minister the Word of faith and minister prophetically to the people.

I had learned, in many ways, to reflect the prophetic mantle that he carried. He entrusted to me not only the physical care of the tent, but also to conduct the crusade. In this position of delegated authority, both my humility and stewardship was exposed. God was measuring my capacity to steward that which was another man's. *"And the Lord said, 'Who is that wise and faithful steward, whom his master will make ruler over his household, to give them their portion of food in due season? 'Blessed is that servant whom his master will find so doing when he comes. 'Truly, I say to you that he will make him ruler over all that he has'"* (Luke 12:42-44).

The last week in August, we traveled across state lines into South Carolina and erected the tent in the town of Estill. At the time, I had no idea that this crusade would define my ministry and open the door for the establishment of my own. From the very beginning, I was the conductor of this crusade. Prophet Johnson had gone with another prophet to Hartford, Conn. for a two week tent crusade there. So, this would be my very first opportunity to open a crusade without his presence. However, it was my constant charge to let the people know that, like John the Baptist, *"There comes one after me who is mightier than I"* (Mark 1:7). And, I conducted the crusade for two full weeks prior to Prophet Johnson's arrival, displaying humility and stewardship. At the end of the first week in Estill, a young prophet walked up to me and gave me the following handwritten prophecy.

September 1, 2001: *"Elder, God spoke these words to me: SEASON, FORE-RUNNER, and PARALLEL. And He said that the sea represents the people and son represents a sonship. In the ministry you are considered a son of the house of Seedtime and Harvest (the name of Prophet Johnson's ministry). God says that a father sends his son to carry out business (ASSIGNMENT). Just as Jesus stated He must go about His Father's business, so must you go about the prophet's business.*

"God says I have set you as the forerunner for the prophet. A foundation must be made in order for the prophetic road to be paved for God's people. God says that's why you operate in the office and ministry of the teacher, although you are doing the work of an evangelist. God is doing this to make full proof of your ministry.

"God said that the word parallel means that because you are a forerunner for the prophet's ministry, the reward of a prophet is going to carry a boomerang effect on your anointing, position, prosperity, providence, and territory. Parallel goes both ways and will never intersect. Why? God said that the anointing on your life is parallel to the prophet. You are on the same length, but yet at a different direction.

"God says that there must be agreement, for how can two walk together except they agree precept upon precept, line upon line. God says this is where My covenant comes in; for the Lord God says a parallel covenant which will never end; it will not divide, intersect in confusion, nor go crooked or perverse; but it will continue to go straight forward and backwards to cover and do the work in which God has ordained it to do."

In this crusade, God really highlighted my teaching anointing. Many of the people that attended this crusade were steeped in religion and legalism, and had only been taught the gospel of salvation. As I taught on the gospel of the Kingdom, I could see that their way of thinking was changing; they became hungry for revelation knowledge. Their minds were being renewed; the word of God was transforming them (see Rom. 12:2). This is where I was when "9-11" occurred. And, by the time Prophet Johnson showed up the following week, they were in anticipation to receive this anointing on an even greater level. We were there for another two weeks. From Estill, we erected the tent in Ridgeland, S. C.

This crusade was totally different from the previous four. Not many local residents showed up for this meeting. Our audience mainly consisted of people from Estill, who were blessed during the crusade there. They consistently drove the 20-plus miles to be in this meeting, which unfortunately lasted only two weeks. What I learned from this crusade is that you cannot expect that, because you had success in prior meetings, all of them will flow the same way, under the same anointing. There was definitely a spirit of resistance in Ridgeland that fought against that crusade. We later learned that some of the local pastors had commanded the people in their congregations not to support our crusade, with one of the reasons being, "We would defile their minds with some new gospel that wasn't holy." The spirit of ignorance was prevalent there.

It was the end of October when that crusade ended. And, that was the last crusade of the year for me. I assisted Prophet Johnson, setting up the tent in Savannah, for a crusade to be conducted by one of his prophetic peers. After that crusade, Prophet Johnson and I disassembled the tent and stored it in the storage facility on my property. We had been conducting crusades for eight months and I needed a break physically. I also needed to be refreshed spiritually.

I knew that Apostle Bradshaw was scheduled to be in Jesup the second week of November for five days of teaching and leadership training in the apostolic and prophetic ministries. I was excited and filled with anticipation as to what God would do and how I would be elevated spiritually and naturally by being in the man of God's presence, listening to his revelatory discourses, learning from his teachings, and participating in his prophetic training exercises. And, I was not disappointed. Two major prophecies concerning my ministry and kingdom assignment were spoken by Apostle Bradshaw during this time, igniting a greater level of fire and intensity in my inner man. His prophetic words came forth as if he was literally painting a picture of my kingdom assignment and destiny on canvas – a blueprint; a step by step notation of what to do and how to do it.

November 11, 2001: *For the Lord said, "Now son, I'm establishing a heartbeat within you;" and the Lord said, "I'm establishing a pace in your life like no pace you've ever known before." For the Lord said, "You've moved for Me; you've gone forth for Me; you've stood for Me. Now I'm going to establish movement with a steady pace. I'm getting ready to give you a step by step notation of what to do and how to* do it," said the Lord of Hosts. "And I'm going to put My foot and your foot together. I'm going to put My hand and your hand together," said the Spirit of the Lord. "And I'm going to begin to cause you to walk into places, and to move into places, and to step into realms, and to walk into realms that you've not been in before." And the Lord said, "Where you set your foot, I'm going to move; and what you put your hand on, I'm going to move. Son, I'm going to stimulate activity; and I'm going to cause activations and movements in areas where things had not moved before."

For the Lord said, "Son, it's going to be supernatural. And what you've tried to do on your own, you've had some success with it. But now watch Me, because I'm getting involved in what you're doing. Now watch Me, because I'm motivating and activating the areas around you." And the Lord said, "It's going to move at My command; and it's going to move at My decree. Son, I'm getting ready to put you into some voice training. I'm getting ready to train you to prophesy. I'm getting ready to train you to speak for Me. And you're going to be saying things that are out of My heart, and out of My soul and out of My mouth."

For the Lord said, "Make no mistake about it – you're a man that's called to this hour and this season. And make no mistake about it – you're a man that I've placed in this flow; and I've placed in this grace." And the Lord said, "I'm going to loose the glory of the psalmist upon you. Even as David, the Sweet Psalmist of Israel began to hear the song of the Lord," the Lord said, "Son, you're going to hear the song of the Lord. And you're going to decree it; and angels are going to move at the sound of your voice, for I the Lord am going to put words in your mouth."

And the Lord said, "I'm sending you to change the atmosphere, and I'm sending you to move in the midst of the dull things. And you're going to stimulate and activate. Son, you're going to sit before Me, and you're going to lay before Me, and you're going to study before Me, and you're going to walk before Me." And the Lord said, "You're going to be in My presence, as well as Me being in yours, for what I'm going to have you to do shall not be the activities of man. It shall not be the work of man. But it shall be supernatural. I am raising you up and I'm placing you in the realm of the prophets," said the Lord God. "And I'm causing you to step into a flow where you're going to know My heartbeat, and you're going to know the pulse.

"And there will be those that will reject you, and those that said you've lost your mind; and those that say you've gone too far." But the Lord said, "Son, if I've put you out there, all you need to know is that I did it, and that I'm with you, and you're in Me, and I'm inside of you. And you're going to know that it's not a thing that you've made up for yourself. You're going to know that it's not a thing that I've made up for you; but it's a thing that I've ordained. I've ordained it," said the Lord. "It's not a quick thing that I simply place upon you at the spur of the moment. Son, I've planned this, and I've ordained this, and I've set it in order. For now," said God, "is a night of activation. Now is a night of stirring, for there is even a wisdom that I'm bringing up from the deep places of your heart and soul."

And the Lord said, "Son, even over your own household, you're going to begin to step into a realm of priesthood where you're going to begin to decree protections, and decree strengths, and decree ordinations and decree ordinances, and decree graces over your own house." For the Lord said, "Son, even as the word husband means house-band, I'm going to cause you to gird up your own house; and, I'm going to cause you to be a band around your house; and, I'm going to cause you to decree protection; there's going to be a strong protective anointing and grace I'm going to put on your household. You're going to begin to pray and intercede; and, you're going to begin to speak some things over your house and over the inhabitants of your house. And you're going to call those things that are not as though they were."

And the Lord said, "Son, the enemy would tell you – you're saying it, and you're saying it, and you're saying it, and nothing's happening." But the Lord said, "It's building up to fulfill the account. It's going to be an activation of new things that will even come into your house. Even as I spoke to your wife and I told her she was coming out of the background, even I'm pulling her forward; and even I'm thrusting you forward the more," said God. "And there are going to be projections where I'm going to pull you forth and push you forth; and pull you forth and push you forth. Some things I'm going to be behind you on, and some things I'm going to be in front of you on. I'm going to push you in some things, and I'm going to pull you in others. But in all of it, you're going to know that I'm there. In all of it, you're going to have the assurance from staying with Me that I the Lord made a promise. And I said I'd never leave you nor forsake you."

So the Lord said, "Now is a time of change; it is a time of thrusting; it is a time *of activity; it is a time of movement. And son, know this, that I'm stirring even now because there's been a removing of some things. And now I'm stirring your gifts. Now, I'm stirring the activity of the prophetic anointing. I'm beginning to bring forth a word out of you that's going to set a fire to the forests of men's lives. Great shall be the flame; and great shall be the flame. And heavy shall be the smoke, for they shall say look – over there is a fire; and over there is a fire. What is causing it? And they are going to follow the smoke; and they're going to see the flame," said the Lord. "And they are going to know surely that a man with a tongue of fire has been in the place." For the Lord said, "I'm setting a fire to the nation. I'm setting flames. And you're going to be a fire starter that I'm going to put in areas, sent to ignite things that have not been ignited before. Where there's been no flame, I'm going to send you. I'm even sending you forth."*

"Brother, I see you going into California repeatedly for ministry. I'm looking at God sending you. I'm looking at the State of Virginia. From the east to the west, God said He's going to span the nation. And even you're going to set foot in many places. I'm looking at Canada. Even in Canada the Lord said, "I'm going to give you territories." The Lord said, "You're going to establish ministry even in Canada. Son, I'm sending you forth. And think it not strange, for now is a time of great preparation and activation for what I shall do," said the Spirit of the Lord!

November 13, 2001: *For the Lord said, "Son, hold fast because the vision shall come to pass. The vision shall come to pass. Though it tarry, wait for it. It shall surely come to pass." The Lord said, "Son, there are things that I'm positioning you for ever so slowly, but ever so steadily. My steps with you are deliberate; they are intricate; they are sure; and, they are pure," I hear the Spirit of the Lord say. And God said, "Son, it's no mistake that you sit under this man (Prophet Johnson). There's no mistake that you hear his words. It's no mistake to the dedications that he's placed in you and provided in you that you have to give space and place to. But, it's not simply a matter of a preacher looking for an opportunity to minister; it's a preacher looking for the heart of God. Son, you're going to find that heart that you search for in Me. You're going to find that place in me to know Me like you've never known Me before," the Lord said.*

The Lord said, "You're coming into a place of sonship that you've never known, that you're going to know. You're going to mentor many young men into sonship – into that place of learning how to gather under leaders and how to serve, and how to be steady. You're going to help teach men how to be men and how to be submitted men; how to be men without compromise. There are so many men who think that to submit to another man means that they have to somehow lose manhood of their own – that they somehow have to be depleted of strength or boldness or creativity." But I hear the Lord say, "You're going to be able to show people how their creativity will fit into that of their leader; and, they're going to learn how to be men of vision – not men of division. There's a great calling and a great work.

"I told you the other day, I saw you in California; I saw you in Virginia; I saw you in Canada. I say it again. You're going to establish works above the Canadian border. I see Saskatchewan; I see Manitoba; I see different areas. I hope cold doesn't bother you. But I'm not saying you're going to move there or live there. But I'm seeing a definite work of God that's going to those regions."

God said, "It's an apostolic tent. I know you've been doing a lot of tent work; but, apostolic tent." I'm hearing that so clearly by the Holy Ghost. But the work of the apostles is coming forth, not only in your pastor, but in you in the season to come. And there are so many different kinds of apostles now that God's going to be raising up. And God said, "You're not going to be limited to that teaching element, or that preaching element. You're going to be issuing into that fathering element, where you're going to actually turn around lives under the anointing of the Holy Ghost.

"And so now, I just loose within you a greater ability to receive what God gives you; a greater ability to digest what you hear from God – what you receive from God; a greater ability to walk in it, that it will be cultivated and stirred; that it will be activated; that it will produce fruit. And I just speak fruitfulness into your life. And I speak grace and strength into you. The Lord just keeps saying, "Hold fast; hold on." The enemy will try to steal the vision some kind of way or another, But I tell you what – God said, "Steadfastness will produce your reward." And the Lord said He's not forgotten about anything that you've sown or given in life. God said, "Son, I'm building you up to a place and a position where you're not going to want for anything but Me," said the Spirit of the Living God! "So I seal you and I speak

grace upon your life, in Jesus' Name. Amen."

*****

God had been speaking to me relative to the launch of my ministry, so I began looking locally for a building that I could rent that would accommodate the ministry I had seen in a vision in 1998. I looked for an entire month, and even tried to get a loan to make something happen. Thank God, I was turned down. Still, I was left with a major problem. I did not have a flock or following of my own. No one was tithing or sowing financial seeds into my ministry. How was I going to afford to even rent a building if I found one? Every door was closed to me and I was beginning to get frustrated. So, I decided upon a five-day consecration fast, which I began on January 1, 2002. I wanted to know the Father's instructions and plans – how to go about establishing my ministry with no building and no money.

On the fourth day of the fast, I decided to take my chainsaw into the woods and cut down a few oak trees for firewood. As I was doing so, I heard a loud crackling sound. I looked up to see black smoke rising high into the sky and it was in the direction of my house. I dropped the chainsaw and began running toward my house. I prayed that my family was okay. I prayed that we wouldn't lose our home. As I got closer, I could see that the fire was indeed coming from my property, but thank God it wasn't our home. My workshop was on fire and I knew that it wasn't going to be saved. It was a total loss. All of my tools and equipment used to refinish furniture were lost, along with several pieces of antique furniture I was storing for several clients. But, the most serious loss for me to deal with was Prophet Johnson's tent.

I completed my fast, constantly thanking God for saving my family and our home. Margie and I, along with our children, did a happy dance and praised God. We did not know how the fire started. Even the fire marshal's report was inconclusive. What we did know was that we had no means of earning any money to sustain us. We barely had enough income, between the crusades and my work as a furniture refinisher, to stay one step ahead of foreclosure on our home. All of our monthly bills were behind, and God was telling me it was time to launch my ministry.

How we made it during the next several months, only God knows. What I know is that this was another season of intense warfare. I had to purposefully and consistently war a good warfare with the prophecies that had been spoken over my life. I found out that what makes the warfare "good" is the fact that you trust God to make a way in spite of what you see and experience. He said that He would never leave you nor forsake you, for with God nothing is impossible.

Throughout each day I would pray in my Holy Spirit language, make proclamations concerning my life, family and ministry, appropriating the scriptures that contained the promises of God. I immersed myself in the word of God, listening to and meditating on faith messages taught by Kenneth Copeland. This was the season when I got the revelation of something Brother Copeland said often in his ministry of faith – "Facts don't change the word of God; the Word of God changes the facts." I spent lots of time in my secret place meditating upon this truth.

From time to time the pressure and stress seemed unbearable. I would walk into the woods and cry, asking God to save us. It was difficult to see my family suffer. But, God was uprooting us. He was about to go extreme on me and my family. He was about to show me that one size does not fit all, and you cannot just say you can do ministry anywhere. I was about to learn that the anointing on my life was ordained for a certain place to launch my ministry.

After we ended our crusade in 2001, I accompanied Prophet Johnson each Sunday evening to Ridgeland, S. C., where he ministered for a local pastor. Each Sunday evening, several of the people who had attended the crusade in Estill, about 25 miles away, would show up. The crusade there had so impacted them that they wanted more.

One day, as Prophet Johnson and I were discussing how God was going to launch my ministry, he suddenly began to prophesy to me. He said that my true ministry was in Estill among the people that I had taught two weeks prior to his arrival, even though it had occurred under his ministry name and crusade. And he said that because I had been a faithful steward of his ministry, God wanted him to release that ministry to me. He said that Estill is where I would establish my ministry, and that God had chosen a few people to join with me and help launch my ministry.

I received that word from Prophet Johnson. And sure enough, several people from that crusade were very much interested in me establishing a church in Estill and becoming their pastor. So, we began having Sunday evening services in the homes of two women who expressed interest in joining my ministry. As this was going on, a couple who had resigned from my father's church heard that we were establishing a ministry and began to follow us to South Carolina. Lamar and Tracy Palmer, along with their two young children and another she was pregnant with at the time, became my first members. I began to pastor them in their home since we still did not have a building.

After the fire destroyed my workshop and the tent in January, I had no direct means of income. Several preaching engagements, along with financial seeds sown to me by people who believed that I had a call of God on my life to minister to people is what I had to sustain my family. However, this was not sufficient to meet our mortgage. We got further and further behind. Still, we were trusting God to save our home or provide a means of acquiring the money to make our mortgage payment current. Creditors and bill collectors would phone us throughout the day telling us how many days or months we were past due, pressuring us to make a payment, or threatening to report us to the credit bureau, and threatening to foreclose on our home. By September, the writing was on the wall. We were at least six months behind.

Our creditor decided to foreclose and gave us one month to move. Where were we going to move to, and with what? We had no money. All of our savings had been depleted. I found myself in a place where the vision looked too big for me. I pondered in my mind whether or not I had actually heard God; maybe I should have kept my job. And, the devil took full advantage of taunting me, telling me that God had abandoned us and that I should just get a job so that I could take care of my family and live like everybody else I knew. But, I knew this was a trick of the enemy to get me to say out of my mouth that I'd missed God and wasn't called into fulltime ministry. He wanted me to abandon my vision by speaking what was going on in my mind.

Just as I was about to waver, Holy Spirit reminded me of the revelation I'd gotten from Kenneth Copeland earlier in the year: "Facts don't change the word of God; the Word of God changes the facts." Holy Spirit reminded me of the prophecies that had been spoken over my life, and the words of Apostle Paul urging Timothy to war a good warfare with his prophecies. The next thing I heard was, **"Don't look at your vision in light of your current state. See it through the lens of faith, which unlocks eternity – the bigness of God. Now, whose report will you believe – Mine or Satan's?"**

I was reminded of how Moses must have felt as he was leading three million stiff-necked people through the wilderness. One of the mandates of his kingdom assignment was to lead the Israelites into their promised land – a land flowing with milk and honey. I learned that, on the way to your destiny, you will encounter opposition that will make your vision look nothing like a land flowing with milk and honey. But, if you are committed and surrendered to God's process, development, and His timing, you will emerge victorious because your purpose has power. It contains the passion to keep you moving forward, to never give up.

When you know your purpose, provision will accompany the vision, though at times it may not seem so. But, as you keep your eyes on the prize, you will see the big picture – the God picture! I knew without a doubt that God had called me into fulltime ministry, given me a vision of it, and several prophecies that not only confirmed the vision, but also painted a picture of my identity in Christ Jesus as a king and priest unto God, *"But he who is joined to the Lord is one spirit with Him"* (1 Cor. 6:17).

"Then Moses said to the Lord, "See, You say to me, 'Bring up this people.' But You have not let me know whom You will send with me. Yet You have said, 'I know you by name, and you have also found grace in My sight.' " Now therefore, I pray, if I have found grace in Your sight, show me now Your way, that I may know you and that I may find grace in Your sight. And consider that this nation is Your people."And He said, "My Presence will go with you, and I will give you rest."Then he said to Him, "If Your Presence does not go with us, do not bring us up from here. So the Lord said to Moses, "I will also do this thing that you have spoken; For you have

found grace in My sight, and I know you by name." (Exo. 33: 12-15, 17;
author's emphasis)

My family and I had to vacate our home by the end of October. We were already into October and still had no idea where we were going to move to. Two weeks into October, after a service I held in the home of one of the ladies who God had appointed to help launch my ministry, a pastor came to me and said that she felt that God wanted her to relinquish her role as pastor, join my ministry and use her ministry building to launch my ministry. This was confirmed by two other prophets. She also told me of a woman she knew who had a home that my family could move into immediately. She phoned the woman and set up an appointment for her to meet me and my family. The very same week, I drove my family to Fairfax, S. C. to meet her.

Mrs. Lawton was a retired educator living in Columbia. She too had driven to Fairfax to meet us. As we sat talking, she told us about the area and told us the names of the power brokers. She really did not desire to rent her home, but as she told us, "I can tell you are a man of God and your family is well mannered." Mrs. Lawton talked on and on for hours. We had met her at 2:00 in the afternoon. It was after 7:00 when we left. But, we left with the keys to her home in our hands and a whole lot of her personal history in our heads – her history as an educator, her family and their influence in the community, and names of people we should contact to make our transition into Allendale County easier once we got settled.

The move from Glenville, Ga. to Fairfax, S. C. was the most difficult move I've ever had to make. First of all, we were losing our home. Secondly, the home we were moving into was much smaller, had only one bathroom, and we did not have access to the master bedroom. Margie and I had to convert a cold, damp garage into our bedroom. Thirdly, we were moving to a less prominent area of a less prominent state. Fourthly, we knew only a few people through ministry and we would have to start over, rebuilding our lives within the community. Finally, I had the charge of building a kingdom-level ministry in a religion-dominated place.

After moving my wife and children to Fairfax, I drove back to our home in Georgia to get a few items that we could not fit into the moving van. Actually,

I had planned to do some light cleaning in the house and spend the time there praying and listening to the prophecies of my life and ministry spoken by Apostle Bradshaw and others. I had recorded them on a cassette tape. I knew that I was in heavy spiritual warfare, and I needed to go to war with my prophecies. I played those prophecies over and over and over. I already knew them word for word, so I spoke them out of my mouth just as they had been spoken to me.

Suddenly, the tears began to pour from my eyes. The tears became a flood accompanied by wailing. I could not stop. The dam of my soul had burst, forcing out all of the sorrow and pain I was feeling. That evening as I left what once had been our home, I stopped by the home of Lamar and Tracy to say goodbye. But, words were nowhere to be found. All I could do was wail. The man and woman of God comforted me as best they could and encouraged me to go forward. Still, I couldn't stop shedding tears. As I left their home, I cried all the way to Fairfax. When I pulled into the driveway, my tears stopped. I knew that another chapter of my life and ministry was about to be written.

The following week, I conducted a meeting at the building that was released to me for the launch of my ministry. During the five nights that I ministered, I could see by the Spirit those who were to join my ministry. Several of them committed to join. And on November 3, 2002, Community Empowerment Ministries, Incorporated was established with Prophet Scottie as its covering. At our ministry dedication I boldly proclaimed: "Community Empowerment Ministries, Inc. is committed to be a ministry of 'excellence with caring.' Our mission is to empower communities through revelation knowledge of the Word of God. Excellence is always a temporary condition. Where there is good, there is always better. Therefore, we set our sights high; for if anything is worth doing, it is worth doing well– 'as unto God and not unto man.'"

Two weeks later my family and I, along with several of our new members, drove to Jesup for three nights to attend services conducted by Apostle Bradshaw. My new members had been excited to meet the man that I had studied and trained under – the man who had spoken powerful prophetic words over my life and ministry. I too, was excited to be in his presence again and to hear the powerful revelations he would share by the anointing of Holy Spirit. It had been a year since I'd seen him. Little did I know, after this meeting it would be eight years before I would see him again. Nevertheless, he didn't leave Margie and me without a lifeline back to him – a prophetic word that would define the ministry I had received from the Lord Jesus.

November 23, 2002: *"Elder Brewton, Sister Brewton – Pastor Brewton now. Man and woman of God join hands. I gave your husband the word of the Lord last night in a private area, some things that God just suddenly laid on my heart. And I just began to speak some things into his life directionally concerning the ministry and the work of God. But God says tonight that He has cancelled some assignments of Satan. He's cancelled them. And God said, "It's important that you believe this and understand that I'm paying attention to your lives."*

The Lord says to tell you, woman of God, "You're not just out there going through the motions. You're not just working until the Lord comes." There have been some things that have happened and it looked as if – "Did we miss God? What went wrong? What happened?" God said, "You've lost nothing. I just have to have ways to motivate you to where I've got to get you. I have to send you into territories of assignment and places of assignment.

"There is a wisdom coming upon the both of you to do the work of the Lord. And your church won't be a conventional house, so don't raise it up to be a conventional house. Just like I said to you last night, pastor, God said start with a spirit of excellence – and the two of you look excellent tonight. Start with a spirit of excellence. Everybody that is training under you enhance them with this. Impress them with this – that even when they are going through – they keep their heads up. Even though they are being challenged, they are keeping their demeanor. I'm not saying they're supposed to lie, but they're to let people know that, "Our trust is in our God.

"God said, He's going to use your ministry to be an example of how to plug in to where the real power is. And man of God, the Lord says, "Son, I'm raising you up as a prophetic voice in the regions I'm sending you to. Not only where you are, but in other places as well." And the Lord said, "I teach you and train you and give you the vocabulary – the vocabulary, the vocabulary of the prophets; the wording of the prophets; the language of the prophetic, I bring to you." I heard the Lord say that,

"Even as I've called you to be a teacher, I'm expanding you beyond simply teaching the Word of the Lord, for great revelation must begin to come out of the wells of your spirit and great explanation for the tenets of life. You're going to be able to explain to people why things happen the way they do." And God said, "Some of this is not something you're going to study upon. But it shall be that you are a ready writer. You shall write the books. And you shall display. I see you making prophetic posters, displaying certain types of prophetic ideas and intentions.

"Woman of God, I see you getting together with somebody – I don't know if you're a seamstress or not, but you're going to get together costumes for the praise dancers and the worshippers. I see a company and a troop of worshipping young women that are going to dance before the Lord in the glory and splendor of the pageantry of God's temple. And they're going to dance before God. If somebody doesn't like it, and thinks it's weird, then that's just too bad because this is what God calls for. And the Lord said, "Much creativity is going to come before you and going to come out of you – creativity and color and design. It's not going to be a dull place. It's not going to be a drab place. You're going to be surrounded by color. You are going to be surrounded by the spirit of excellence. And you're going to give people a chance to come alive again. And there are some that just need a thrust."

"Even as I told you last night, brother, God has called you to some who are intellectual. And some who are well-studied and well-behaved. But you will have the Word of the Lord for them, for God says He's putting you in such a position that He's entrusting the lives of people who have made it in society unto your hands.

The Lord said, "There are many changes coming even to your relationship as husband and wife – many changes of new understanding of one another; new understanding of one another's behavior patterns; new understanding of one another's secret desires. I see the two of you entering a new season of intimate talk; intimate communications that is for your ears only. This is the secret place for you two. It's a realm that God said He wants to put His hand upon." God said, "The example of marriage is going to be an example of ministry. It is going to be a prototype for some people to look upon. There is an anointing on this one.

"Woman, I'm going to tell you now, God didn't create you to be a woman of lack. God created you to be a woman of splendor and design. You're going to live like you

know God and look like it. It's going to go both ways. Yes, there are times when you may wish you had more than you have. But just wait; and watch; and develop the servant's heart. God said, "Press, even beyond those times where you don't feel like doing anything. Do it anyway. Do it anyway.

"What I heard last night, and I said this to the man of God, is that there's a relocation coming for where the church is physically located right now because God said that He's ushered you into certain areas, and God said look at the kinds of people that are coming to your service. Have another meeting, a larger meeting, and have a kind of a survey. God said, "Survey the soil." I remember Him saying that last night. "Survey the soil of the territories that He's placed you in and called you to. You're going to begin to see how to set up your intercessors for what they need to be praying about and what they need to be praying for. But I speak this word over your lives that you develop a new sensitivity. And I speak an impartation of grace to you for leadership.

"Pastor, prophet of God, come and lay hands with me on this man of God as we assign you; as we speak over you; as we declare to you the purpose of God in your life – that you should go and teach, and raise up people, and release the prophetic voice of God over them with the revelation of God. We decree that you will hear the Lord speak; and that you will give the people divine purpose and planning of God; that you will have stamina, and ability, and courage to defend the Church of God against the adversary; that you will have the drive, and the strength to destroy the works of the devil. Manifest Jesus! Manifest the presence of the Lord! Destroy the works of the devil – with boldness, with power, with virtue! I speak strength to your soul; strength to your life; covering to your household – to your family, your children, to your automobile, to all that belongs in your hand. And I speak courage to you; that God will settle you, and strengthen, and establish you and your wife, and your family, in the name of Jesus!

"We send you into that arena with apostolic ability and prophetic power, and pastoral grace; a teacher's anointing, and an evangelistic purpose. All five-fold operations shall come out of your ministry. All five-fold operations shall work in the midst of you. All five-fold operations shall function there, in the name of Jesus.

"Woman of God, not stuck as a praise and worship person; not stuck as an inter-

154

cessor. But a leader shall begin to arise out of your bosom; and begin to come forth, and reflect, and gather the women, and teach them, and train them to be free – not religious bondage, but freedom; subject to your husband and honoring him, but free to be the woman God has ordained of you.

"Not a bondage ministry, man of God. There will be some that will say, "What is this thing he brings." But the Lord said, "I've transitioned you and I'm sending you forth with apostolic power to do the will of God." God said, "Let your purpose carry you; ride on your purpose. When you don't see or feel anything else, ride on your purpose, for I the Lord shall do this thing." "All things work together for good to them that love God; to them who are called according to His purpose." Hold on to purpose. Ride on purpose, because purpose stays anointed; purpose stays on fire; purpose stays in power. God said, "Your purpose will never dry out. Latch on to it. Hold on to it; pray for it; fast for it; seek Me for it. I'm giving you visitation this day."

And you've often wondered, woman of God, "Lord, are You sure I'm the one you want to do this with?" God said, "I have not made a mistake in whom I've chosen. You are indeed the handmaiden of My choice. You're going to help establish the course for many others. Don't just look at what's going on now. Get a vision for the future. Keep your hope and your faith in Me and watch what I shall do to supply your lives."

The Lord said, "Stay in the place where My presence is. Invite Me into your worship. Don't even try to be traditional in worship because that's a stronghold. Teach your people to be worshippers. Bring them into the presence of the Lord. Break the old tradition. Decorate the altar with splendor. Bring in those that will worship and dance before the Lord." And the Lord said, "I shall be your God."

*****

As you become a steward of God – a steward of the Word of God, you will learn to steward your kingdom assignment in the same way. Your stewardship will require humility and faithfulness to that which is another man's, before God will give you that of your own. Learn to become a follower before you become a leader. If you can steward well that which belongs to another man, you are well on your way to become a steward of your kingdom assignment. Walking in humility and being a faithful, loyal servant will prepare you for delegation. As my pastor and covering for over 10 years, Prophet Johnson delegated or entrusted to me his tent crusade ministry. Many times, I represented him when he could not make an engagement. He sent me as a representative of himself and his ministry. My faithfulness to steward well his ministry prepared and helped to equip me for my own.

Dr. Bradshaw states in his book, *The Technology of Apostolic Succession*, that delegation and destiny work hand in hand. "The challenges that leaders give their people reflect on how well they are going to function in the future. Nothing tests a person for the future like delegation. Leaders can observe their people to see how they function under pressure, how well they work with others and how developed their problem-solving skills are. Doubtless, they will make mistakes, but that is where the proper spiritual parenting skills come in. Spiritual parents must be able to guide their people through those seasons of miss-steps and mistakes with the person's destiny in mind. **"Delegation and Destiny"** work hand in hand to sharpen the individual and to prepare him or her to become the kingdom-level masterpiece that God has designed. Without delegating or challenging the individual to increasingly higher levels of function, we doom them to the stagnation of a powerless existence, robbing them of their future." (Kingdom House Publishing, Inc., 2010, pg. 291)

God will require you to give an account of your stewardship to your kingdom assignment. This is your foundation for success: *"If you're honest in small things, you'll be honest in big things; If you're a crook in small things, you'll be a crook in big things. If you're not honest in small jobs, who will put you in charge of the store?"* (Luke 16:10-12, MSG)

CHAPTER NINE

TRUSTING GOD'S PERFECT TIMING

"I have seen the God-given task with which the sons of men are to be occupied.
He has made everything beautiful in its time.
Also He has put eternity in their hearts..." (ECCL. 3:10-11)

Probably, the most important component of process that God uses to equip you for Kingdom deployment is time. The first mention of the word **time** in the Bible also involved the word **process**. The kingdom assignment that you are being prepared for will come to pass in the process of time. *"And in process of time it came to pass"* (Gen. 4:3, KJV). Also, you must understand that God sets time – appointments – *"At this set time in the next year"* (17:21); *"At the time appointed"* and, God does things according to time - *"According to the time of life"* (18:14).

The Hebrew word translated **time**, as in process of time, is *yowm (yome).* It literally means, from one sunset to the next. Figuratively, it denotes a space of time defined by an associated term – days, years, age, perpetually, or season. **Time**, as it relates to being set as an appointment, is the Hebrew word translated *eth (ayth)*, meaning now, when, continually, (due) season, what time. **Eth** more clearly refers to a **now** season or a **due** season **when** something should or must take place, as used in Eccl. 3:1 – *"To every thing there is a season, and a time to every purpose under the heaven"* (Strong's).

In your pursuit to become equipped and established for deployment into your kingdom assignment, you must understand time the way God uses it in alignment with your developmental process. Doing things outside the timing of God has proven to have negative consequences. Like Abraham and Sarah, you can birth an Ishmael instead of an Isaac – Ishmael being a child of the flesh and Isaac being a child of God's promise.

However, it is common for believers, during their development of spiritual maturity, to cry out to God, "When, God, when?" This is a commonly-asked question when waiting for a manifestation of some sort from God. At some point in the process of development, you will probably ask God, "When?" "How long will it take or how long will I have to wait before I get my breakthrough?"

Throughout the Bible, we find instances where individuals – heroes of faith – asked, "When, God, when?" And there were times when these heroes of faith failed to receive God's best because they could not abide in God's perfect timing. Again, Abraham and Sarah serve as examples of how you can end up with an Ishmael (the son of self-effort) or an Isaac (the son of promise) if you do not heed God's perfect timing. In another instance, God stripped King Saul of his throne because he did not abide God's timing as relayed to him through Samuel, the prophet/priest. His focus was on the people and not on God. Prior to Samuel's arrival at Gilgal, where there was to be a sacrifice made on behalf of Israel for victory in battle against the Philistines, King Saul foolishly offered a sacrifice, a role God had expressly given to priests. His excuse was that the people were scattered from him in fear of the Philistines.

> *"He waited seven days, **the time set** by Samuel; but Samuel did not come to Gilgal, and Saul's men began to scatter. So he said, "Bring me the burnt offering and the fellowship offerings." And Saul offered up the burnt offering. Just as he finished making the offering, Samuel arrived,*

*and Saul went out to greet him. "What have you done?" asked Samuel. Saul replied, "When I saw that the men were scattering, and that you did not come at **the set time,** and that the Philistines were assembling at Mikmash, I thought, 'Now the Philistines will come down against me at Gilgal, and I have not sought the LORD's favor.' So I felt compelled to offer the burnt offering." "You have done a foolish thing," Samuel said. "You have not kept the command the LORD your God gave you; if you had, he would have established your kingdom over Israel for all time."* (1 Sam. 13:8-13, author's emphasis)

Even David, as he fled for his life from King Saul – a process of his surrender, struggle and suffering that prepared and equipped him for his kingdom assignment – asked God on several occasions, *"How long, O Lord? Will You forget me forever?"* (Psa. 13:1). But, David grew spiritually mature by enduring the process that equipped him for the palace, to rule as king. Later in his life, he could write: *"I waited patiently for the Lord; And He inclined to me, And heard my cry. He also brought me up out of the horrible pit...**Blessed is the man who makes the Lord his trust.***" (Psa. 40: 1-2, 4, author's emphasis)

What all of this boils down to is trusting God instead of focusing on the "when" question. You will need to grow in this area because you want all good things to happen in your life. The problem you will have to overcome has to do with your flesh – its unquenchable appetite for now. God has a season, a "set time", to manifest every purpose. This will require you to trust His perfect timing, not knowing **how** He is going to accomplish what needs to be done and not knowing **when** He will do it. And, because God uses times of waiting – periods, seasons – to stretch your faith, He usually won't be early. But, He is never late.

You must learn to wait with patience. Your patience is a sign that you trust God. You want positive change and good things in your life, but you will have to embrace the process of waiting with patience and trusting God's perfect timing in order to experience your kingdom transformation. Trusting God's perfect timing, the set time, for your Isaac to be birthed, is a part of the process that will equip you for your kingdom assignment. So, you will have to wait. The real issue is how you wait. There is a wrong way and a right way to "wait."

Waiting wrongly produces misery and sorrowful pain. But, waiting God's way is a process of patience that produces your desires perfect and entirely, where you lack nothing. **Patience teaches you how to legally possess those things you desire without the stress and losses that come with being impatient.** *"But let patience have her perfect work, that you may be perfect and complete, lacking nothing"* (James 1:4, KJV).

It costs to be patient. It costs in terms of bringing fleshly lusts under spiritual subjection because your flesh wants no part of that. It wants only to be gratified – and immediately. And, when flesh is allowed to go unchecked, the end result is wantonness with no limitations. You see, patience is developed under trial. That means you will go through some difficult situations prior to a manifestation from God. And, this "trial of faith" period will require total trust in God, because timing and trust work together.

There is a difference between "due time" and "do time." Due time is God's time – when He knows you are ready and not when you think you are ready. Do time is what you actually do and how you do it, in alignment with God's word while you wait. The waiting process often causes agitation. This is a critical spirit that can leave you frustrated. While you are waiting, Satan will attempt to make you speak wrong words that can abort the timing of your blessing. You must refuse to allow words of discouragement to come out of your mouth.

To take a quote from Solomon's wisdom, *"The race is not to the swift, Nor the battle to the strong, Nor bread to the wise, Nor riches to men of understanding, Nor favor to men of skill; But **time** and **chance** happen to them all"* (Eccl. 9:11, author's emphasis). Since I have already defined time, let's focus on the word **chance** as it is defined in the Hebrew language. *Pega (peh-gah)* means impact: chance, occurrent. **Pega** is taken from *paga (paw-gah)*, which means to impinge by importunity: make intercession, pray, reach, cause to entreat (Strong's). This use of the word "chance" has less to do with luck – a chance happening or occurrence upon something desirable (Merriam-Webster), and more to do with the deliberate timing of God for the manifestation of a specific event, activity, or request upon your life, brought on by the impact of your preparation, persistence, and demand.

"Time and chance happen to them all." In other words, Solomon is saying to you that **time** – God's process of a set time or appointed time — will manifest a **now** season or a **due** season **when** something should or must take place to advance your life and kingdom assignment. **Chance** is the occurrence, at a particular time or place, of something you've entreated or sought favor from God by being overly persistent in your requests or demands, prayers and petitions, forcing an impression upon your kingdom assignment in the mind of God and causing it to become current in time – IMPACT! Solomon said that this should happen to us all. Therefore, as you continue to trust God's perfect timing to manifest the "REAL YOU", IMPACT IS IMMINENT!

The wisdom that Solomon seems to be sharing is that events and occurrences are controlled by God. You simply have to take advantage of God's opportune times for your advancement. Preparation, persistence, and patience place a demand on the original plan of God for your life which leads to opportune times or God's set time to elevate you. Preparation takes place prior to elevation. You are responsible for discovering your God-ordained purpose for your life on earth. You must prepare yourself to accomplish your purpose in a manner that will bring glory to God and advance His Kingdom in the earth. And, since only God knows the process that will lead to your spiritual maturity and equipping to carry out your kingdom assignment, you must endure the process – surrender, struggle, suffering, persisting in trials, tribulations, persecutions, etc. with patience – not by your might or power, but by His Spirit (see Zech. 4:10). Be strong in the Lord and in the power of His might (Eph. 6:10), for through faith and patience you will inherit God's promises.

Patience is defined as the capacity, habit, or fact of being patient, which is inclusive of bearing pains or trials calmly or without complaint (Merriam-Webster). How many people do you know who habitually endure trials and pain without complaint? My guess is probably only a few, if any. Yet, this is the sacrifice God requires of you in order to reap the rewards He's ordained for your life, *"For you have need of endurance, so that after you have done the will of God, you may receive the promise"* (Heb. 10:36). Patient endurance is required! **You have need of patience.** The Greek word translated **patience** is *hupomone (hoop-om-*

on-ay). It means cheerful, hopeful endurance, constancy: enduring, patience, patient continuance (waiting). Also **hupomeno (hoop-om-en-o)**, which means to stay under; to undergo or bear trials, have fortitude, persevere, endure, and suffer (Strong's). Patience is imperative not only to do God's will, but also to receive God's promises. To receive God's best, His goodness, you must undergo or bear trials with fortitude and perseverance.

You must accept God's timing because patience (waiting) has rewards. Patience produces favorable responses from God, because "patience is a seed. It is the season between sowing and reaping" (Mike Murdock). If you knew how long it would take for God's perfect manifestation of your desires, you would probably give up. However, when you trust God, you keep your eyes on the rewards – the reality of your desires. Secured in this mindset, you never give up. You are *"fully persuaded that, what God had promised, He was able also to perform"* (Rom. 4:21, KJV). The waiting period is simply God's training period that requires your obedience to His word without questioning or trying to figure out "when." As God directs your steps, you will sometimes be led in ways that make no sense to your natural mind. You will not always understand. If you try to use human reason or logic to try and figure things out, you will open the door to experience unnecessary struggle, suffering, confusion and misery.

Remember, humility is the foundation for stewardship. Through impatience, you will make the mistake of "giving place" to the devil, opening the door for the spirit of pride to overtake you. From that point, you will try and figure out everything yourself. King David said, *"I trusted in, relied on, and was confident in You, O Lord; I said, You are my God. My times are in Your hands"* (Psa. 31:14-15, AMP). Peter the Apostle said, *"God resists the proud, But gives grace to the humble"* (1 Pet. 5:5). Humility is a covering that draws the protection of God into your life. You do not succeed in God unless you are leaning and relying on Him. The sooner you understand this principle, the sooner God can work His plan in your life.

You must learn how to traverse the "time of waiting" that is between seed-time and harvest by trusting God's Word and His perfect timing. Since relatively few of us live in the same season at the same time, you should never be jealous or compare yourself with someone who is enjoying their harvest while you are still planting or waiting. The in-between-time is a time of learning God's will and obeying Him. This is where you learn to choose God's will instead of your own. You cannot allow yourself to be drawn into the world's system of doing every evil thing for immediate satisfaction of your fleshly lusts. However, when you learn to trust and obey God, all kinds of good things happen in the spirit realm that you cannot see. In God's perfect time, your seeds of obedience suddenly break forth into a magnificent manifestation of God in your life. When harvest time comes, the desires of your heart begin to manifest and all kinds of good things appear. Your profiting appears to all (see 1 Tim. 4:15). God causes things to manifest at exactly the right time – His perfect time. To quote Maya Angelou – "All great achievements require time!"

So, whenever you get impatient, waiting for the promises of God to manifest concerning your kingdom assignment, focus on the function – the intended fulfillment of your kingdom assignment – and not on the fruit. Avoid the "when, God, when?" question and trust God completely for His perfect timing, when the fullness of the harvest is released and your profiting appears to all. *"For when God made promise to Abraham, because He could swear by no one greater, He swore by Himself, saying, 'Surely blessing I will bless you, and multiplying I will multiply you.' And so, **after he had patiently endured, he obtained the promise**"* (Heb. 6:13-15, author's emphasis).

*****

Unbeknownst to me, apparently something happened that night, after the service in Jesup, which led to Prophet Johnson severing ties with his "spiritual father," Dr. Gordon E. Bradshaw. And for the next eight years, I would remain loyal to Prophet Johnson and to his ministry, not contacting Apostle Bradshaw as I was commanded. But, God knows how to rejoin on earth what He put together in eternity. Over an eight year period, I saturated my spirit with the messages and training sessions taught by Apostle Bradshaw that I had recorded. I wrote all of his prophecies to me on a legal pad and memorized each one, consistently waging spiritual warfare with them. In the meantime, Community Empowerment Ministries, Inc. was taking shape and growing into the Kingdom of God dimension as per the prophecies, but not without struggle.

Starting a new ministry in a new place from "scratch" is never an easy task. The challenges I was met with as the founder and pastor were of monumental proportions. Most of the pastors that I know never would have embarked upon this "uncertain" journey, especially at the cost I'd paid to be there. It was much easier for them to walk into a ministry position in a local church that had been established for decades and affiliated with some prominent association, denomination or assembly of churches.

But, God transitioned me. And, He gave me the grace and patience to face and endure the difficult challenges and tasks I faced as I began to transition the people's mindset from religion to kingdom. All they had ever been taught was religion – legalism. "The Lord will make a way." "All my appointed time, I'm gone wait 'til the Lord comes." Seemingly, they couldn't wait for Jesus to part the clouds and take them to Heaven, where their new life of no more troubles, burdens, pains or tears would begin. They had no idea or revelation that they could have heaven on the earth.

The gospel of the kingdom, properly ministered by mature believers who understand and minister under the prevailing grace and power of Jesus' governmental authority, carries a divine influence that changes mindsets, atmospheres and environments to the heavenly pattern of the kingdom. This is exactly what needed to be infused within the people if I were to successfully get my ministry established. But, that would only take place through grace, time, and personal sacrifice.

I found myself teaching rudimentary aspects of learning prior to teaching the gospel of the kingdom. I had to meet the people where they were and adhere to the foundation of the gospel – love. God is love (1 John 4:8), and love is God's drawing card. *"Yes, I have loved you with an everlasting love; Therefore with lovingkindness I have drawn you"* (Jer. 31:3). And, I had to show a lot of love given the condition of the people God sent me to minister to. At that time, the region of the state I'd been sent into had the lowest educational attainment level, lowest per capita income, highest poverty rate, highest teenage pregnancy rate, highest infant mortality rate, highest unemployment rate, highest illiteracy rate and the highest percentage of children living in poverty in South Carolina (U. S. Census, 2003; S. C. Kid's Count). The Lord called and ordained me to minister in the midst of this magnitude of poverty factors.

Meeting people where they were, in this type of environment, was an arduous task. It was slow and time consuming, which required a great level of patience. But, I didn't complain because the grace of God was upon me to meet those challenges, even though I had not perceived the depth of the challenge. What I did know is that the prophecy spoken over my life in 2000 by Apostle Bradshaw concerning having my own ministry had come to pass (refer to Chapter 7 for prophetic word, Feb. 17, 2000).

I knew that this was a prophecy of confirmation even as Dr. Bradshaw was ministering it to me. All I had ever done prior to becoming a pastor was counsel and teach low income, underprivileged, underachieving high school students. And, I simply loved it. I was at my best when I could reach seemingly hopeless students and turn their lives around by building their self-concept and self-esteem, respecting them and patiently teaching them. To see these kinds of students go on to college and graduate was a most fulfilling and rewarding accomplishment. God bestowed His grace upon me relative to my divine assignment and equipped me for this type of ministry, which displays love, faith, humility, compassion, integrity, respect, and patience abundantly – all are a part of that grace.

It was this type of environment, the condition of the people I was sent to minister to, which became a classroom that God used to teach me that His timing is the absolute best time, since it is He who has "made everything beautiful in its time." So, I resigned myself to faithfully teach and meet the people right where they were. I had to learn to persevere during the difficult times. I had to persist in being a faithful steward of the ministry I received from the Lord to minister grace to His people. I had to do what is right as opposed to what was easy. I had to indulge trivial offenses and poverty mindsets when I didn't want to. I had to discipline myself to solve other people's problems, even when my personal problems exceeded theirs. I believe in values over feelings.

God was teaching me about character. Holy Spirit was training and developing me with godly character in line with His fruit (see Gal. 5:22-23). I was learning to be passionate in service to God. He was developing in me a spirit of excellence and a spirit of leadership. He was teaching me how to persevere and become a strong finisher. For over eight years, God did some amazing things to keep my ministry afloat, even when it seemed as if we weren't advancing.

This was the magnitude of what I was faced with in ministry. Besides this, the scope of what I was confronted with at home, the daily care and support of my family, was even larger.

As I stated in an earlier chapter, I moved my family from Tattnall County in southeast Georgia to Allendale County, S. C. the last week of October, 2002 – through the process of elimination. As the story goes, God uprooted us; a ministry I had no idea I'd started during a tent crusade August 20 – September 16, 2011; a fire that destroyed our means of living in January, 2002; and, foreclosure of our home in October, 2002.

For several months leading up to October, I conducted church services in the homes of two prospective members while searching for a house to rent and a building to rent for the ministry. I had no success finding either. Then, at one of our meetings, an evangelist who was also a pastor said that God told her to sublease her building to me and study under my ministry. She also knew where we could find a house for immediate occupancy, but only for six months. This is how my family and I ended up in Allendale County, population 11, 362 – over 8,000 African-Americans.

Margie and I had no idea of the county's history, and when we announced to her relatives who resided in Lexington, S. C., our decision to move to Allendale, they bombarded us with stories of how poverty-stricken the county was; we were also informed that the state's Department of Education had taken control of the county's school district in 1999. In spite of the negative publicity, Margie and I, along with our teenaged daughter and son visited the county's middle and high schools. And, it was very obvious that there were major disciplinary problems.

I think that we all experienced culture shock, especially our children. They did not want to attend these schools. We had a decision to make. We were either going to be part of the problem or part of the solution. I was convinced that God had sent us to such a place as this to be part of the solution. And, after much prayer, we enrolled our children in the Allendale County School District. It was difficult to see our children struggle to adapt to their new environment, and they really never did.

I promptly became involved in the community, becoming a member of the Sheriff's Task Force which focused on curbing gang-related activity within the community as well as the middle and high schools. I began to frequent the county library to learn about the community and what events led to its current state. After discovering many of the root causes leading to the county's problems I understood clearly that transformation would be a slow process requiring commitment of time, effort, wholehearted devotion and lots of resources in order to bring forth solutions.

Over the course of our six-month lease of the house in Fairfax, we searched for housing in adjacent counties whose community and schools were much better. My wife and children were far less enthused about living in Allendale County than I was. Actually, my enthusiasm had more to do with obeying God and accepting my kingdom assignment than living in Allendale County. Nevertheless, at their behest, we looked for the neighborhood, house, and price we thought would be best for us. Nothing opened up for us.

Desperate, we turned our attention back to Allendale County and directed our search within the town of Allendale, the county seat. Weeks went by and we could find nothing. We had one week to vacate our current home. That Sunday after our church service, I felt compelled to drive back to Allendale to a neighborhood where we had looked for a house just two days prior. There was a feeling deep in my spirit that Allendale was where we were supposed to live. I had gotten involved in a community effort to help improve the county's image and standard of living, which actually lined up with the mission statement of my ministry.

I drove again through this neighborhood and, lo and behold, there was a sign advertising the sale or rent of a house we'd seen two days before, only the sign was not there. I immediately phoned the owner, who did not hesitate to set up an appointment to show us the house. That meeting led to an agreement, and that is how we ended up living in the town of Allendale. I extended my involvement in the community by joining other community organizations, volunteering at the county's alternative school, and coordinating the community's summer recreation program, volunteering as a counselor. By the end of 2004, I had done so much research on the county that it led to the publication of my first book, *A Slave of Circumstance*, 2005 by BookSurge, LLC (Createspace).

It had been three years since I'd seen or had any contact with Apostle Bradshaw. I knew this man was to be my spiritual father and mentor. I knew that I had this man's spiritual DNA, yet I was alienated from him. I felt as if I'd become stagnant in ministry partly because I was not receiving the level of ministry, training, or divine connections that would accentuate my ministry and move it into the dimension I'd seen in the vision God had shown me. And, since the prophet who supposedly was covering me had no covering of his own, I felt stagnant. I couldn't take off; I was just hovering. As I was to learn later, **it is extremely unwise to be under someone who is completely void of accountability to others.**

Dr. Gordon E. Bradshaw writes:

"I have had the unfortunate learning experience of having spiritual sons who were pastors and who were completely underdeveloped in foundational truth. I did not mentor these people from within my ministry. There were individuals who said they believed that God has placed them under my care for mentoring and personal development. Needless to say, I offered them "*covering*" and received them into the network family. It didn't take long for them to say all of the regular "speeches" that come with network "covenants." ***"God sent me to you!" "I'm not going anywhere...this is the right place to be!" "I'm not trying to start a network of my own yet...I'm not ready for that!" "I just know that I'm supposed to sit under you for as long as it takes!"***

"Hearing those confessions, I began the mentoring process by asking those leaders who were within a reasonable traveling distance to attend a monthly session on ministry development. Many of them showed up for a period of time. There was a friendly relationship there, and we would see each other fairly often. I would often go to their churches to "*observe*" their services. To my dismay, I discovered that they didn't possess the foundational "*engines*" to energize their churches at Kingdom levels. Many of them claimed to be Apostles... and some were. But, their technologies were not yet developed enough to adequately affect their members or the atmospheres and areas in which they functioned.

"A few of them would make an attempt to "*impress*" me when I came, but I could see that they were missing vital elements from their operational structure. After all of the "***rehearsals***" ...then came the "***reversals!***" Some came to me and described how it was time for them to leave because the Lord had given them the "name" for their own network and they had pastors who wanted to follow them. Bear in mind, these individuals were barely functional in the most basic aspects of relationships and ministry work! But, they wanted to be "***Chief Apostles!***"

"These same individuals couldn't seem to figure out why they had trouble getting people motivated and activated. They couldn't "*take off*" into the height of the Spirit so they spent a great deal of time just "*hovering*!" I even had some who went to other cities under the "*assignment*" to plant and establish ministries. Well, two and three years into the process, nothing had happened. ...More "*hovering*!" People who "*hover*" don't move up or down. They just sort of "*float*" in midair waiting for something to suddenly "blow" them into their destinies! They are saturated with indecision and indifference. They actually do expect the impossible! **BUT IT WON'T HAPPEN!** ...At least not like they are expecting.

"After going through this process for awhile, I questioned God about what was wrong. He told me that I should not be providing a "*Covering*" for people who were just "*Hovering*!" Each time I spoke to the leaders it was one excuse after another! I eventually told some of them to *"**either build a ministry or go join one!**"* I discovered that only superficial amounts of my spiritual DNA had ever been transferred to these people to begin with." (*The Technology of Apostolic Succession,* Kingdom House Publishing, Inc., 2010, pp. 178-179)

I attended a prophetic service in November, 2005 held at my father's church. There, God was to refresh me and reignite the flame that burned inside of me concerning my kingdom assignment. I had listened to Dr. Bradshaw's messages on cassette tapes so often until some of them were barely audible. During spiritual warfare, I had consistently warred with the prophecies that had been spoken over my life. I had asked the man of God, the prophet, to renew his covenant with his "spiritual father," all to no avail. And, the signs of being unaccountable were beginning to show. There was no movement forward. I needed a refreshing. That night, God used a young lady, prophetess LaTara Hunter-Tillman, to reignite the flame and blow passion back into the sails of my kingdom assignment. Here is what she prophesied to me.

November 4, 2005: *"Pastor, I hear the Lord say, "There is another book that's being birthed." And, as I see another book that's being birthed, it's getting ready to go to bestsellers. God says, "I'm getting ready to put you on a platform." I see you on a platform with distinguished people and educated people.*

"Resources are going to be able to flow in, and even the things that you desire. I see a youth center being raised up; I see the extension of a church; I see a lot of work going on; a lot of work taking place. God's going to begin to bring in the resources. God is setting you up; even now, He's setting you up. Even as He put you over the airwaves and you begin to speak the Word of the Lord, even over the airwaves, God is getting ready to give you regions.

"I see you getting on a plane. I see you getting on a plane more and more, and traveling to California, and traveling all over this place – to Hawaii; I see you traveling all through the airways. And I hear the Lord say, "Tell him, son, I've given you the airways." He said, "There's an opening in the airways. In this life, I've allowed you to speak through the radio. It is the airwaves. And I've given you the airwaves to

enter in My atmosphere and even in the heavens." God said, "You're going to begin to fly.

"I see you going to colleges. I see you beginning to speak to people." He said, "And as you begin to speak to Yale students, and as you begin to speak to these students, those people are going to be impacted by your ministry. I see you eventually building. And as you build, that ministry is going to grow by leaps and bounds." He said, "Even as you share where I brought you from and what I brought you out of; even as you open your mouth and share it, you're going to find people in towns and certain places that are going to run to your counsel.

"I see a strong men's ministry. And He's giving you – He's developing in you a strong men's ministry. I see a strong boy's ministry. God said that He's going to raise that ministry up in a strange land; a strange place. But, He's getting ready to raise it up. And, even as your family steps out and begins to possess the things that you have longed for – the house and the cars – as you begin to possess these things, God said, "Because you're going to be building My house, I'm going to build yours." I see you becoming a wealthy man. And, what could not happen in the secular world, God said, "I'm getting ready to give you what you're owed."

He said, "There is something that is on the inside of you that is still there that was imparted in you, even from your schooling. And I'm getting ready to give you the world! You need a refreshing. And as you receive the refreshing, I hear the Lord say, "Tell My son to receive My refreshing right now. Receive My strength. I've given you wings now. I've given you the ability to fly now. Go forth, son, and endeavor everything. If you put your hand on it, I'm going to bless it."

"I'm going to open the heavens. It's going to be like a Jacob's ladder effect – going up or coming down. I'm going to open it up. And when I open it up, recognize it; speak it; and it will come." And it's going to be a repeat; it's going to be a repeating affect. God is going to work on your behalf. Peace is going to be on your children. It's a new season, a fresh anointing. I see prosperity; you're walking in your new season."

*****

Over the course of the next five years, Margie and I kept our hands to the plow. We had grown in our faith, but the ministry wasn't growing in the normal way ministries grow. God was building a foundation in my ministry to raise kingdom-level leaders. Those who deemed the teaching and training too long, too deep and not progressively in tune with other ministries that they considered to be "blessed" had walked away. They could not discern the depth of what was being released into their lives and how they were being prepared and equipped to accomplish their kingdom assignment and enjoy success in life.

By 2010, I had become a bit anxious. I was feeling ill at ease because things just weren't moving forward. Again, I felt stuck – trapped. I wanted to renounce the prophet of God as my covering and walk away. But, I understood completion. I understood waiting on God's perfect timing. Plus, where would I go? There was no one else I knew as versed in teaching revelation knowledge of the Scriptures and as accurate prophetically. And, I knew no one that I could reach out to who would understand the ministry that I'd been called to; no one who understood what it meant to give up everything to pursue it; no one who understood what it meant to live by faith each day.

I prayed again and again that the man of God would reunite with Dr. Bradshaw. Some in my ministry implored me to walk away before the ministry crumbled under the weight of maintaining its relationship with a man of God who was not accountable to others. Spiritually, I could see the seams of his ministry start to pull apart. Still, he remained defiant and I remained faithful. God was about to show up on time once again and bring deliverance.

On New Year's Day, 2011, as I was surfing the web, I saw a pop-up of a website advertising a book that totally caught my attention. The title of the book was *The Order of Melchizedek* by Dr. Francis Myles. I had never heard any extensive teaching on the subject although I loved to read about this eternal king/priest after whom God had established Jesus as Royal High Priest. The word that caught my attention was order. What was Melchizedek's spiritual and natural order, class, genus, hierarchy or kingdom?

As I pondered that question, I begin to look at other books being offered on this site. And lo and behold, a very familiar name stood out. It was Dr. Gordon E. Bradshaw, and he'd just published a book called, *The Technology of Apostolic Succession*. I was elated. That's the kind of title that really stirs my inner spirit.

Immediately, I ordered his book.

The site said that I should allow two weeks for delivery. Well, four weeks passed and I still had not received the book. Having paid by debit card, I emailed a heated letter to Dr. Francis Myles' website demanding the product that I'd purchased and attached the receipt showing that the bank had charged my account and payment had been made to the site four weeks earlier. I expected a reply along the lines of an apology and an oversight. What I received was a total surprise and the breakthrough I'd been waiting on for over eight years.

Apparently, Dr. Francis Myles informed Dr. Bradshaw of the letter stating my displeasure in not having received my book within the stated timeframe. Dr. Bradshaw recognized my name and remembered me from the ministry in Georgia that had once been apart of his network. The day after I'd sent the email, I received an email from Dr. Bradshaw, apologizing for the delay and any inconvenience it had caused me. And, because of my inconvenience, he also gave me a free download of two of his prophetic training e-books. His personal cell phone number was included in the email, which he concluded with this happy statement: "CALL ME"!

I knew that this meant a reconnection with the man of God, whom I knew was my spiritual father even before I'd met him. Satan had tried to sever the bond of the father/son relationship that had been ordained by God, but the spiritual DNA was too powerful. I had prayed fervently for over eight years for this breakthrough, and Dr. Bradshaw had not forgotten me. He'd said to me that his assignment to the man of God in Georgia had a great deal to do with meeting me and pouring into me his apostolic and prophetic gifts and anointing. I had stayed the course; I had remained faithful; and, I had been a steward of another man's ministry, honoring his word. In short, I had trusted God's perfect timing.

As you learn the will of God by obeying His Word, you will also mature in your position in Christ to trust and depend upon God to lead you through the 'period of waiting,' "For we walk by faith, not by sight" (2 Cor. 5:7). You will develop patience to keep your focus on the function of God (the eternal) rather than the fruit (the temporal). Patience has rewards – breakthroughs, the perfect time for the beautiful things that God has ordained for your life and the accomplishment of your kingdom assignment. In God's perfect timing you will receive the fullness of God's harvest and you will be blessed to be a blessing as you advance His kingdom in the earth.

So, whenever you get impatient as you wait for the promises of God to manifest, focus on the function – the intended performance of your divine purpose – and not the fruit. Avoid the "when, God, when?" question and trust God completely for His perfect timing, when the fullness of the harvest is released – the beauty of His timing. *"Therefore we do not lose heart. Even though our outward man is perishing, yet the inward man is being renewed day by day. For our light affliction, which is but for a moment, is working for us far more exceeding and eternal weight of glory, while we do not look at the things which are seen, but at the things which are not seen. For the things which are seen are temporary, but the things which are not seen are eternal"* (2 Cor. 4:16-18).

SECTION FOUR:

FROM FOOTMEN TO HORSEMEN

"In order to restore Earth, God had to raise the 'standard' and give mankind supernatural ability and clear marks for the territories and assignments we are to undertake. Our authority isn't ambiguous, random or undefined. It is authority for assignment – specific and focused. We are empowered to 'press into success' by re-"forming" planet Earth's cultures and spheres of influence" (Dr. Gordon E. Bradshaw, *I See Thrones! Igniting & Increasing Your Influence In The Seven Mountains Of Culture*, 2015, Kingdom House Publishing, Lakebay, WA, p. 259).

"If you have run with the footmen, and they have wearied you, Then how can you contend with horses? And if in the land of peace, In which you trusted, they wearied you, Then how will you do in the floodplain of the Jordan?" (JER. 12:5)

"My anger burns against your shepherds, and I will punish these leaders. For the LORD of Heaven's Armies has arrived to look after Judah, his flock. He will make them strong and glorious, like a proud warhorse in battle. From Judah will come the cornerstone, the tent peg, the bow for battle, and all the rulers. They will be like mighty warriors in battle, trampling their enemies in the mud under their feet. Since the LORD is with them as they fight, they will overthrow even the enemy's horsemen." (ZECH. 10:3-5, NLT)

CHAPTER TEN

THE RISE OF COMMISSIONED, KINGDOM-LEVEL LEADERS

"Go through, Go through the gates! Prepare the way for the people;
Build up, Build up the highway! Take out the stones,
Lift up a banner for the peoples!" (Isa. 62:10)

The royal rule of the Kingdom of God and His righteousness is that saints should live in the manner that displays Jesus' character and His acts. At the on-set of the New Testament Church, the apostles did just that, as documented in the Acts of the Apostles. In doing so, the Bible teaches that multitudes were added to the faith and the churches grew. *"And believers were increasingly added to the Lord, multitudes both of men and women"* (Acts 5:14). *"So the churches were strengthened in the faith, and increased in number daily"* (Acts 16:5).

In those early years of the church's infancy, the standards of moral character were high, the supernatural power of God was being manifested by the apostles and many believers, and the quality of spiritual life and purity of doctrine was in alignment with Jesus' Words and what He had taught His disciples.

However, years of Roman persecution during the second and third centuries eventually led to the Christian religion being outlawed. It was re-sanctioned by the Emperor Constantine in 313 A.D. By then, however, the spiritual, supernaturally-charged church had faded into obscurity and the structural church, based on sense knowledge, began to dominate, especially after the fall of Rome in A.D. 476. This domination of the structural church continued until the Reformation of the 1500's.

The 1,000-year period prior to the Reformation was known as the "Dark Ages" of the Church. This was the time of the apostate church – an empty form with virtually no life, love, or sympathy for suffering humanity. It was a Church filled with corruption, immorality, bribery, bloodshed, and counterfeits without faith in Jesus Christ. But, God raised Martin Luther to light the flame for the restoration of the church in 1517, which led to the Protestant Movement. This movement was the open door for the spiritual church to come forth and emerge from the flesh-led structured church. Of course, the Church has experienced several restoration movements since the Protestant Movement, including the Holiness Movement of the 1700's and 1800's, and the Pentecostal Movement of the early 1900's. The latter half of the 1900's ushered in the restoration of the office of the prophet, and finally, the restoration of the office of the apostle during the last decade of the 20th Century.

"Every time a new truth is to be restored, the Holy Spirit supernaturally opens the mind of man to new understanding and ways of worship. That truth has been in the Word of God all the time, but until the time of revelation and refreshing comes from the presence of the Lord, man does not grasp its meaning…The church has been a sleeping giant, but it is now awake and on the move. It is now being prepared to begin its conquering march as the Army of the Lord" (Dr. Bill Hamon, *The Eternal Church*, Christian International Publishers, 1981, Santa Rosa Beach, FL, pp. 159 & 303).

The Church is now living in the 21st Century. God has re-established the apostles and prophets as the foundations of the Church (see Eph. 2:20). And God is requiring the full measure of the stature of Christ to arise within the Body. This is the season of the manifestation of the sons of God, the Army of the Lord full of love, spiritually mature, doing exploits and subduing earthly kingdoms. The standard has been raised for citizens of the Kingdom of Heaven.

The requirement is that we are standard-bearers who carry the flag, ensign, or banner that displays the territories that God has decreed are His. This is the season of supernatural manifestations which can only take place through accelerated movement of the Church for supernatural lift into the realm of *"all spiritual blessings in heavenly places in Christ"* (Eph. 1:3, KJV).

The spearheads – apostles and prophets – of this Army of the Lord are challenging believers to live above the systems of the world through the grace of the Lord Jesus Christ and God's faithfulness to His Word, for "The just shall live by faith" (Rom. 1:17). As members of the universal Body of Christ, we must now put into practice the governmental principles of the Kingdom of Heaven that produce spiritual, physical and materialistic prosperity and wealth for advancing God's kingdom on earth. *"The earth is the Lord's, and all of its fullness"* (Psa. 24:1).

The new standard of the kingdom requires that you be purified by the fire of the Holy Spirit, refined and tested in the furnace of affliction (see Isa. 48:10) so that everything that isn't of God (flesh/natural) can be shaken and that which cannot be shaken (spirit/supernatural) may remain (see Heb. 12:27). *"Who is she that looks forth as the morning, Fair as the moon, Clear as the sun, Awesome as an army with banners?"* (Song of Solomon 6:10, KJV). *"And the Lord shall utter his voice before his army: for his camp is very great: for he is strong that executeth his word: for the day of the Lord is great and very terrible; and who can abide it?"* (Joel 2:11, KJV).

Yes, the standard of the kingdom has been raised for believers to ascend, by supernatural lift, into the Holy Spirit realm of righteousness, and peace, and joy (see Rom. 14:17). **If you know that God has called and ordained you to be commissioned as a kingdom leader, then you must arise to that level.** Isaiah 62:10 is a major directive of your kingdom mandate, *"Go through, go through the gates; prepare ye the way of the people; cast up, cast up the highway; gather out the stones; **lift up a standard for the people**"* (KJV, author's emphasis).

My assertion is that there is a difference between simply a "kingdom leader" and a "commissioned, kingdom-level leader." Therefore, I will distinguish between the two. The commissioned, kingdom-level leader has arisen to the "**standard**" – that is, he or she prioritizes the pattern and government of the Kingdom of God as taught by Jesus and the apostles of the 1st Century Church, especially Apostle Paul. Paul's ministry stands out as the standard of the Kingdom and he held himself accountable to it and fathered other sons and daughters to adhere to that standard. This standard – commissioned, kingdom-level leaders – separates those leaders who have endured the God-process to spiritual maturity and whose priority it is to advance the government of the Kingdom in the earth, as opposed to simply "have church" or have inspirational meetings that make people feel good, teaching them how to acquire things and have a good life without prioritizing Matt. 6:33.

Kingdom leaders, on the other hand, do things and make things happen by their might and power – the abundance of their resources, along with their ability to influence others in order to achieve their personal goals and desires. They may call themselves kingdom leaders. In other words, they associate the word "kingdom" with their ministry, but their message never reflects the government of the Kingdom, nor do they raise spiritual sons and daughters who prioritize the Kingdom. With their mouths they talk about the Kingdom of God, but their heart is far from it. Jesus said, *"For even the Son of Man did not come to be served, but to serve, and to give His life a ransom for many"* (Mark 10:45). I contend that this statement is the distinguishing factor between a "kingdom leader" and a "commissioned, kingdom-level leader." The Church, the end-time army of God, representing His Kingdom, must be led by those who prioritize His plans and purposes – commissioned, kingdom-level leaders – servant leaders, not "served leaders."

Standard is defined as a conspicuous object (as a banner) formerly carried at the top of a pole and used to mark a rallying point especially in battle or serve as an emblem; something set up and established by authority as a rule for the measure of quantity, weight, extent, value, or quality. Standard applies to any definite rule, principle, or measure established by authority (Merriam-Webster). The Hebrew word translated *standard* is **nec (nace)** from **nacac (naw-sas)**. It means, a flag, sail, a flagstaff, a signal; a token: – banner, pole, sail, ensign, standard. Primarily, it means to gleam from afar, i.e., to be conspicuous as a signal through the idea of a flag as fluttering in the wind; to raise a beacon: – lift up as an ensign.

God wants to commission you as a standard-bearer – a commissioned, kingdom-level leader. **Commissions are not given; they are earned.** Your earnest commitment to endure God's process of development toward spiritual maturity, being equipped and deployed for success into your kingdom assignment, all play a role in your rise to the place of being commissioned. A **commission** is an authorization or command to act in a prescribed manner or to perform prescribed acts: A CHARGE; authority to act for, in behalf of, or in place of another (Merriam-Webster). The Hebrew word translated **commission** is *dath (dawth)*, meaning a royal edict or statute: commandment, commission, decree, law, and manner. Its Greek companion is *epitrope (ep-ee-trop-ay)*, which means to give permission, i.e., by implication full power; allow; give leave, liberty, license, let, and permit: commission (Strong's).

Again, a commissioned, kingdom-level leader is a standard-bearer. You have been called and ordained by God to be a commander. God wants to give you a charge and authorization to act on behalf of His Son, Jesus. God wants to give you full authority and power as an ambassador for Christ (see 2 Cor. 5:20). As such, you become one who bears or carries a standard or banner; one that leads an organization, movement, party or corporation on behalf of the Kingdom of Heaven. The standard of the Kingdom is the Word of God. And, the Word of God as contained in the Bible is the constitution of the Kingdom of Heaven.

There is a major difference between the constitution of a country and the constitution of the Kingdom of Heaven. For example, I am a citizen of the United States. Our form of government is a democracy – government by the people, for the people; rule of the majority. Therefore, its constitution was drafted to conform to that of a democracy. **God is the Sovereign King of the Kingdom of Heaven, and the constitution that governs His kingdom is government of His people, for His people.** God has the final word. Therefore, heaven's form of government is a theocracy. *"Where the word of a king is, there is power; And who may say to him, 'What are you doing?'"* (Eccl. 8:4). If you are a believer then you are first and foremost a citizen of the Kingdom of Heaven. Your earthly citizenship is secondary. Through Jesus you have access to the Father by the Holy Spirit. *"Now, therefore, you are no longer strangers and foreigners, but fellow citizens with the saints and members of the household of God"* (Eph. 2:19).

As a commissioned, kingdom-level leader, you are a **commander**! A commander is one in an official position of command or control: COMMANDING OFFICER. The presiding officer of a society or organization; **a commissioned officer** (Merriam-Webster, author's emphasis). The Hebrew word translated **commander** is ***tsavah (tsaw-vaw),*** which means to constitute, enjoin: appoint, give a charge, send with a charge: commander, send a messenger, put (set) in order (Strong's). *"And Moses did as the Lord commanded him: and he took Joshua, and set him before Eleazar the priest, and before all the congregation: **And he laid his hands upon him, and gave him a charge, as the Lord commanded** by the hand of Moses"* (Num. 27:22-23, KJV, author's emphasis).

Commissioned, kingdom-level leaders are commanders sent forth by the authority of the King of kings and given a charge to put or set things in kingdom order. David was a commander, a kingdom-level leader whom God commissioned and sent forth, giving him a charge to subdue nations and put things in order as per the Kingdom of Heaven.

> *"Incline your ear, and come to Me. Hear, and your soul shall live; And I will make an everlasting covenant with you – The sure mercies of David. Indeed **I have given him as a witness to the people, A leader and commander for the people.** Surely you shall call a nation you do not know, And nations who do not know you shall run to you, Because of the LORD your God, And the Holy One of Israel; For He has glorified you."*
> (Isa. 55:3-5, author's emphasis)

As a commissioned, kingdom-level leader, you are a soldier in the Lord's army who protects and defends the Kingdom of Heaven in the earth. Your assignment is to carry out the plans and purposes of God, your commander in chief, and to please your commanding officer, Jesus. ***"You therefore must endure hardship as a good soldier of Jesus Christ.*** *No one engaged in warfare* *entangles himself with the affairs of this life, that he may please him who enlisted him as a soldier"* (2 Tim. 2:3-4, author's emphasis).

As you carry out your kingdom assignment as a commissioned, kingdom-level leader, you will realize supernatural manifestations of the Holy Spirit's gifts, along with miracles and prophetic manifestations in every area of your life. But, in order to realize and experience this supernatural thrust, you must step up – climb, elevate, assign and avail yourself to greater heights and altitudes in the Spirit. You will need to take a quantum leap into your destiny. **Quantum** is a quantity, amount, portion or part; any of the very small increments or parcels into which many forms of energy are subdivided; a large significant portion, quantity or amount. **Quantum leap** signifies an abrupt change, sudden increase, or dramatic advance. An example of this is Joseph's quantum leap from prisoner to Prime Minister of Egypt.

God has called you to a higher standard of love, faith, humility, surrender, character and stewardship through trust and dependence upon Him for greater wisdom and revelation to have understanding of the times and to know what should be done. You are living in the Issachar age. That means that you too are *"of the sons of Issachar who had understanding of the times, to know what Israel ought to do"* (1 Chron. 12:32).

God wants to give you the spirit of wisdom and revelation in the knowledge of Him, so that you can experience the richness of His glory as a saint who receives your kingdom inheritance. *"That the God of our Lord Jesus Christ, the Father of glory, may give to you the spirit of wisdom and revelation in the knowledge of Him, the eyes of your understanding being enlightened; that you may know what is the hope of His calling, what are the riches of the glory of His inheritance in the saints"* (Eph. 1:17-18). When you receive the spirit of wisdom and revelation in the knowledge of Him, revelation is released from the intelligence of God that has the potential to instantly transform you to hear and receive supernatural downloads from Holy Spirit and process it quickly, for this is the Kingdom Age in which God has accelerated your movement into the Holy Spirit realm through supernatural lift.

As a standard-bearer, you hoist the banner of the Kingdom of Heaven and display the power of an all-powerful spiritual army through godly character and actions, as you subdue societal cultures and nations, conquering all things for the King of kings. *"You have shown Your people hard things; You have made us drink the wine of confusion. **You have given a banner to those who fear You,** That it may be displayed because of the truth. Selah"* (Psa. 60:3-4, author's emphasis).

> *"**Lift up a banner** on the high mountain, Raise your voice to them; Wave Your hand, that they may enter the gates of the nobles. **I have commanded My sanctified ones**; I have also called My mighty ones for My anger – Those who rejoice in My exaltation. The noise of a multitude in the mountains, Like that of many people! A tumultuous noise of the kingdoms of nations gathered together! **The Lord of hosts musters The army for battle.**"* (Isa. 13:2-4, author's emphasis)

Something transitory has taken place in the Body of Christ during the Jewish year of Rosh Hashanah 5776 that will define the magnitude of the Church's spiritual maturity and fullness of the stature of Jesus Christ for the next seven years. The "**Shanah Shift**" (© 2015 by Dr. Gordon E. Bradshaw, *"I See Thrones,"* Kingdom House Publishing) – the breath of Holy Spirit, the Ruwach, the wind of change – has blown in the saints' direction for breakthroughs, new realms, new doors, new opportunities, and new assignments to take more ground for Kingdom advancement. The Ruwach has blown and swept in demonstrations of the miraculous with abundance of resources for fulfillment of divine assignments.

Encased within the word Hashanah is the Hebrew word, *shanah (shawnaw)*. It means to duplicate, to do again, double, repeat, and do the second time (Strong's). In other words, what Heaven has planned, the earth is going to yield to. God said to me, "**Events and Moments will determine the Shift.**" God will use events and moments to advance the Church from potential to manifestation. God has raised the standard by raising kingdom leaders who have been commissioned by way of their faithfulness and stewardship, and have walked in a spirit of complete loyalty and devotion to their commanding officer, Jesus Christ. As a saint, you must decree Luke 11:2 (KJV) fervently, "THY

WILL BE DONE, AS IN HEAVEN, SO IN EARTH." You must consistently make the decree, "DO IT AGAIN, LORD!"

Like Queen Esther, you must realize that you have come to the Kingdom for such a time as this (see Est. 4:14)! As you ascend to your earthly throne, you must understand that there is a divine assignment for that throne. "**As we accept our assignments and become equipped with the tools of the trade we take on yet another level of competence and stability. Today we are called, not only to sit upon thrones, but to become as 'living thrones' in our assignments…We are equipped with supernatural tools to stand in our official assignments**" (Dr. Gordon E. Bradshaw, *I See Thrones! Igniting & Increasing Your Influence in the Seven Mountains of Culture*, 2015, Kingdom House Publishing, Lakebay, WA, p. 61).

Also, you must define the next level of your assignment according to God's standard for this season. You must understand the shift – moments and events will dictate the shift that will move you from potential to manifestation. **Potential** means existing in possibility: capable of development into actuality; something that can develop or become actual. **Manifestation** is defined as Materialization: an outward, visible expression; a public demonstration of power and purpose (Merriam-Webster). The Greek word translated **manifestation** is *phanerosis (fan-er-o-sis)*, which means very apparent, plainly, clearly, publicly, expression (Strong's).

I am convinced that your shift into your kingdom assignment – place of prominence – where you sit on your earthly throne as a king is what God has ordained for this season. You must know, without a doubt, that you have an earthly throne and that it is your right as a saint of God to occupy it, as an ambassador for Christ. *"Now to you, O profane, wicked prince of Israel, whose day has come, whose iniquity shall end, 'thus says the Lord God: "Remove the turban, and take off the crown; Nothing shall remain the same. Exalt the humble, and humble the exalted. Overthrown, overthrown, I will make it overthrown! It shall be no longer, Until He comes whose right it is, And I will give it to Him"'* (Ezek. 21:25-27).

Even Jesus had to be shifted into His kingdom assignment; the breath of the Ruwach blew in the events and moments that would thrust Him into His destiny. You see, God had to raise the standard, so to speak, in order for Jesus to fulfill His divine assignment. And, He used events and moments to accomplish this. **The shift caused by the breath of the Spirit of God always involves increase!**

In his gospel, Luke tells the story of how Joseph and Mary took Jesus to Jerusalem for the annual Feast of Passover celebration (an event), and how Jesus stayed behind after the feast without their knowledge. They had gone a day's journey from Jerusalem before realizing that Jesus was missing. Joseph and Mary went back to Jerusalem to find Him. And, they eventually found Jesus, after three days, in the temple among doctors both receiving and giving revelation.

Mary questioned Jesus about his behavior, saying *"Your father and I have sought You anxiously"* (2:48). *"And He said to them, 'Why did you seek Me? Did you not know that I must be about My Father's business?'"* (vs. 49). Jesus' response was a Holy Spirit moment of divine revelation. Although Joseph and Mary did not understand the scope of Jesus' response, Mary kept all these things in her heart. And Jesus went back with His parents to Nazareth and was obedient to them. *"And **Jesus increase**d in wisdom and stature, and in favor with God and men"* (vs. 52, author's emphasis).

Jesus' obedience, being subject to His parents, led to His increase in **wisdom** and **stature**. And He gained favor with God and men. Take a closer look: At 12 years of age, Jesus needed parental oversight – no matter how brilliant He was. Jesus needed to subject Himself to the order of God so that He could obtain the wisdom of His Father, for *"though He was a Son, yet He learned obedience by the things which He suffered. And having been perfected, He became the author of eternal salvation to all who obey Him"* (Heb. 5:8-9). This is how Jesus increased in wisdom.

Again, at 12 years old, Jesus' physical body – His stature – wasn't developed so as to take upon it the contemptuous and brutal beating He endured at age 33, when Jesus was in the prime of His physical strength. So, from age 12 to age 33, Jesus matured both spiritually and physically. But, His shift from potential to manifestation took place at the age of 30. He was shifted into His divine assignment and destiny by His mother, Mary.

In John's gospel, Mary was invited to a wedding in Cana of Galilee. Jesus and His disciples were also invited. Now, remember, I stated earlier that God said to me, **"Events and Moments will determine the shift."** Well, here it is. The *event* was a wedding. The *moment* was Jesus' willingness to act on a word spoken by Mary *that was predetermined in the Mind of God before He created the world. God knew that this word from Mary would literally shift time and release Jesus into His destiny.* Mary said to Jesus, *"They have no wine."* Jesus said to her, *"Woman, what does your concern have to do with Me? My hour has not yet come"* (2:3-4, author's emphasis). Jesus didn't realize that His hour was Mary's concern.

Remember, Mary had kept in her heart many things concerning Jesus – words that angels and prophets had spoken over Him. And, at this wedding event, the Holy Spirit quickened Mary to release them. She confidently told the servants, *"Whatever He says to you, do it"* (vs. 5). After Jesus turned water into wine, Apostle John wrote: *"This beginning of signs [miracles, KJV] Jesus did in Cana of Galilee, and **manifested** His glory; and His disciples believed in Him"* (vs. 11, author's emphasis). Jesus was shifted from potential to manifestation. He was commissioned to perform multitudes of miracles and release multitudes into their destiny.

In this season of the "shanah shift," Holy Spirit is commissioning kingdom-level leaders with His gift of a word of knowledge – words that God had spoken in His mind from before the foundation of the world, but has held them in His heart until such a time as this, specifically for you, *"Declaring the end from the beginning, And from ancient times things that are not yet done, Saying, 'My counsel shall stand, And I will do all My pleasure'"* (Isa. 46:10). This is your breakthrough season. It's your time to arise to the place of your commission as a kingdom-level leader – from potential to manifestation. That is who you are. You are a member of Christ's body, Who is the Head of the Church. And, as the Head goes, so goes the body. This is your season to evict ungodly kings and authorities from your earthly throne!

Let's take a look at how Esther, a Jewish girl, became queen and sat on her earthly throne in the palace. Again, remember that the palace is also a place of divine assignment. Events and moments will determine the shift. The King of

Persia held a feast (event) and called upon Queen Vashti to perform a dance before all his princes and servants, and to show off her beauty. Vashti refused to do so, which made the king very angry. Therefore, he used his royal power as king to make a royal commandment that dismissed Vashti as queen (moment). The **event** of a feast led to a **moment** where a **shift** took place, the removal of Vashti as queen. The queen's throne became vacant.

A shift represents a change in place, position, or direction. A shift orchestrated by Holy Spirit leads to another shift, and another... for greater kingdom manifestations. The event and moment that led to the dismissal of Vashti as queen led to another event – the gathering of beautiful young virgins from 127 provinces within the king's empire, *"Then let the young woman who pleases the king be queen instead of Vashti"* (Est. 2:4). Esther is chosen as one of the fair young virgins. This is a moment.

After 12 months of purification with sweet perfumes and oil of myrrh, each young woman had opportunity to go into the king's house. And, she was given whatever she desired to take with her from the women's quarters. Each one had her night and was dismissed from the king's house and into the house of the concubines the next day.

But, when Esther's time came to be with the king, she requested nothing but what the king's eunuch advised. She did not rely upon her own wisdom, but sought the wisdom of the one person who knew what pleased the king. The shanah shift was on. What was ordained in the mind of God in eternity had to manifest in the earth. Esther is anointed with the favor of God because she is a Jew, called to save His chosen people. *"And Esther obtained favor in the sight of all who saw her. So Esther was taken to King Ahasuerus, into his royal palace... The king loved Esther more than all the other women, ...so he set the royal crown upon her head and made her queen instead of Vashti"* (3:15, 17).

Years later, the king promoted one of his chamberlains, Haman, and made him head of all the princes. The king commanded that all royal officials bow to Haman. But Mordecai, Esther's guardian, would not bow, nor did he reverence Haman. Because of this, Haman decided to destroy not only Mordecai but all the Jews throughout the kingdom. When Mordecai found out that Haman had tricked the king into signing this death warrant into law, he sent word to Esther of Haman's plot, commanding her to go to the king to make supplication and plead for her people. But, Esther replied to Mordecai that the law stated that anyone who goes into the inner court to the king, who has not been called, is put to death, except the king holds out the golden scepter so that person may live. *"I myself have not been called to go in to the king these thirty days"* (4:11).

Mordecai's response was sharp and to the point. It was a reminder to Esther of why she was even in the palace. His words shifted her into her destiny as queen so that she would have power, influence and favor with a king who would have destroyed the Jewish people had she not been his queen. *"Do not think in your heart that you will escape in the king's palace any more than all the other Jews. For if you remain completely silent at this time, relief and deliverance will arise for the Jews from another place, but you and your father's house will perish. **Yet who knows whether you have come to the kingdom for such a time as this"*** (vss. 13-14)? Esther heeded the words of Mordecai and, using wisdom, asked that all the Jews who were present in Shushan fast for three days and nights with her and her maids. Then she made a decree, committing to her kingdom assignment. *"And so I will go to the king, which is against the law; and if I perish, I perish!"* (vs. 16)

On the third day Esther put on her royal apparel and stood in the inner court. When the king saw her, she obtained favor in his sight and he held out to her the golden scepter. *"And the king said to her, 'What do you wish, Queen Esther? What is your request? It shall be given to you – up to half the kingdom!'"* (5:3). Eventually, Esther exposed Haman's plan to the king and he hung Haman on the gallows that he had prepared for Mordecai. So, not only did Esther advance in her position as queen, but also the king rewarded Mordecai and gave him Haman's ring and his house. *"For Mordecai the Jew was second to King Ahasuerus, and was great among the Jews and well received by the multitude of his brethren, seeking the good of his people and speaking peace to all his countrymen"* (10:3). Events and moments determine the shift. Esther's shift led to Mordecai's shift, which led to the shift of the Jewish people from a death sentence to a position of honor and respect, not only for them but also for their God.

God commissioned Esther and Mordecai as kingdom-level leaders – commanders – who were given a kingdom assignment and were prepared and equipped to carry it out successfully. They understood the purpose for their time in the palace and trusted God's timing of deliverance and honor for His people. Events and moments led to several shifts that prepared and equipped Esther to become queen and Mordecai to become second to King Ahasuerus so that they could fulfill their kingdom assignment. Your God-orchestrated shift will involve certain people who will assist in preparing and getting you equipped for your kingdom assignment. And, the shift will usually include a change in place, position or direction. God will use anointed men and women to speak a word over your life, shifting you into your destiny. And, your kingdom assignment will lead many saints into their "palace."

If you are going to successfully accomplish your kingdom assignment, you must be bold and courageous, for success does not come without persecutions, dangers and hazards. However, divine favor shows up when you are commissioned by God as a kingdom-level leader, and trust Him completely as you carry out your kingdom assignment at all costs.

Your commission requires that you use your influence and authority as a king and priest unto God to love, respect, honor and advance other saints into their kingdom assignment. Your commission requires that you steward well the resources God entrusts to you to empower people and not to abuse them. Your commission requires that, as a kingdom-level leader, a commander in the Lord's army, you are loyal and devoted to advancing the Kingdom of Heaven in the earth.

This is your season of enlargement. You are being shifted by God-orchestrated events and moments for your next level – from potential to manifestation. Define your next level and program your mind to receive, achieve and advance God's kingdom by fulfilling your kingdom assignment as a commissioned, kingdom-level leader who arises and commits to walk before God in a spirit of complete loyalty and devotion – a faithful and wise steward. *"For the eyes of the Lord run to and fro throughout the whole earth, to show Himself strong on behalf of those whose heart is loyal to Him"* (2 Chron. 16:9).

*****

After reconnecting with my spiritual father, Dr. Gordon E. Bradshaw, in February 2011, my life and ministry went from stagnation in a local place to steady movement and advancement internationally. That is the scope of the vision that God had engraved upon my heart in 1998. But, first, I needed to be properly mentored apostolically and aligned prophetically. This was yet another process I had to commit to, if I was to become commissioned as an apostle – a kingdom-level leader.

I was glad that I had already been trained by Dr. Bradshaw years earlier. So, I was somewhat familiar with the strenuous exercises he exerts and commands mastery of in his training sessions. However, I had stepped into a higher dimension of spiritual maturity and this was, without a doubt, a higher standard of training. Dr. Bradshaw would test, periodically, my dedication and motive to determine whether I was seeking "asylum" or "assignment."

He'd said to me, "Never build an army with folk whose loyalty has not been proven." He said that people who seek "asylum" are basically running from accountability and reliability. Their motive is never about "assignment" because it costs too much. "But, the good experiences and temperaments that are forged through relationships, mentoring and molding cannot be created any other way. There are No substitutes for "discipleship" and sonship in the kingdom!"

Dr. Bradshaw made sure that there were no short circuits between us due to distance and lack of opportunity to meet physically, as he lives in Chicago and I live in South Carolina. Many lessons, prophetic trainings and other teaching sessions were given by way of phone calls, video, e-mails, electronic presentations and books. But, he knew at some point we would have to have physical contact. Until that time, Dr. Bradshaw trained and developed me according to what he calls "the mountain of apostolic development," seven divisions that could be subdivided into several experiences that take place during the development of those levels. Each experience contributes to the main character and nature of how one will function as an apostle.

The mountain contains these levels, beginning at the foundation and leading to the summit:

1. **Anointing** – *The calling and consecration to begin studying the mandates of the office.*

2. **Alignment** – *Positioning and placement into the "flow" of the activities of the office.*

3. **Assignment** – *Understanding the purpose, principles and practices of the office.*

4. **Activation** – *Being commissioned, recognized, activated and released into the office.*

5. **Application** – *Performing the application of those purposes, principles and practices of the office.*

6. **Authority** – *Learning how to apply the governmental anointing of the office.*

7. **Apostleship** – *Fully functioning in an assigned sphere of ministry within the office.*

(Dr. Gordon E. Bradshaw, *The Technology of Apostolic Succession,* Kingdom House Publishing, Lakebay, WA, pp. 80-81)

I found out during the training process that I had already been operating in apostolic ministry for some time and did not know it. Therefore, it did not take long for me to grasp the intangibles and add them to my Holy Spirit-tool belt and arsenal of weaponry. After six months of intense teaching, training and mentoring me in the government and office of the apostle, Dr. Bradshaw commissioned me an apostle in August, 2011. I had arisen as a commissioned, kingdom-level leader, going from a foot-soldier, to a disciple, to a commander – a horseman, one who leaps; rapid in flight; a driver; a warrior charging in to battle (Strong's).

Kingdom-level leaders, ARISE! GO FROM FOOTMEN TO HORSE-MEN. *"If you have run with the footmen, and they have wearied you, Then how can you contend with horses?"*

"My anger burns against your shepherds, and I will punish these leaders.

For the LORD of Heaven's Armies has arrived to look after Judah, his flock. **He will make them strong and glorious, like a proud war-horse in battle.** *From Judah will come the cornerstone, the tent peg, the bow for battle, and all the rulers.* **They will be like mighty warriors in battle, trampling their enemies in the mud under their feet. Since the LORD is with them as they fight, they will overthrow even the enemy's horsemen.** *"* (Zech. 10:3-5, NLT, author's emphasis)

CHAPTER ELEVEN

UNDERSTANDING YOUR AUTHORITY AS A KING-PRIEST

"And from Jesus Christ, who is the faithful witness,
the firstborn from the dead, and the ruler over the kings of the earth.
To him who loved us and washed us from our sins in His own blood,
and has made us kings and priests to His God and Father,
to Him be glory and dominion forever and ever. Amen." (REV. 1:5-6)

Your authority as a believer must be appropriated from your supernatural position in Christ. Remember, a commissioned, kingdom-level leader is a commander; and commanders possess authority delegated to them by a commanding officer – in your case, Jesus. As a kingdom commander, you will take things by force with a righteous justification; you will commandeer or seize people, places and things that do not align themselves with the constitution of the kingdom. As a kingdom commander, you never act out of your flesh or self-righteousness. You understand that your authority has been delegated to you by Jesus Christ. And, God Himself is the power behind your authority, *"For though we walk in the flesh, we do not war according to the flesh. For the weapons of our warfare are not carnal but mighty* *in God for pulling down strongholds, casting down arguments and every high thing that exalts itself against the knowledge of God, bringing every thought into captivity to the obedience of Christ"* (2 Cor. 10:3-5).

Unfortunately, there are still many Christians who fail to recognize and appropriate their identity in Christ. Many of these believers are "baby Christians." But, we've already established the fact that baby Christians can never become wise master builders. If you are spiritually immature, you will fail to realize and never fully appreciate your position in Christ, along with the authority that comes with it. And the results are woeful – loss of authority and dominion, loss of victory in life, loss of miracles and the joy of God's presence. Not knowing who you are in Christ could cost you dearly. On the other hand, recognizing who you are in Christ by Holy Spirit revelation of Scripture and acting upon or becoming that person can turn a lifetime of spiritual mediocrity and stagnation into a life bent on excellence and consistent victories, spiritually and naturally, through the spirit of advancement. *"And Jesus increased in wisdom and stature, and in favor with God and men"* (Luke 2:52).

During His earthly ministry, Jesus exemplified authority. **Authority** is defined as power to influence or command thought, opinion, or behavior (Merriam-Webster). The Hebrew word translated **authority** is ***rabah (raw-baw)***. It is a primary root word meaning to increase (in whatever respect): [bring in] abundance, be in authority, enlarge, excel, exceedingly full of, make great, grow up, increase, be more in number, much greater, make to multiply, nourish, plenteous, process [of time], very thorough (Strong's Hebrew). The Greek word translated **authority** is ***exousia (ex-oo-see-ah)***. It means ability, privilege, force, capacity, competency, freedom, mastery, magistrate, superhuman, potentate, token of control, delegated influence: authority, jurisdiction, liberty, power, right, strength (Strong's Greek).

There was a huge distinction between how the scribes of Jesus' day taught and how Jesus taught the people. *"And so it was, when Jesus had ended these sayings, that the people were astonished at His teaching, for He taught them as one having authority, and not as the scribes"* (Matt. 7:29). Obviously, Jesus' authority, which was delegated to Him by His Father and Commander-In-Chief, induced or brought forth increase in whatever respect – it enlarged people, moved them into a state of excellence, made them grow up spiritually and become more in number, much greater. His authority made people multiply; it nourished them and made them plenteous over a process of time; it was very thorough. Jesus' authority was given as a privilege, and it carried force, capacity, competency and freedom; it was a delegated influence that He used as a potentate, as magistrate within His jurisdiction. His authority showed forth mastery and superhuman ability in liberty, power, right, and strength. And, Jesus exercised His authority fearlessly, knowing that the power of God was backing Him.

In order to know, understand and activate your authority "in Christ," you must understand your dual citizenship. Physically, you live on the earth but spiritually you are seated together in the heavenly places in Christ Jesus. *"And raised us up together, and made us sit together in the heavenly places in Christ Jesus"* (Eph. 2:6). Your old condition, prior to salvation, was one that was dead to God. However, your new condition in Christ makes you alive to God. *"But God, who is rich in mercy, because of His great love with which He loved us, even when we were dead in trespasses, made us alive together with Christ (by grace you have been saved)"* (vss. 4-5). Therefore, your new condition (your supernatural heavenly citizenship) supersedes your old condition (simply living in this world as a citizen of a nation) where by nature you fulfilled the desires of your flesh and of your mind, according to the prince of the power of the air and the spirit who now works in the sons of disobedience, children of wrath just as the others (vss. 2-3).

Your position in Christ is one of authority. Prior to Jesus' ascension into heaven, He told the 11 remaining apostles that all power had been given to Him in heaven and in earth (Matt. 28:18). *"But this Man, after He had offered one sacrifice for sins forever, **sat down at the right hand of God,** from that time waiting till His enemies are made His footstool"* (Heb. 10:12-13, author's emphasis). *"And what is **the exceeding greatness of His power toward us who believe according to the working of His mighty power which He worked in Christ** when He raised Him from the dead and seated Him at His right hand in the heavenly places, far above all principality and power and might and dominion, and every name that is named, not only in this age but also in that which is to come. And He put all things under His feet, and gave Him to be head over all things to the church which is*

His body, the fullness of him who fills all in all" (Eph. 1:19-23, author's emphasis).

The same power that God used to raise Jesus from the dead is available to any believer who knows, understands and activates that power by faith. The Greek word translated **power** here is ***dunamis (doo-nam-is)***, and it refers to the force of miraculous power and ability (Strong's), and it is available to be put to use by you for the fulfillment of your kingdom assignment. God gives His authority (exousia) and power (dunamis) as gifts to the spiritually mature – commissioned, kingdom-level leaders – commanders. *"Behold, I give you the **authority (exousia)** to trample on serpents and scorpions, and over all the **power (dunamis)** of the enemy, and nothing shall by any means hurt you"* (Luke 10:19, author's emphasis).

Now, let's incorporate your role as a king-priest with the authority and power given to you by God because you've been commissioned as a kingdom-level leader. From Scripture, we know that Jesus exercises authority and power in heaven and in earth. Jesus is your Royal High Priest who sits on the right hand of the Majesty on high (see Heb. 1:3). He exercises His authority and power in the earth through you, as a member of the church – His Body. As a member of His Body, you contain the same *"fullness of Him who fills all in all."* In order to exercise this awesome royal quality, you must agree with the constitution of the Kingdom of Heaven by giving God your permission to use you to reflect it in the earth. *"The heaven, even the heavens, are the Lord's; But the earth He has given to the children of men"* (Psa. 115:16). Therefore, you must invite God to work through you so that you initiate the same prayer that Jesus taught His disciples, *"Thy kingdom come, thy will be done, as in heaven, so in earth"* (Luke 11:2, KJV).

Through Christ, you are a king and a priest unto God, not unto men. Kings and priests unto God must express His heart. Only commissioned, kingdom-level leaders are mature enough to express the heart of God because they have been transitioned from the old church leadership structure (religion) into a new wine, servanthood leadership, *"Just as the Son of Man did not come to be served, but to serve, and to give His life a ransom for many"* (Matt. 20:28). God has raised servant leaders, kings and priests that will express His heart – His kingdom plans and purposes in the earth, using His authority and power to accomplish them.

Let me reiterate that kings and priests unto God exemplify the heart of God.

Their heart has been developed from godly character because they submitted to God's timed process of spiritual maturity, as opposed to being driven by their quick fix, high profiled, celebrity status, independent leadership model based on personality. Personality leadership is based upon an independent mindset. The basic thrust is "I," and it is selfish in nature. The old church leadership model is an outward approach. It says, "I built this." "These are my people." "I am self-reliant." "I worked myself up from nothing, pulling myself up from my own bootstraps."

Statements like these are self-serving. Yes, leaders who have been independent of trusting God have accomplished a lot through their own effort (might and power). But, how much more can be accomplished when leaders become servants who express the heart of God through their works, and are distributors of the grace of God because they possess a godly character?

On the other hand, servant leadership is the character of kings and priests unto God. Kings and priests use authority wisely and express God's heart through love, humility, integrity, respect, and justice. These are the qualities that you must possess as a king and priest unto God, and acquiring them comes through the principle of process – the sequential, incremental, highly integrated stages of growth and development based on grace and time.

As a commissioned, kingdom-level leader, who is a king and priest unto God, you are a man or woman after God's own heart. David purposed in his heart to do the will of God and fulfill his kingdom assignment at all costs. When you purpose in your heart to fulfill your divine assignment at all costs, you too are a man or woman after God's own heart. GOD IS A COMPLETER! And He always finishes strong! "*The Lord has sought for Himself a man after His own heart, and the Lord has commanded him to be commander over his people*" (1 Sam. 13:14, author's emphasis). "*I have found David the son of Jesse, a man after My own heart, who will do all My will*" (Acts 13:22, author's emphasis).

Kings and priests unto God – servant leaders – possess the heart of David. As a king and priest unto God, your primary desire should be to do all God's will, seeking first His kingdom and His righteousness (Matt. 6:33). God has raised 21st Century leaders who possess the "sure mercies of David," through His everlasting covenant, and has qualified them as servant leaders who possess the same qualities David possessed as king over Israel – that of a **witness**, a **leader** and **commander** to the people; a king and priest unto God who uses his authority wisely. *"...And I will make an everlasting covenant with you – The sure mercies of David. Indeed I have given him as a witness to the people, A leader and commander for the people"* (Isa. 55:3-4).

The Hebrew word translated **witness** is *ed (ayd)*, taken from the word uwd (ood), which means a testimony; a recorder, i.e. prince. It also means to duplicate or repeat a process, and testify (as by reiteration) (Strong's). Kings and priests, servant leaders, are witnesses who reflect Jesus' leadership model. As a king and priest under the sovereignty of God, you record the testimony of Jesus, duplicating, repeating and reiterating the process by which Jesus led.

The Hebrew word translated **leader** is *nagid (naw-gheed)*, taken from nagad (naw-gad), which means a commander (as occupying the front). Other honorable themes are: captain, chief, governor, noble, prince, ruler, excellent thing, i.e. stand out boldly (Strong's). As a king and priest unto God, you stand boldly out front as a commander of excellent things. Through godly character, you have acquired honorable themes such as captain, chief, governor, prince, and ruler – the sure mercies of David.

Finally, as a king and priest, a servant leader who understands the authority that has been delegated, you are a **commander**. The Hebrew word used in translation is *tsavah (tsaw-vaw)*. It means to constitute, enjoin: appoint, give a charge, send a messenger, and set in order. As a king and priest unto God, you are a servant leader who is a commander commissioned with authority from God to set things in order, not only in the church but also in the earth. You are to raise sons and daughters who can reflect and duplicate your servant leadership as a king and priest, and appoint them, charge them, and send them forth as kings and priests who possess the authority of the Kingdom of Heaven. To be a witness, a leader, and a commander requires godly character.

Character never forms in isolation from outside influences. It grows out of the crucible of challenge, difficulty, hardship, struggle, and pain. It is a transformation of the whole person from the inside out, led by your submission to Holy Spirit and allowing His precious fruit to take root in your spirit to produce a consistent outward flow of godly character. Again, this doesn't happen overnight. This process will challenge everything in you. It will require love, faithfulness, obedience, humility and patience – a willingness to wait on the Lord, trusting His perfect timing.

Oswald Sanders said, "True disciples are not manufactured wholesale. They are produced one by one because someone has taken the pains to discipline; to instruct and enlighten; to nurture and train one that is younger." As a king and priest unto God, you must be willing to invest time in training those who hunger to learn from you. As a servant leader, a component of your kingdom assignment will involve solving a problem for someone else – this is how you express the heart of God.

As a king unto God, you have a throne or thrones in the earth within the Seven Mountains of Culture. As a priest unto God, you have an altar or altars in the earth also within one or more of the Seven Mountains of Culture. An altar is simply any place where dedication, consecration, intercession, prayer, offerings and sacrifices are made unto God. These two roles must work together in harmony in order for the authority of God to manifest in your life as a commander. You must understand the role you play as a king, as well as the role you play as a priest.

Our sovereign King and Royal High Priest give us this model of the King-Priest working together in harmony. From His throne in the spiritual Mt. Zion God is the Supreme ruler (King), and Jesus is the express image of His person (Heb. 1:3) who sits on the right hand of God's throne making intercession (Priest) for us (Heb. 7:25). Therefore, kings and priests inhabit the same throne. *"Yes, [you are building a temple of the Lord, but] it is He Who shall build the [true] temple of the Lord, and He shall bear the honor and glory [as if the only begotten of the Father]* **and shall sit and rule upon His throne. And He shall be a Priest upon His throne, and the counsel of peace shall be between the two [offices – Priest and King]"** (Zech. 6:13, AMP, author's emphasis). So, then, both offices – king and priest – exercise authority from the same throne.

Now let's examine your role as a king, and your role as a priest. **Role** means a character assigned or assumed; a socially-expected behavior pattern usually determined by an individual's status in a particular society; a function or part performed especially in a particular operation or process (Merriam- Webster). Your position in Christ is to function as or to take on the character of a king and a priest. To do this, you must understand the difference between the two roles. **Kings make decrees. Priests pray and make petitions.**

As a king and priest unto God, you are His servant, representative, and ambassador for Christ who inhabits the earth in His stead (see 2 Cor. 5:20). You make decrees in Christ's stead. You pray for people in Christ's stead. In your role as king, you make a decree or give a command, in Jesus' Name, toward something or someone on behalf of God. As you function in your priesthood, you pray to make petitions – requests and supplication – to God on behalf of someone or something. For example: When I make a decree, I simply command something or someone. "**In the name of Jesus, I command…**" When I pray or make a petition, I simply pray, "**Father, in the name of Jesus, I petition You on behalf of…**" This is the authority of the king-priest.

Jesus is King of kings – the blessed and only Potentate (1 Tim. 6:15), and our Royal High Priest, called a high priest forever after the order of Melchizedek (Heb. 5:10). These two roles operate as One, just as Melchizedek was both king and priest, *"For this Melchizedek, king of Salem, priest of the Most High God"* (Heb. 7:1). The two offices work together in peace and harmony. By understanding your role as a king and priest unto God, from your position in Christ, you can be confident that when you make a decree or a petition, it is from your heavenly position where you sit with Christ Jesus on the right hand of God. This is the seat of power, dominion and glory.

And, since the heavenly Mt. Zion is the dwelling place of God, it is higher than any earthly mountain. Your decrees and petitions, voiced through your faith in Jesus, echo from Mt. Zion, and the things of the kingdoms of this world must submit to the Supreme power and authority of the King of kings. When you have faith in God's faithfulness to His Word, His faith expressed through your decrees and prayers are just as authoritative as if Jesus had spoken them. Like Jesus, you are seated in heavenly places far above all principality, and power, and might, and dominion.

Kings and priests wear clothing that is symbolic of their respective offices. A part of a king's royal attire is a crown. A part of a priest's garmet is an ephod. Don't forget to put on your spiritual garments. In other words, make sure that when you make a decree, you make it as a king. When you pray or make petitions, make them as a priest. When it is necessary to make decrees and pray or make petitions, you are aware, by the Spirit, that you are wearing both styles of garments. For example, a king understands that his crown symbolizes rulership, enlargement and protection. A priest understands that his ephod symbolizes the presence and glory of God for answers. The reality is that God is backing your authority, and that authority is available to you from two realms – heaven and earth. You are seated together in heavenly places with Jesus on His throne as a king and priest with God, and you are positioned in the earth within the Seven Mountains of Culture to sit on a throne as a king and priest unto God. That is your position in Christ, and that's a one up on the devil.

"And Jesus came and spoke to them, saying, 'All authority has been given to Me in heaven and on earth'" (Matt. 28:18). And when Jesus ascended to Heaven, He transferred His authority to the Church – His body of kings and priests, servant leaders, commanders whom He commanded to carry out "The Great Commission." Jesus is seated at the right hand of the Father, the position of authority, and you are seated with Him NOW! So, you must realize that the authority that Jesus has also belongs to you as an individual member of Christ's Body, and is available to you NOW! You are one with Christ. *"But he who is joined to the Lord is one spirit with Him"* (1 Cor. 6:17). But, Jesus is not here in the earth physically. Therefore, all of His authority that can be exercised on earth must by exercised by you, a member of His Body.

"…He who is in you is greater than he who is in the world" (1 John 4:4). As a king and priest unto God, the authority that you possess is greater than that of the devil. Jesus expressed the greatness of his authority many times as He cast demon spirits out of people. He did not ask His Father to cast them out. He possessed that authority because it was delegated to Him by His Father. You, too, must do the same. Don't leave it up to God to do what He has given you the authority to do it. He has conferred His authority on you, so use it. *"Truly I tell you, **whatever***

you forbid and declare to be improper and unlawful **on earth must be what is already forbidden in heaven**, and **whatever you permit and declare** proper and lawful **on earth must be what is already permitted in heaven**" (Matt. 18:18, AMP, author's emphasis). This is your position in Christ Jesus. Through Jesus, your authority is authorized to be used on earth in alignment with what has already taken place in heaven. This is why it is imperative that, as a king and priest unto God, you know and understand the constitution of the Kingdom, the Word of God.

Do not underestimate the role that your faith plays in exercising God's authority. And your faith is always based on the Word of God. When exercising the authority of God, you must stand on the Word of faith, and not be moved by what you see. Smith Wigglesworth said, "I'm not moved by what I see. I'm not moved by what I feel. I'm moved only by what I believe." As kings and priests unto God, you are empowered to use your authority to enforce Jesus' victory.

In Jesus' Name, you exercise authority over the devil. This is the first sign mentioned to follow any believer. *"And these signs will follow those who believe: In My name they will cast out demons"* (Mark 16:17). Yes, Satan has authority; but his is an evil authority of darkness. Through faith in Jesus, you have been delivered from Satan's authority and translated or conveyed into His glorious kingdom of light (Col. 1:13). Therefore, you have the right to speak to the authority of darkness and command him what to do. Again, your authority as a king and priest unto God is yours whether or not you feel like it. But, you must exercise it.

Jesus has delegated His authority over Satan to you on earth. If you don't use it, nothing will get accomplished, except you will be devoured by your adversary, the devil. *"Look, I have given you the authority to trample on snakes and scorpions and over all the power of the enemy; nothing will ever harm you"* (Luke 10:19, Passion). *"Be sober! Be on the alert! Your adversary the Devil is prowling around like a roaring lion, looking for anyone he can devour. Resist him, firm in the faith…"* (1 Pet. 5:8-9, Passion). You will defeat Satan only as you use your authority as a king and priest, exercising it by faith in alignment with God's Word.

Now that you understand your authority as a king-priest unto God, and exercise it by faith in His Word, you reign as a king in life. You identify your rightful throne and exercise dominion in whatever societal mountain you are called to. You have grown from a footman to a horseman, so to speak. You have become a commander, a servant leader, modeling the life and acts of Jesus. You can now train spiritual sons and daughters to whom you may delegate any of the details of your leadership, and they, too, will reflect the kingdom pattern of living as kings and priests unto God with the authority of Jesus Christ.

As you come to an even greater understanding of who you are and what you are in Christ, you will stand in the king's palace – the place of your kingdom assignment where enlargement takes place and resources abound. You are a royal seed planted by God. As royalty, you exude and exhibit majesty, nobility, glory and grace. You have been ordained to live in a higher standard, above the systems of the world. Like Daniel and the three Hebrew boys, your royal spiritual DNA code in Christ is that you are without blemish, well-favored and skillful in all wisdom, discernment, and understanding, apt in learning knowledge, and competent to stand and serve in the king's palace (Dan. 1:4, AMP).

As you appropriate your position in Christ, you will use your authority as a king and priest to advance the kingdom of God, reaping the end-time harvest of souls, preparing the way for Christ's return and kingdom rule in the earth. *"For unto us a Child is born, Unto us a Son is given; And the government will be upon His shoulder...Of the increase of His government and peace There will be no end, Upon the throne of David and over His kingdom, To order it and establish it with judgment and justice From that time forward, even forever. The zeal of the Lord of hosts will perform this"* (Isa. 9:6-7).

Chapter Twelve

THE JUST SHALL LIVE BY HIS FAITH

"For the vision is yet for an appointed time; But at the end it will speak, and it will not lie. Though it tarries, wait for it; Because it will surely come, It will not tarry. **Behold, the proud, His soul is not upright in him; But the just shall live by his faith.***"*

(HAB. 2:3-4, AUTHOR'S EMPHASIS)

As I stated in Chapter Six, God said to me that He wanted me to teach His people faith. Of course, I had no idea what that meant, and I could not fathom what it meant to live by faith. But, God put me on the path of life that not only taught me how to live by faith but also how to teach others to live by their faith – a faith that is settled in the Word of God.

I remember God asking me in early 1994, **"What would you be willing to give up to show that you trust Me with your life?"**

At that time, this was a very powerful and sobering question because the only thing I had of any significant value to me was my amazing album collection – the only thing that I had salvaged from my turbulent, defiant years as a backslider. After thinking on that question for a long while, I finally managed to ask the Lord what He wanted me to do with it.

He said, **"I want you to donate them to the music emporium downtown."**

I was living in Augusta, Ga. at the time. I said, "Yes, Lord. I trust You. I'll do it."

I drove my sister's car downtown to Broad Street and after several trips from the car into the store, finally got my collection inside. When the proprietor came over to inspect my collection, his eyes widened. As he looked carefully at the condition of many of the albums he could not contain his enthusiasm. His huge grin told me that he was very pleased, not only with the condition of the albums but also with the quantity. He could sell them and make a 100% profit since they were donated.

As I signed the collection over to him, I felt a little queasy. I had just given away everything I owned. And, to be honest, it did not feel good. But, as I left the store, the Lord said, **"Because you've honored Me, I will give you another collection of even greater value."**

After hearing that word I felt a little better. However, what I didn't know was this would be the first of many sacrifices that God would ask of me as I surrendered my life to Him. Other sacrifices over the years would include working in a low-paying job outside of my degree field, leaving the secular job market for full time ministry, giving up my new vehicle, giving up my family's home and property, losing my reputation as a college professor, and putting my own ministry vision on hold in order to faithfully steward someone else's. There are many more, some of which are too personal to talk about in the context in which I'm writing.

Father was teaching me how to live by my faith, how to trust Him completely. Probably the most challenging test came after Christmas in 1999. I heard the Lord say, **"I've called you and ordained you to lead a debt-free ministry. I'm going to teach you how to live by faith to become debt-free. Will you cut up your credit cards and trust Me to supply and sustain your life?"**

My initial thought was how would I be able to take care of my family without credit? Very little money was coming in from my full time ministry. But, at least enough money flowed through my hands to make a minimum monthly payment. I said, "Yes Lord, I'll do that."

He said, **"I'm going to make you debt-free and your ministry. It will be a standard representing the economy of My Kingdom."**

Since that time, I have not had a credit card. As I write this book, it has been 18 years since I left the secular job market in obedience to God. He'd said to me at that time, that if I would humble myself and trust Him, He would raise me to a place and position where I would not want for anything but Him. I still stand on the Word of God by my faith. I have faith in God's faithfulness to His Word. Holy Spirit gives me His gift of faith, one of the power gifts. And, today I teach others internationally this abiding faith in God and the finished work of His Son, Jesus. God has been faithful to His Word. He has never left me nor forsaken me. Yes, it has been difficult most of the time, but the supply always showed up. If I were to sum it all up, I'd have to say like my grandmother used to: "My soul looks back and wonders how I got over."

*****

The stories of the Old Testament heroes of faith who achieved greatness will attest to the fact that they were first broken by God prior to being prepared for His use. Generally, God grinds to powder first those whom He uses in a great way to express His glory. The book of Job teaches that when you have achieved greatness outside of God's will, you will possess a degree of arrogance being confident in your prosperity, success, and security. You become carefree and uninhibited – at ease. In this state of self-reliance, you become more and more dependent upon your resources and less dependent on your God. God's will is that you are totally dependent upon Him through your faith in His faithfulness to His own Word, *"The just shall live by his faith"* (Hab. 2:4). A large portion of Apostle Paul's epistles consist of his teaching on faith. Three times in the New Testament, he quotes Habakkuk: Romans 1:17, Galatians 3:11, and Hebrews 10:38, concluding with this statement: *"But if anyone draws back, My soul has no pleasure in him. But we are not of those who draw back to perdition, but of those who believe to the saving of the soul"* (vss. 38-39).

"Forever, O Lord, Your word is settled in heaven" (Psa. 119:89) reveals a very

powerful truth that must be taken seriously, if you are going to live according to the constitution of the Kingdom of Heaven. This word has to proceed out of a faith that has been developed into complete, absolute trust in the Word of God. In other words, you must possess a "mature faith" that is also settled in the Word of God. Let's look at a couple of definitions of faith as stated in Scripture. Faith is, *"The fundamental fact of existence is that this trust in God, this faith, is the firm foundation under everything that makes life worth living. It's our handle on what we can't see"* (Heb. 11:1, MSG). *"NOW FAITH is the assurance (the confirmation, the title deed) of the things [we] hope for, being the proof of things [we] do not see and the conviction of their reality {faith perceiving as real fact what is not revealed to the senses]"* (AMP).

The Greek word translated as **faith** is ***pistis (pis-tis)***, meaning persuasion, i.e. credence; moral conviction of religious truth, or **the truthfulness of God**, especially reliance upon Christ for salvation; constancy in such profession: assurance, belief, fidelity (Strong's, author's emphasis). A study of the definition of faith from the Amplified Bible helped me break it down into four major categories: 1) Assurance (confidence), 2) Hope (earnest expectation), 3) Proof (evidence or demonstration), and 4) Conviction (certainty).

All believers have been given a measure of faith by God. Yet, Jesus taught that some of His disciples had *"no faith"* (Mark 4:40), *"little faith"* (Matt. 8:26), and He taught that certain ones had great faith (Matt. 15:28). *"But without faith it is impossible to please Him, for he who comes to God must believe that He is, and that He is a rewarder of those who diligently seek Him"* (Heb. 11:6). In this verse there are five revelations that are pertinent to our topic of faith. 1) Faithlessness leads to impossibilities; 2) God is pleasured when you use your faith; 3) You must come to God believing that He is the God of His Word; 4) As a believer, you are required to diligently seek God; and, 5) Faith carries with it a guaranteed reward. **Your faith in God will manifest God's faithfulness to you. Faith that is genuine must mature through hearing the Word of God, speaking it, acting on it, and persisting in it. "The just shall live by His faith."**

However, in this fast-paced, multifaceted, technology-fueled society, bent on government-sanctioned laws that oppose the Word of God, combined with an unstable world economy, many believers have found themselves in a place of unbelief or lack of faith and trust in God. They find themselves living according to the systems of the world instead of from the sure economy of the kingdom. This can easily happen within the context of the kind of society I just mentioned. It screams immediate gratification. People are consistently accumulating more and more stuff, which requires more and more of their time. Many of these people will tell you that their life depends upon having, possessing or owning this or that.

None of these desires of the flesh are oblivious to the least of believers. And, during a lengthy season of unanswered prayer or whenever the thing that they desired did not manifest within the time they felt God should have given it, immature believers find themselves weakening in their faith in God's Word. Their faith is not developed enough; their faith is not settled in the Word of God. *"Take heed and beware of covetousness, for one's life does not consist in the abundance of the things he possesses"* (Luke 12:15).

God already knew, in His eternal mind, what your society would look like today. He is not now, never has been, and never will be shocked or surprised at how things are or the evil atrocities that take place in our worldly societies. Jesus was quite aware of this also when He prayed for those who were His disciples during His earthly ministry and for all Believers.

> *"I have given them Your word; and the world has hated them because they are not of the world, just as I am not of the world.* ***I do not pray that You should take them out of the world, but that You should keep them from the evil one.*** *They are not of the world, just as I am not of the world.* ***Sanctify them by Your truth. Your word is truth.*** *As You sent Me into the world, I also have sent them into the world. And for their sakes I sanctify Myself, that they also may be sanctified by the truth.* ***I do not pray for these alone, but also for those who will believe in Me*** *through their word; that they all may be one, as You, Father, are in Me, and I in You; that they also may be one in Us, that the world may believe that You sent Me."* (John 17:14-21, author's emphasis)

Your faith must be settled in the fact that, in the mind of God, you are not of this world. You are first and foremost a citizen of the Kingdom of Heaven. You'll never get a Holy Spirit revelation of this if you haven't learned to think eternally. But, God has ordained that you live out your kingdom citizenship on earth – in the world. Why? So that the world may believe that God sent Jesus to save the world, as you expressed salvation through your lifestyle. And, God did not leave you unprotected against the evils of the world. Jesus prayed that the Word of God – truth – would sanctify or set you apart from the world (conforming to the evil systems of the world).

In order to be set apart from the world though the Word of God, your faith must be settled in the Word. **The just shall live by his faith!** Satan knows whether or not your faith is settled in God's Word. That's why he tempts you with the things of the world to find out your true allegiance. God does not tempt, He tests your heart for loyalty birthed out of humility or total dependence upon Him. Apostle James teaches that the testing of your faith produces patience, and a double-minded man is unstable. You cannot serve God and systems of the world which are driven by Mammon.

> *Let no one say when he is tempted, "I am tempted by God"; for God cannot be tempted by evil, nor does He Himself tempt anyone. But each one is tempted when he is drawn away by his own desires and enticed. Then, when desire has conceived, it gives birth to sin; and sin, when it is full-grown, brings forth death. Do not be deceived, my beloved brethren. Every good gift and every perfect gift is from above, and comes down from the Father of lights, with whom there is no variation or shadow of turning. Of His own will He brought us forth by the word of truth, that we might be a kind of firstfruits of His creatures"* (James 1:13:-18).

Once the devil tempts you through your fleshly desires and you fall for it or you get hooked on your evil desires, they are conceived in your mind. And of course, from the mind things are produced. Once this happens, the devil simply applies pressure to the situation. His mission then is to keep you grounded and settled in fear. And, when fear sets in, religion shows up. You become impatient and make the decision, from your mind of fear, to improve your dilemma by taking matters into your own hands, forgetting God's promises to you if you continue in the faith. *"If ye continue in the faith grounded and settled, and not moved away from the hope of the gospel…The blessing of the Lord makes one rich, And He adds no sorrow with it"* (Col. 1:23, KJV; Prov. 10:22, NLT).

Because you are a believer, God has given you a measure, a ***metron*** or a determined extent of faith, the same measure that He's given to all saints, *"as God has dealt to each one a measure of faith"* (Rom. 12:3). Still, God requires you to mature in your faith, which means you must consistently hear the Word of God. *"So then faith comes by hearing, and hearing by the word of God"* (Rom. 10:17). A consistent dose of the Word of God will feed and fuel your faith for growth or increase. So, then, the measure that you were originally dealt by God increases as you consistently hear the Word. The more Word you actually hear, the more mature your faith becomes and this is how your faith becomes settled in the Word of God; and, as a just or righteous person, you now live by your faith.

Let's take a look at two words and their meanings because they are pivotal to your understanding of this. Your original measure of faith grows, increases and becomes mature – a sustained faith, as in *"the just shall live by his faith."* First, let's define "hearing" as used in the text above. The Greek word translated **hearing** is ***akoe (ak-o-ay)***, taken from ***akouo (ak-oo-o)***, which means the act, the sense or the thing heard: to give audience to, come to the ears, and understand (Strong's). Next, let's define the word "settled." David expresses the Word of God as such, *"Forever, O Lord, Your word is settled in heaven"* (Psa. 119:89). Paul said that your faith should be grounded and settled. The Hebrew word translated **settled** is ***natsab (naw-tsab)***, a primary root word meaning to station: appoint, erect, establish, pillar, make to stand upright, best state; fixed (Strong's). The Greek word translated **settled** is ***hedraios (hed-rah-yos)***, which means to sit: sedentary, i.e. immovable: settled, steadfast, and grounded (Strong's).

From these definitions, you should be able to understand that faith is a continuous exercise of sensing what has been heard, understanding it, and acting on it. The more Word that you sense or get a divine revelation of enters into your heart and you have understanding of it. Understanding the Word that you consistently hear makes it easier to act or obey the Word by faith or total trust in God. As you act on the Word that you know or understand, your faith becomes stationary, erect like a pillar upholding a structure; it becomes steadfast, grounded and immovable. This is what I called a sustained faith, and a sustained faith is a faith that has increased, grown and matured.

As you learn to live by your faith, *"For we walk by faith, not by sight"* (2 Cor. 5:7), you will be enlarged within the sphere which God appointed you – your kingdom assignment. As your faith increases, and it becomes an evident testament of your advancement and success within your field of assignment, others should be greatly enlarged in their field of assignment because of your mature faith, which further opens doors in regions beyond your own for the gospel of the kingdom to be released. *"We, however, will not boast beyond measure, but within the limits of the sphere which God appointed us – a sphere which especially includes you…not boasting of things beyond measure, that is, in other men's labors, but having hope,* **that as your faith is increased, we shall be greatly enlarged by you in our sphere"** (2 Cor. 10:13, 15; author's emphasis).

So, then, when your faith is increased, the measure that God initially dealt to you has been developed, strengthened, settled, and can result in having a visible and tangible effect on the lives of others. The apostles of Jesus never could have reflected His leadership after His ascension into heaven if their faith had not increased, and they were wise enough to ask Jesus for help. *"And the apostles said to the Lord, 'Increase our faith'"* (Luke 17:5).

Like Abraham, you become *"strong in faith, giving glory to God"* (Rom. 4:20), which means that you are not a weak, immature believer who simply does nothing "waiting on the Lord." You're not just shuffling along in unbelief or doubt expecting God to do something for you. This is the kind of "misguided faith" that has led too many believers to the escapist mentality. They can't wait for Jesus to hurry up and rapture the Church out of this world. Meanwhile, they do nothing. Instead of standing their ground with a faith that is settled in God's Word, they dilute the purity of God's Word and overlook the simplicity that is in Christ Jesus by making their situations and circumstances more complex and extremely religious. The end result is that they abort the beautiful blessing God had appointed for them in its season.

If you don't remain steadfast, living by your faith in God's Word, you may get weary and faint or give up on your life of faith. *"If you fall to pieces in a crisis, there wasn't much to you in the first place"* (Prov. 24:10, MSG). *"So let us not become tired of doing good; for if we do not give up, the time will come when we will reap the harvest"* (Gal. 6:9, GNB).

God never does anything apart from your faith, even in the severity of need, *"for without faith it is impossible to please Him"* (Heb. 11:6). There has to be a faith connection to God. Believing and receiving work together in the Kingdom of God. When faith cries out, God answers. This is why it is so important that you spend quality time with God on a daily basis. In His presence, you receive answers. God's assurance to anyone who diligently abides in His presence is that he will receive answers. *"He shall call upon Me, and I will answer him"* (Psa. 91:15).

If you live by your faith, then your faith has matured. It is a faith that is grounded, settled and immovable. You have learned to trust God's faithfulness to His Word. Your faith walk began from a committed heart, being constantly aware of your kingdom assignment. Your focus and passion has been centered on the fulfillment of your divine assignment, which has been driven by acting on your faith. You have been able to bear up under pressures and not give in to the storms of life. But, what about those saints who have not increased in their faith? **Faith that is not increased can actually fail.**

I liken some of them to Apostle Peter, prior to Pentecost. He wrestled with negative thoughts and fears, at times appearing schizophrenic. I say this because in the gospels we find Peter's behaviors and attitudes to be both contradictory, even antagonistic at times. And, such can be your behavior and attitude if you are a faithless Christian. One day you're happy and professing faith in God, and the next you are sad and can't believe God for a bacon, lettuce, and tomato sandwich. This is the point of unbelief that opens the door for Satan to destroy what faith you once had.

The devil sought to take advantage of Peter's unbelief, but Jesus stepped in to ensure that his faith would not fail. *"But I have prayed for you, that your faith should not fail; and when you have returned to Me, strengthen your brethren"* (Luke 22:32). God had to increase Peter's faith and He did so by testing it. Peter was called by God to be a commissioned, kingdom-level leader, a commander. Prior to Pentecost, Peter's faith was described as "little," even though he actually walked on water. But, after Pentecost, when the Holy Spirit had fully come to dwell in him, Peter became a bold witness for Christ, teaching with authority as Jesus had done; and 3,000 souls were added to the Church that day (Acts 2:41). Peter continued to go forth, preaching the gospel of the kingdom, performing miracles, even raising the dead.

The story pertaining to Peter's walk on the water to meet Jesus is told in Matthew's gospel. Between three and six o'clock in the morning Jesus approached the disciples' boat walking on the water. When they saw Him, they were terrified and cried out in fear that it was a ghost. But, I love Jesus' peace response: *"Be of good cheer! It is I; do not be afraid"* (14:27).

Peter discerned the voice of Jesus and said, *"Lord, if it is You, command me to come to You on the water"* (vs. 28). Well, what was Jesus going to tell Peter, "It's not Me?" No. Jesus said, "Come." Peter's faith and courage are displayed upon leaving the boat. None of the other disciples made the slightest move to get out of the boat. And, I imagine that more than one of them tried to convince Peter to stay in the boat. You see, the boat is a source of natural security. But, Peter was willing to risk failure to experience a supernatural relationship with Jesus. He left his natural security and entrusted himself to Jesus' supernatural power.

Heeding the command of Jesus to "come," Peter actually walked on the water which is a testament to the "little" faith that he had; and, which indeed was enough. *"So the Lord said, if you have faith as a mustard seed, you can say to this mulberry tree, 'Be pulled up by the roots and be planted in the sea,' and it would obey you"* (Luke 17:6). But, God is too wise to promote Peter before he had proven, in the form of a sustained faith, his true allegiance to Jesus and the Kingdom of Heaven.

When Peter saw and realized the severity of the waves produced by boisterous wind, he became afraid. What you see and experience as fact can affect your faith. What Peter saw and believed through fear caused him to begin to sink. Thank God for His compassion. Peter had the presence of mind to call on Jesus to save him. And, Jesus protected Peter and kept him from drowning. In the end, Peter learned an invaluable lesson that all believers should learn as they endeavor to increase their faith: **You must take faith-risks in order to increase your faith, even if it seems that you've failed in previous efforts to achieve a thing.**

More often than not, fear will accompany growth. Jesus pointed out to Peter that it wasn't the boisterous waves that caused him to begin to sink, which seemed like failure, since he never made it to Jesus walking on the water. It was his lack of sustained faith that kept him from completing his walk on the water to Jesus. Therefore, Jesus referred to Peter's faith as "little." Peter doubted Jesus' faithfulness to His word. He'd told Peter to "Come." And, Jesus' word had the final authority. Had Peter not succumbed to what he saw, no doubt he would have made it all the way to Jesus.

God could have allowed Peter to walk to Jesus with no visible threat; however, He allowed the roughness of the wind to further challenge Peter's faith. Like Peter, your loyalty to God and His kingdom must be proven through your life of faith, prior to the release of His glory upon you for the fulfilling of your kingdom assignment. And remember, what you see and experience as facts can affect your faith. Nevertheless, be assured that **"Facts don't change the Word of God; the Word of God changes the facts."**

God's way of doing things that challenge your faith may sometimes seem to make no sense to your natural understanding. The reason is because your natural understanding of God's will is limited. You must seek to understand God's will from an eternal perspective – the supernatural realm where you seek the guidance of Holy Spirit, who searches the deep things of God that you might know the things that are freely given to you by God (see 1 Cor. 2:9-12). God does not want you to yield to "faith-fatigue" while He's challenging you to increase your faith, for He desires that you possess the full measure of faith required to complete your kingdom assignment.

The epistle to the Hebrews was written, in part, to encourage believers who had grown weary in their faith to stand their ground and not give up or faint. The theme is very clear: God's actions toward believers through Jesus' finished work on the Cross. Your heavenly Father wants you to come into possession of the victorious life achieved for you through Jesus' victory over death and hell.

Jesus is: *"the brightness of His glory and the express image of His person, and upholding all things by the word of His power"* (1:3); the destroyer of *"him who had the power of death, that is, the devil"* (2:14); *"the Apostle and High Priest of our confession"* (3:1); *"a great High Priest who has passed through the heavens…let us hold fast our confession"* (4:14); *"called by God as High Priest according to the order of Melchizedek"* (5:10); *"the forerunner…entered for us, even Jesus, having become High Priest forever according to the order of Melchizedek"* (6:20); He who *"always lives to make intercession for them"* (7:25); *"also Mediator of a better covenant, which was established on better promises"* (8:6); *"the Mediator of the new covenant, by means of death, for the redemption of the transgressions under the first covenant, that those who are called may receive the promise of the eternal inheritance"* (9:15); *"a High Priest over the house of God…for He who promised is faithful"* (10:21, 23); *"a rewarder of those who diligently seek Him"* (11:6); *"the author and finisher of our faith, who for the joy that was set before Him endured the cross, despising the shame, and has sat down at the right hand of the throne of God"* (12:2); *"the same yesterday, today, and forever…For He Himself has said, 'I will never leave you nor forsake you,' So that we may boldly say: 'The Lord is my helper; I will not fear. What can man do to me?"* (13:8, 5-6).

The writer of Hebrews encourages believers to come boldly to the throne of Grace to obtain mercy in times of need (4:16). The Kingdom of Heaven is a kingdom of grace. This is leverage for the believer who commits to a life lived by faith. Through Jesus you can always approach God without condemnation and receive mercy and grace any time you need it. So, then, *"Let us hold fast the profession of our faith without wavering; (for he is faithful that promised)"* (10:23, KJV).

In order to receive these truths, you must possess faith that is active and sustained. Your sustained faith keeps you from getting in God's way as well as keeps you on the Way. The posture of faith is to *"Stand fast therefore in the liberty by which Christ has made us free, and do not be entangled again with a yoke of bondage"*

(Gal. 5:1). "The just shall live by his faith!"

Whenever you are faced with difficulties and uncertainties as you are being developed and equipped for your kingdom assignment, know that your faith is settled in God's Word. Know that your life of faith is rooted, grounded, established and settled on what God has said concerning you in His eternal mind. Make the commitment now to live by faith the rest of your life. Trust God's faithfulness to His Word and rest in the assurance of knowing that God's goodness is all about making all things go well for you.

Settle it in your mind right now! **"I am a love person; I am a faith person, and I am a Word person."** Faith is expressed through love (see Gal. 5:6). Be strong and mature in your faith life, which makes you strong in the Lord and the power of His might. Put on the whole armor of God each day and stand your ground on the truth – His Word is truth. Stand by faith on the righteousness you have obtained through faith in Jesus; stand by faith on the gospel of peace; stand by faith on the helmet of salvation and the rhema of the Holy Spirit. Above all, know that your faith is a shield. It will protect you against the day or season of surrender, struggle, and suffering for Christ as long as you are sustained in God's faithfulness to fulfill His words spoken over your life from His eternal mind. *"For the vision is yet for an appointed time, but **at the end it shall speak, and not lie:** Though it tarry, wait for it; Because it will surely come, it will not tarry"* (Hab. 2:3, KJV, author's emphasis).

God determines the events of life, and moments will manifest the shift that will lead you into your destiny. Your vision, your sphere of influence, in whatever mountain within the cultures of society it may be, **will speak and not lie – in the end!** It will speak in the end (God's perfect timing of making all things beautiful in its time) because God spoke it in the beginning (in His eternal mind). *"Declaring the end from the beginning, And from ancient times things that are not yet done, Saying, 'My counsel shall stand, And I will do all My Pleasure'"* (Isa. 46:10). God is faithful to His Word. Put the Word of God in your heart every day and live by it. ***"The just shall live by his faith!"*** This is the lifestyle of a commissioned, kingdom-level leader. ARISE!

SECTION FIVE:

KINGDOM-LEVEL ACCOUNTABILITY

Accountability to the King of kings should be your standard of living in every position and function of your kingdom assignment.

*"And **that servant who knew his master's will, and did not prepare himself or do according to his will,** shall be beaten with many stripes.*
*But he who did not know, yet committed things deserving of stripes, shall be beaten with few. **For everyone to whom much is given, from him much will be required;** and to whom much has been committed, of him they will ask the more."*
(Luke 12:47-48, author's emphasis)

CHAPTER THIRTEEN

EMBRACING THE NEW 21ST CENTURY APOSTOLIC MODEL

*"Paul, a bondservant of Jesus Christ, called to be an apostle,
separated to the gospel of God...concerning His Son Jesus Christ our Lord...
Through Him, we have received grace and apostleship for obedience to the faith
among all nations for His name, among whom you also are the called of Jesus
Christ."* (ROM. 1:1, 3, 5-6)

I cannot overstate the importance of the role that apostolic fathering plays in the development of true apostles, modeled after the original apostles of the New Testament Church as recorded in the Acts of the Apostles. Their apostleship was global in scope, a testimonial to the fact that the apostleship is a model of ascension into a greater level of accountability, order, and kingdom assignment in alignment with the plans and purposes of God through Jesus Christ.

After I was reunited with my spiritual father, Dr. Gordon E. Bradshaw, in 2011 he immediately began to "father" me into the apostleship – the order, government, model, and office of the apostle – its position within the Kingdom of God and the Body of Christ to become the foundation of the Church and equip other believers through "spiritual ascension" to carry out their kingdom assignment, *"having been built on the **foundation** of the apostles and prophets, Jesus Christ Himself being the chief cornerstone...in whom you also are being built together for a dwelling place of God in the Spirit"* (Eph. 2:20, 22, author's emphasis). In other words, the architect of the apostleship is a position which places the apostle at the bottom, as a foundation upon which to build, rather than the top. Apostles and prophets are foundations upon which the church is built by the Spirit of God with Jesus as its cornerstone.

The apostle is a foundational office to the Body of Christ. As such, the true nature of an apostle must be one of concern for the generation of believers that will be raised up to function as commissioned commanders – apostles – who lead the charge of advancing the Kingdom of Heaven in the earth. The Greek word translated **foundation** is ***themelios (them-el-ee-os),*** which means something put down, i.e. a substruction (of a building, etc): - foundation; to lay a basis for, i.e. erect or consolidate: lay the foundation, ground, settle. The Greek word translated **apostle** is ***apostolos (ap-os-tol-os),*** meaning a delegate; specifically, an ambassador of the Gospel; officially, a commissioner of Christ with miraculous powers: apostle, messenger, he that is sent (Strong's).

Apostles are commissioned commanders sent by the King of kings as a delegation of ambassadors, possessing miraculous power to consolidate the Body of Christ by laying the substructure or foundation upon which Holy Spirit builds for a dwelling place for God. Actually, apostles are military generals. The word apostle was a secular term used long ago to describe those who were sent out by their respective kingdoms for the purpose of expanding their kingdom by subduing weaker kingdoms and incorporating or assimilating them into their culture, under their laws. These new converts or conquests to the kingdom had to be trained and acclimated into the systems, policies, doctrines, culture and rules of the kingdom of dominion.

As apostles of Christ, we have a similar task. We are given power and authority to accomplish the same task for the kingdom of God. We are commissioned and sent into regions, territories, and nations to convert people, incorporate them into the kingdom of God and lead them into their kingdom destiny. In order to do this, we must adhere to the apostolic model of the 21st Century, here and now. We can no longer function under the mandates of an "old" apostolic model. **The new apostolic model is a technology of change, as apostles are agents of change, calibration and adjustment.** This requires a high level of transitional responsibility.

Believers are the building stones for the foundation of Christ, which means believers have to be built up supernaturally to become the "superior material" apostles use to build upon the foundation, which is Jesus, *"For no other foundation can anyone lay than that which is laid, which is Jesus Christ"* (1 Cor. 3:11). *"You also, as living stones, are being built up a spiritual house, a holy priesthood, to offer up spiritual sacrifices acceptable to God through Jesus Christ"* (1 Pet. 2:5). This suggests that the new apostolic model of the 21st Century Church is one of transformation and reformation.

The root word for transformation is **transform,** which means to change in composition or structure; to change in character or condition. It implies a major change in form, nature, or function (Merriam-Webster). The Greek word translated **transform** is *metamorphoo (met-am-or-fo-o),* taken from the prefix *meta (met-ah)* and root word *morphe (mor-fay),* meaning to transform: change, transfigure; association, succession, transfer or sequence through the idea of adjustment of parts; shape; nature, fashion or form (Strong's). *"And do not be conformed to this world, but be transformed by the renewing of your mind, that you may prove what is that good and acceptable and perfect will of God"* (Rom. 12:2). The Body of Christ cannot allow itself to get stuck in this current timeframe, bogged down in a quagmire of tradition, legalism and disunity.

According to the writer of the epistle to the Hebrews, there is a time of reformation when old ways of doing things must become new. We will entertain that analogy with the new apostolic model of the 21ˢᵗ Century shortly. The root word for reformation is **reform**, which means to put or change into an improved form or condition; to amend or improve by change of form or removal of faults or abuses; enforcing or introducing a better method or course of action (Merriam-Webster). The Greek word translated **reformation** is *diorthosis (dee-or-tho-sis)* taken from a compound of *dia (dee-ah),* the channel of an act; through - by reason of or for the sake of; and, *orthos (or-thos),* meaning honest, level or direct: straight, upright. Together, the meaning is to straighten thoroughly; rectification, restoration: reformation (Strong's).

> *"The Holy Spirit indicating this, that the way into the Holiest of All was not yet made manifest while the first tabernacle was still standing. It was symbolic for the present time in which both gifts and sacrifices are offered which cannot make him who performed the service perfect in regard to the conscience – concerned only with foods and drinks, various washings, and fleshly ordinances imposed **until the time of reformation.**"* (Heb. 9:8-10, author's emphasis)

Let's draw an analogy between these Scriptures, based upon old covenant sacrifices which were only symbolic in nature and the 21ˢᵗ Century apostolic leadership model, based on the grace of Jesus Christ, *"who has come, **not according to the law of a fleshly commandment,** but according to the power of an endless life"* (Heb. 7:16, author's emphasis). You must understand the 21ˢᵗ Century apostolic model is one of transfer, sequence and adjustments. Jesus is the Mediator of the New Testament, a better covenant established on better promises. *"For if that first covenant had been faultless, then no place would have been sought for a second"* (Heb. 8:6-7).

Under the old covenant, the people did not have direct access into the presence of God. Under the new order, we all have access to God through Jesus. Under the old covenant, only the high priest could enter the Holy of Holies once a year on the Day of Atonement. Under this covenant, people could not truly come to God through the blood of animal sacrifices. Under the new covenant, believers can come boldly to enter into the holiest, the presence of God, by the blood of Jesus, who offered His body as a sacrifice for sins one time for all people forever.

These "better promises" let us know that Old Testament worship was symbolic, a copy of the true pattern to come – the way to God is through Jesus Christ. Under the old covenant, the high priest stood to offer sacrifices. But, Jesus sat down, indicating a new order. By this transformation, the Old Testament order of offering sacrifices was no longer the standard of being cleansed from sin. It was replaced with a new order, a new standard that was inclusive of change – the succession of a form – and reform, the channel of an act to straighten thoroughly, honestly and rectify a form calibrating and adjusting it to meet the current standard.

This calibration and adjustment requires a new perspective on how apostolic leaders view those that they are or should be fathering. In this context, **calibration** means to adjust precisely for a particular function; to measure precisely; to measure against a standard (Merriam-Webster). Since there are so many different kinds of apostles (especially marketplace apostles) being raised by God and commissioned as kingdom commanders in this season, the apostles who have been the pioneers and largely assigned to an ecclesiastical role, tend to develop a system to differentiate between the new order of apostles and themselves, promoting themselves above others and using the title of apostle as a position of power to lord over the offices of the prophet, evangelist, pastor and teacher. Clearly, this is a misunderstanding and misapplication of the apostleship. Many "old school" apostles have tried to relegate the apostolic office only to the religious mountain culture, which has led to a misappropriation of the grace and purpose of the apostleship. (See Dr. Bruce Cook, *Aligning with the Apostolic: An Anthology of Apostleship, Vol. 1,* in this regard; Kingdom House Publishing, Lakebay, WA, 2013.)

I am in no way suggesting that the "old order" is no longer useful. On the contrary, the new apostolic model is a combination of the old and new, calibrated and adjusted to conform to the standard of God for harvesting souls in this end times season. It showcases the diversity within the Body of Christ because it embraces the many diverse global networks and alliances, along with their applications and experiences of the apostleship.

I am convinced that Daniel saw God's ever-increasing, everlasting kingdom unfold before his eyes, as he was elevated in the Spirit of God. I believe he saw the technologies of the 21st Century apostolic model, the many changes and transformation of people's mindsets and attitudes along with the succession of ideas and technologies required for commissioned, kingdom-level leaders to meet the standard of God's end-time army to fulfill its mandate to harvest the souls of the world for the Kingdom of God and advance the Kingdom in the earth prior to Christ's return.

Daniel said, *"knowledge shall increase."* He spoke of a progressive knowledge in alignment with the process of time, civilization, industrialization, and technological advances. This is why he was instructed by the angel of God to *"shut up the words, and seal the book, even to the time of the end"* (vs. 4). The Message Bible says it this way, *"In the interim there is going to be a lot of frantic running around, trying to figure out what's going on."* But, verse 3 actually reveals to spiritually mature saints – commissioned, kingdom-level leaders – the 21st Century apostolic model of the Kingdom of God. *"Those who are wise shall shine Like the brightness of the firmament, And those who turn many to righteousness Like the stars forever and ever."*

This verse is referring to the commissioned, kingdom-level leaders of the end times. How do I know this? Jesus links the two together in His Olivet Discourse. *"And the gospel of the kingdom will be preached in all the world as a witness to all the nations, and then the end will come. Therefore when you see the 'abomination of desolation,'* **spoken of by Daniel the prophet,** *standing in the holy place"* **(whoever reads, let him understand)"** (Matt. 24:14-15, author's emphasis). "Whoever reads" refers to 21st Century commissioned, kingdom-level leaders who know and understand the Kingdom of God and its gospel message of good news. The assumption is that kingdom-level leaders – the commissioned, apostolic commanders – would know what Daniel's hidden reference means.

One of the problems that the Body of Christ faces today is fear of the unknown. People, generally, don't like uncertainty. But, for believers, this fear is fueled by unbelief or lack of trust and dependence on God, and it has caused many to remain spiritual babies unable to increase in the knowledge of God and of His Son. It would seem that 2 Cor. 5:7 is simply a frequently-used phrase without any significant meaning to them, *"For we walk by faith, not by sight."* The Church must embrace the eternal in order to walk or live by faith. *"While we do not look at the things which are seen, but at the things which are not seen. For the things which are seen are temporary, but the things which are not seen are eternal"* (2 Cor. 4:18).

Growth requires change. And, change is difficult to embrace when ignorance is present – where there is a lack of pursuing God's wisdom. Thomas Carlyle, a 19th Century Scottish author said, "That there should one man die ignorant who had capacity for knowledge, this I call tragedy."

There is indeed a new apostolic leadership model for 21st Century saints, instituted by God in alignment with the standard of how leaders of the Kingdom should be prepared and equipped to carry out their kingdom assignment. This new wineskin is comprised of true disciples, kingdom-level leaders who have been commissioned by God because they have believed in and been processed by Jesus' Word, *"If you abide in My Word, You are My disciples indeed"* (John 8:31). The Greek word translated **new** is ***neos (neh-os),*** which signifies new in respect of time, that which is recent; it is used of the young, and so translated, especially the comparative degree "younger," **accordingly what is *neos* may be a reproduction of the old in quality or character. It stresses the fact of the believer's new experience, recently begun, and still proceeding** (Vine's Expository, author's emphasis).

> *"And no one puts new wine into old wineskins; or else the new wine will burst the wineskins and be spilled, and the wineskins will be ruined. But new wine must be put into new wineskins, and both are preserved. And no one, having drunk old win, immediately desires new; for he says, 'The old is better'"* (Luke 5:37-39).

What this means, in the context of which I write, is that people are not easily freed from old habits, religious mindsets, and denominational prejudices.

Nevertheless, Jesus implied that when one is instructed concerning the Kingdom of Heaven, he is like a householder (a commissioned, kingdom-level leader who manages all things well) who brings forth the older and younger generations together to form a complete and functional family lineage. "Therefore every scribe instructed concerning the kingdom of heaven is like a householder who brings out of his treasure things new and old" (Matt. 13:52).

So, then, this new 21st Century apostolic leadership model is a patterned process of transformation and reformation. Why? Because God is meticulous about building things that are strong, durable, and sustainable; in other words, generational. Our Father has used time to process true disciples, who have committed to being "handled" by Him. They have allowed the transformation and reformation of the new wine apostolic leadership model to mold and shape them for the current standard of the Kingdom. They are servant leaders who committed to the sequence of advancements required for the renewing of their mind. These are the commanders who understand that commissioned, kingdom-level leadership requires interdependence, embracing and involving the old and the new. They no longer boast of "I," but "we."

The Kingdom process to commissioned, kingdom-level leadership is indeed a gradual transformation which requires total commitment from the one who is seeking to know and understand his kingdom assignment, and he will stay on the kingdom path (the narrow path) at all costs until he finds it. The new 21st Century apostolic model is patterned after this level of servant leadership. *"But he who is greatest among you shall be your servant. "And whoever exalts himself will be humbled, and he who humbles himself will be exalted"* (Matt. 23:11-12). *"Strive to enter through the narrow gate, for many, I say to you, will seek to enter and will not be able"* (Luke 13:24).

The new 21st Century apostolic leadership model is one which requires leaders to "occupy the narrow place for the benefit of the many" (conversation with Steve McVickers, 2015). It is a model of servant leadership. Jesus did not come to be ministered to, but to minister (Matt. 20:28). This is the call and the cry of God's heart to His people. The commanders of the Kingdom must now arise to the challenge of teaching and fathering the young people of the world. The youth of the world, those under 25, make up almost half of the world's population. Many of them have no moral foundation and they live in a world ravished by crime, violence, abuse, sanctioned promiscuity, and suicide. Social media outlets fuel their mindsets from the framework of their worldview.

And, since the Church has not understood the makeup of a unified Body built on the foundation of the apostles and prophets, it has lacked the kingdom authority to confront this demonic technology and take back the youth of the world for the Kingdom of God. As a result, the youth of the world have no point of reference for right or wrong. Kingdom-level leaders must arise to deter this demonic technology of Satan and bring reformation of moral character back to the youth of the world through the new apostolic leadership model.

True apostles are commanders. They are the master builders of the Church. Their kingdom assignment is to raise spiritual sons and daughters into a functional body of kingdom citizens who reflect the pattern or government of the Kingdom. This is why apostolic parenting is so important in this season. Apostolic parents serve as the schematic representation of the structure to be built. The office of the apostle represents the law of first things. *"And God has appointed these in the church: first apostles, second prophets, third teachers…"* (1 Cor. 12:28). The Greek word translated **first** is ***proton (pro-ton),*** meaning first in time, place, order or importance (Strong's). Apostles are reformers, who come first to initiate new grace for the work of the Kingdom.

Apostles possess the spirit of a reformer, a grace to initiate a sequence of events and successions that lead to restoration and reformation. In this sense, apostles are radical representatives of the Kingdom of God – defenders of the Kingdom; defenders of the name of Jesus; defenders of the Word of God; defenders of the faith; and, defenders of the Church. The process toward reformation is a radical process, which calls for radical people – apostles, commanders who bring correction, rectification, restoration, salvation, deliverance, and spiritual growth to the sons and daughters whom they parent.

The Church is in a season of revolutionary change. Certainly, it is uncomfortable but very necessary if we are going to witness and partake in the end time revival that will harvest untold multitudes into the Kingdom. Jesus was a radical revolutionary. He had to teach His disciples the costs associated with discipleship. *"If anyone comes to Me and does not hate his father and mother, wife and children, brothers and sisters, yes, and his own life also, he cannot be My disciple"* (Luke 14:26). Believers who have not committed themselves to true discipleship generally become a breeding ground for religion. Nothing is required of the saint who relegates himself to simply being a pew-warmer.

The Church has to be radical because of its kingdom assignment. It was created to be a launching pad for the Kingdom of God in the earth. It was designed by God to become the foundational dimension that gives the saints full access to Him. We are the Kingdom citizens whose mandate is to carry out the conquest of earthly kingdoms, subduing the mountains of culture. This is a radical assignment. Therefore, the new 21st Century apostolic model has to be about form and function, not one or the other. The old order was more about form, a basic blueprint of design. It produced a basic understanding of the apostleship, a basic grasp of the outer framework of the office of the apostle. However, it failed to reveal the inner workings or functions of the apostolic office. It represented a title, "Apostle," without displaying the function. Function goes beyond form. One has to fully understand the office in order to carry out the function.

The new 21st Century apostolic order is about form and function. Apostles must function as commanders, servant leaders, fathers, defenders of the faith, who exercise kingdom authority and boldness to war against the demonically-influenced world systems. *"And through the hands of the apostles many signs and wonders were done among the people"* (Acts 5:12). In this season of the Church's kingdom assignment, God is identifying true apostles – those that are His – because they are the foundation of the Church, sealed or certified by God. *"Nevertheless, the solid foundation of God stands, having this seal: 'The Lord knows those who are His'"* (2 Tim. 2:19).

True apostles – commissioned, kingdom-level servant leaders, commanders – are emerging on the scene and are carrying the indisputable marks that distinguish them as apostles. The sent ones whom the Lord knows are His. *"I know your works, your labor, your patience, and that you cannot bear those who are evil. And you have tested those who say they are apostles and are not, and have found them liars; and you have persevered and have patience, and have labored for My name's sake and have not become weary"* (Rev. 2:2-3). True apostles will have the evidence of authenticity. They will wear the seal of authenticity through their having fathered sons and daughters who are also reflecting the Kingdom, producing still other disciples. *"And the things that you have heard from me among many witnesses, commit these to faithful men who will be able to teach others also"* (2 Tim. 2:2).

True apostles adhere to the "apostles' code of conduct," instructions for holy living as stated in 1 Thess. 5:12-23; they adhere to the rules of the Kingdom as stated in Luke 6:27-38. They exhibit the signs of an apostle, the definite characteristics of true apostles. Beware of charlatans, those who claim to be apostles but never exhibit the grace or godly character to walk in the apostleship, *"For such are false apostles, deceitful workers, transforming themselves into apostles of Christ"* (2 Cor. 11:13). The good news is that false apostles are being exposed for the impostors they are.

The following are some of the definite characteristics that authenticate true apostles as stated by Roger Sapp in his book, *The Last Apostles on Earth* (1995, Companion Press).

1. Signs, Wonders, and Miracles – *"Truly the signs of an apostle were accomplished among you with all perseverance, in signs and wonders and mighty deeds"* (2 Cor. 12:12).

2. Revelation of the Calling to Independent Witnesses – *"Now in the church that was at Antioch there were certain prophets and teachers: Barnabas, Simeon who was called Niger, Lucius of Cyrene, Manaen who had been brought up with Herod the tetrarch, and Saul; As they ministered to the Lord and fasted, the Holy Spirit said, 'Now separate to me Barnabas and Saul for the work to which I have called them"* (Acts 13:1, 2).

3. Ministers Are Given to Apostles – *"And Sopater of Berea accompanied him to Asia – also Aristarchus and Secundus of the Thessalonians, and Gaius of Derbe, and Timothy, and Tychicus and Trophimus of Asia. These men, going ahead, waited for us at Troas"* (Acts 20:4, 5).

4. Full Functioning Churches – *"If I am not an apostle to others, yet doubtless I am to you. For you are the seal of my apostleship in the Lord"* (1 Cor. 9:2).

5. Serious Resistance from Evil Prince Angels – *"And lest I should be exalted above measure by the abundance of the revelations, a thorn in the flesh was given to me, as a messenger of Satan to buffet me, lest I be exalted above measure."* (2 Cor. 12:7)

The new 21ˢᵗ Century, apostolic model is represented by the many diverse global alliances and networks of apostles and prophets, young and old, authenticating their true apostleship in alignment with the Scriptures, and applying new apostolic technologies in the form of applications and expressions for diversity and full function of the Body of Christ. The Church must embrace it because this is yet another fresh wave of God's glory. It is heaven's dance upon the earth, a time of celebration when the eternal "Now" faith "is" is manifesting in the form of breakthroughs involving new areas of increase, favor and new assignments to the saints and servant leaders who have been forerunners and stewards of the apostleship, leading the way and building up the Body of Christ. This is a kairos time when the eternal mind of God is being manifested in the earth through the saints.

God is shaking the earth, but He is also shaking heaven so that an old move of God can be replaced with a current move of God, unifying the Body of Christ. Many saints are "praying down revival." While this is a good thing, and we are seeing pockets of revival in isolated places, many saints still don't have a revelation of the fresh oil that is being poured into the Body of Christ that will provide the fuel that will produce the global wildfire revival that cannot be contained nor put out. The problem is that too many saints want revival of this magnitude but are not willing to be transformed; they want reformation without transformation. They want to remain spiritual babies but eat adult food; they want to be spiritual giants overnight, but they haven't committed themselves to the process of spiritual maturity; they want to be the ones who lead, but have never been good followers; they talk about the love of God toward all people, but continue to support racism within the Body of Christ. As James the Apostle says, *"Out of the same mouth proceed blessing and cursing. My brethren, these things ought not to be so"* (3:10).

Let's take a look at what Scripture says about this great shaking of heaven and earth. *"Be careful, then, and do not refuse to hear him who speaks. Those who refused to hear the one who gave the divine message on earth did not escape. How much less shall we escape, then, if we turn away from the one who speaks from heaven! His voice shook the earth at that time, but now he has promised, 'I will once more shake not only the earth but heaven as well.' The words "once more" plainly show that the created things will be shaken and removed, so that the things that cannot be shaken will remain"* (Heb. 12:25-27).

God is not only shaking the earth, but heaven as well. Not because heaven needs shaking; there is nothing out of order in heaven. Rather, **God is shaking from heaven (the eternal mind of God to His sons and daughters on earth as per their kingdom assignment) the Kingdom pattern that cannot be shaken or removed by ungodly people and the demonic world systems that seduce them.** God is shaking from heaven, the new 21st Century, apostolic model that the Church must embrace in order to become the catalyst of the greatest revival of souls for the Kingdom of God of any time in history.

Not surprisingly, however, there are some saints who fear this shaking. I believe it is because so many have compromised with the world's way of living and accomplishment. They have never known the power of their true identity as a king and priest in the royal family of God. They have never committed to living by their faith, trusting God, taking Him at His Word. They never experienced the benefits of the Kingdom. The wealth of the King and His Kingdom determines the quality and quantity of the benefits available to its citizens. *"Bless the Lord, O my soul' And all that is within me, bless His holy name! Bless the Lord, O my soul, And forget not all His benefits: Who forgives all your iniquities, Who heals all your diseases, Who redeems your life from destruction, Who crowns you with lovingkindness and tender mercies, Who satisfies your mouth with good things, So that your youth is renewed like the eagle's"* (Psa. 103:1-5).

If I stopped with this short description of the benefits available to citizens of the Kingdom of Heaven, it would constitute greater benefits than any earthly kingdom could ever supply. What earthly king can forgive your sins or heal all your diseases? Only the King of the Kingdom of Heaven daily loads the citizens of His kingdom with benefits (Psa. 68:19), gives them richly all things to enjoy (1 Tim. 6:17), and it is His good pleasure to give them the kingdom. *"But seek first the kingdom of God and His righteousness, and all these things shall be added to you"* (Matt. 6:33). *"Do not fear, little flock, for it is you Father's good pleasure to give you the kingdom"* (Luke 12:32).

As God shakes the heaven and the earth, He protects those that are His. Saints who are His live lifestyles of faith, according to the Father's divine pattern; they pattern their lives after the life of Jesus. They believe, honor, respect and emulate their spiritual parent(s); and, they do the work of advancing the Kingdom of God in the earth. These are the front-liners and forerunners, spiritually mature believers who trust God and rely on His grace and goodness through their faith in His faithfulness to His Word. *"God is not a man, that he should lie; neither the son of man, that he should repent; hath he said and shall he not do it? Or hath he spoken, and shall he not make it good"* (Num. 23:19, KJV). Over the course of almost 25 years as an ordained minister, I have found that many people who call themselves Christians do not believe the Word of God sincerely. Their words and actions, through unbelief, rob them of the benefits of the grace available to them as believers. Saints really do need to grow in grace and in the knowledge of our Lord and Savior Jesus Christ (2 Pet. 3:18).

The shaking of heaven and earth is for the benefit of Kingdom citizens! We should be celebrating – dancing before the Lord in thanksgiving of what He is doing for the advancement of our lives and kingdom assignments. Instead, there are many believers who are steeped in unbelief and fear associated with this great end-times shaking. Much of this fear is due to the fact that these saints "refuse to hear him who speaks." Not hearing the Word of God leads to having no faith in the Word of God because faith comes or increases by hearing the word of God (Rom. 10:17), *"For therein is the righteousness of God revealed from faith to faith; as it is written, THE JUST SHALL LIVE BY FAITH"* (Rom. 1:17, author's emphasis).

The refusal to hear and trust God's Word completely leads to a place and position of no escape. If saints trust in their money and the things that they possess, prioritizing them over their faith in God, they will not escape God's shaking of those things that can be shaken. Having acquired them according to the demonic systems of the world – out of the will of God – they are shaky. Remember, created things will be shaken and removed so that the heavenly things, built in the will of God by trusting His Word, will remain.

I believe that through this shaking, heaven's patterns are falling upon the shoulders of those spiritually mature, commissioned, kingdom-level servant leaders – commanders, front-liners and forerunners – who have walked faithfully in their kingdom assignments, preparing and equipping the saints for their kingdom assignments within the Body of Christ. These are faithful and wise stewards who know how to manage the King's resources, and who will feed the flock of the Great Shepherd, providing them with their portion of meat (spiritual equipping) at the proper time (see Luke 12:42).

The new 21st Century apostolic model is being shaken from heaven to commissioned, kingdom-level leaders so that the Church can embrace it and not be shaky. I believe that this current shaking is unleashing an even greater anointing and positioning of the Church than the 1st Century Church experience. They trusted God to deliver and protect them from the evils and tyranny of their day. They prayed, power flowed, and finances flooded the Church. Their faith-filled words were honored by God and the Holy Spirit poured out His gifts upon them which were manifested in mighty demonstrations – signs, wonders, and miracles.

In like manner, this shaking is ushering in a flood of prosperity and resources that will be the foundation for the success of the new assignments, new territories, new realms and greater levels of breakthrough God is releasing onto the Body of Christ. If we stand on the Word of God and trust Him completely, we shall see His glory manifested in every area of our lives. God has instructed and dispatched angels of breakthrough, angels of financial provision, angels of wisdom, angels of protection, and angels of grace because we are positioned as the righteousness of God through faith in Jesus, who has given us the victory. *"But thanks be to God, who gives us the victory through our Lord Jesus Christ. Therefore, my beloved brethren, be steadfast, immovable, always abounding in the work of the Lord, knowing that your labor is not in vain in the Lord"* (1 Cor. 15:57-58).

Let's embrace the new 21ˢᵗ Century apostolic anointing with outstretched hands in thanksgiving. As God shakes heaven upon earth, rewards will manifest according to what we have done in service to God as servant leaders. As we submit our emotions and actions to the Lord and walk by faith, not in unbelief and fear, the shaking that's taking place not only protects us but also showers us with supernatural manifestations that will further us in Him to fulfill our kingdom assignment.

Let's celebrate, then, and dance as heaven dances upon the earth. We are about to receive a kingdom that cannot be shaken. We should be grateful as we reverence and worship The King in a new and exciting way that pleases Him. *"Let us therefore, receiving a kingdom that is firm and stable and cannot be shaken, offer to God pleasing service and acceptable worship, with modesty and pious care and godly fear and awe"* (Heb. 12:28, AMP).

CHAPTER FOURTEEN

EMPOWERING SAINTS FOR KINGDOM CONVERSION

"The kings of the earth stood up, and the rulers were gathered together against the LORD, and against his Christit..."The kingdoms of this world are become the kingdoms of our LORD and of his Christ; and he shall reign forever and ever."
(ACTS 4:26; REV. 11:15, KJV)

My elevation into the apostleship, through spiritual fathering and mentoring, was an internal transformation that brought forth the reformation, the calibration and adjustment required to bring me into alignment with the current standard of the Kingdom. Likewise, the Body of Christ is being transformed from within – internally but eternally. A powerful conversion is taking place among the saints as God releases the new 21st Century, apostolic/prophetic order to the Church, powered by the Holy Spirit. God is confirming and strengthening the saints as the Church positions itself for "the great end-time harvest." To this end, God is in the process of uprooting the dominant religious spirits that the devil has used to infiltrate the Body of Christ and keep it in a continuous pattern of divisiveness, i.e. religion, deception, self-righteousness, self-centeredness, rebellion, dishonesty, jealousy, apathy, slothfulness, disunity, pride, racism and strife.

Satan has sought to destroy the Church by using *"rulers of the darkness of this world"* and *"spiritual wickedness in high places"* (Eph. 6:12, KJV). He wants the church to be immature and impotent, but really that is a vain thing. The Church has its victorious inheritance through God's anointed One, Jesus Christ. *"Why do the nations rage, And the people plot a vain thing? The kings of the earth set themselves, And the rulers take counsel together, Against the LORD and against His Anointed, saying, 'Let us break Their bonds in pieces And cast away Their cords from us...The Lord shall hold them in derision...And distress them in His deep displeasure'"* (Psa. 2:1-5).

All of the devil's work against the Lord and His Christ, which includes the Body of Christ, is a vain thing. I'm convinced that Satan has a very short memory. Apostle John both saw and wrote the revelation of Jesus Christ which emphasizes that the kingdoms of this world will become the kingdoms of our Lord and of His Christ. Also, prior to Jesus' public ministry, Holy Spirit led Him into the wilderness to be tempted by the devil for 40 days. One of the temptations used by Satan had to do with the kingdoms of this world, which he said he would give to Jesus if Jesus would worship him. *"Jesus refused, again backing his refusal with Deuteronomy: "Worship the Lord your God and only the Lord your God. Serve him with absolute single-heartedness"* (Luke 4:8, MSG).

The victory of the Church has already been prophesied in the revelation of Jesus Christ to Apostle John. The Church is now experiencing God's reordering – restoration and reformation – of His original interdependent Church *"on earth, as it is in heaven."* "Make no mistake! The Apostolic/Prophetic Kingdom Church order and lifestyle will reestablish the Father's ultimate intention to possess, on earth, a Holy Church and redeemed world finally and totally prepared for His return. The Kingdom Church will bear no resemblance to the present illustrations of the earth-bound Church!

"It will carry no identification signs of compromise with anything or anyone that bears the evidence of "man-made" and /or man-centered! Oh No! It will look like, act like, and talk like Christ, Who lives in each one, and is therefore, the image of the whole Body! Their vocation will be "…the simplicity and devotion to Jesus," and together, bringing in the astounding end-time harvest. Their avocation will be anything related to their own personal needs." (Paul Bersche, *"The Return of the Kingdom Church,"* July 26, 2014, Kingdom Congressional International Alliance [KCIA] Newsletter).

The kingdom conversion process that God is using to restore His one original Church in the earth is one of progression. Conversion is a type of progression because it is revolutionary. The Greek word translated **conversion** is *epistrophe (ep-is-trof-ay)* taken from *epistrepho (ep-ee-stref-o)* which means to revert: come (go) again, convert, return, turn about again; reversion, i.e. revolution (Strong's). This is a season of conversion by revolution. **Revolution** is the fundamental change in the way of thinking about or visualizing something: a change of paradigm (Merriam-Webster). Kingdom conversion is revolutionary. This is a revolutionary new season for the Church, a reversion, a turning about again, returning to the original plan for the Church as God has seen it in His eternal mind. *"So being sent on their way by the church, they passed through Phoenicia and Samaria, **describing the conversion of the Gentiles;** and they caused great joy to all the brethren"* (Acts 15:3, author's emphasis).

The kingdom conversion process is a gradual advancement to raise the saints to a state of evolutionary change patterned after the Kingdom of Heaven. Our strategies for advancing this Kingdom in the earth must be a progressive technology of improvement beyond the last season of restoration of the five-fold ministry offices to the Church. Since the Body of Christ has received the ministry of reconciliation, we must *"make full proof"* of this ministry. *"Now then, we are ambassadors for Christ, as though God were pleading through us: we implore you on Christ's behalf, be reconciled to God"* (2 Cor. 5:20).

True Kingdom ambassadors must hunger for the heart of God and pursue God's heart. True Kingdom leaders must endure seasons of preparation. The Church must commit to Jesus' servant leader model. This is how we become empowered for kingdom conversion – back to the future, the original mind of

God as it relates to the Body of Christ. Knowledge is power; sharing knowledge is empowerment. "People who choose to mature, mature." Commissioned, kingdom-level leaders must follow Apostle Paul's example and train the saints, especially the youth of our generation, to become ambassadors for Christ.

Paul spent quality time, going from church to church in many regions, confirming and strengthening the souls of the disciples. *"And when they had preached the gospel to that city, and had taught many, they returned again to Lystra, and Iconium, and Antioch,* **confirming the souls of the disciples,** *and exhorting them to* **continue in the faith,** *and that* **we through much tribulation** *enter into the kingdom of God"* (Acts 14:21-22, KJV, author's emphasis). *"After he had spent some time there, he departed and went over the region of Galatia and Phrygia in order,* **strengthening all the disciples"** (Acts 18:23, author's emphasis).

The Kingdom Church Age order is that the saints are disciples who disciple. Apostles and prophets are the servant-leader foundations of the Church who train the saints for kingdom conversion. They train the trainers who, in turn, train other trainers, thereby creating a generational succession of well-trained, kingdom-level leaders, commissioned to fight for the conversion of earthly kingdoms to the kingdoms of our Lord and of His Christ, as God ordained in His eternal mind.

As commissioned servant leaders, apostles and prophets must "transfer" their anointing to those that they father, mentor and train to be commissioned, kingdom-level leaders. The only effective and transferable anointing is a tangible anointing – a mantle – that is seen on the recipient through their character and behavior. "The only anointing that is a lasting anointing is the anointing that activates the mind." The Hebrew word translated **mantle** is **addereth (ad-deh-reth),** meaning something ample (as a large vine); a garment, glory or robe (Strong's). In the Bible, mantles are symbolic of one's ministry or office. It is the symbol of a person's anointing that can be transferred through mantles bestowed on others. *"He also took up the mantle of Elijah that had fallen from him, and went back and stood by the bank off the Jordan. Then he took the mantle of Elijah that had fallen from him, and struck the water, and said, 'Where is the Lord God of Elijah?'"* (2 Kings 2:13-14).

242

Mantles are sources of power and are a representation of the power God entrusts spiritual fathers and mothers to operate with. The mantle that is transferred is infused with the divine pattern of a kingdom assignment that God has ordained to be accomplished through whoever the mantle is passed on to. However, of a surety, the transfer of the mantle carries with it the transfer of the relationship the mentor or spiritual parent has with God, for it is God who is the source of power behind the mantle. This is the kind of apostolic and prophetic anointing that affects and influences people, leading them to behavior modification and actions that transform them and change the way they think and what they believe.

A lasting anointing will move you to the place of conversion. True conversion doesn't take place within your spirit until there is a total surrender of self to God – His Word, His Will, His Way. You must be truly committed to being taught and trained in the government of God's Kingdom. This is how you will acquire strength and confirmation as a true disciple. Jesus made it clear to Peter that he had some more growing to do. Jesus wanted Peter to come up to His standard of spiritual maturity through a conscious act of total surrender, where he would be strengthened in his faith and confirmed as the apostle to the Jews. *"Simon, Simon! Indeed, Satan has asked for you, that he may sift you as wheat. 'But I have prayed for you, that your faith should not fail; and when you have returned to Me, strengthen your brethren'"* (Luke 22:31-32). The King James Version says, *"and when thou art converted, strengthen thy brethren."*

Apostolic and prophetic leaders must be converted and strengthened before they can convert and strengthen the saints. Conversion is basically the result of exchanging one thing for another. In this case, the saints are exchanging their outdated religiosity, self-righteous and divisive ways for an anointing that is tangible and lasts for kingdom conversion. The saints are learning how to wear the "mantle of misrah," a phrase coined by my spiritual father, Dr. Gordon E. Bradshaw. It means strength to prevail. This mantle or apostolic and prophetic anointing is the prevailing grace and governmental authority of Jesus Christ to change atmospheres and environments, and transform mindsets from unbelief and religion to faith in the kingdom of God's government. This is the "lasting anointing" that, when operated in faith by a commissioned kingdom-level leader, will operate by the power of Holy Spirit in ministry, the marketplace, and municipalities to transform lives and position the Church to reclaim the Seven Mountains of Society for the Kingdom of God.

The commanders, apostles and prophets, will lead the way for the conversion of earthly kingdoms to become the kingdoms of our Lord and of His Christ, as the saints – the army of God – usher in the end-time harvest. Saints who wear the mantle of misrah — for this Kingdom Age anointing is not only for the commanders, it is a believer's anointing, as Dr. Bill Hamon has written about in *The Day of the Saints* — have received a lasting anointing that will empower other saints for kingdom conversion; and these will empower others and so on. It is imperative that you, a believer through faith in Jesus Christ, embrace this current order and Kingdom standard, *"For the devil has come down to you, having great wrath, because he knows that he has a short time"* (Rev. 12:12).

This is the Kingdom Age season of the Church's reformation. It is a revolutionary season of apostolic and prophetic power. It is a season of acceleration that will unfold from the wisdom of God, strategies for victorious spiritual warfare along with the many new technologies that God is releasing in record time. These Kingdom technologies are necessary in order for the saints to keep pace with the current move of God. As the saints begin to add to each other through their specific gifts and anointing, an impenetrable force is being formed – an invincible, end-time army.

When God sees our unity and support for each other, a revolutionary standard, He will send His power of revolution to confirm our discipleship. This Kingdom Age revolution is going to change how unbelievers and world systems see the Church, as it begins to influence the activities of governments, corporations and organizations. The Church is taking a quantum leap into her end-time assignment. Remember, Jesus was a revolutionary.

This third great awakening – Kingdom Age Awakening – of the Church is being spearheaded by a remnant of kingdom-level leaders, whom God has prepared and commissioned to be the standard of maturity representative of the Body of Christ. This faithful, Holy Spirit-dependent, five-fold ministry company have successfully completed God's process for development which has led to *"equipping the saints for the work of ministry, for the edifying of the body of Christ, till we all come to the unity of the faith and of the knowledge of the Son of God, to a perfect man, to the measure of the stature of the fullness of Christ"* (Eph. 4:12-13).

The substance of this Kingdom Age Awakening of the Church is the new 21st Century apostolic model, accompanied by a misrah governmental mantle to do exploits that will eradicate the divisions within the community of God's people so that we are calibrated, adjusted and brought into alignment with God's kingdom purposes, as one perfect man. This new apostolic model is an interdependent reality in which the Church is being mobilized and deployed as the army of God, having all things common as one perfect man, the Body of Christ.

Paul didn't say, "till we all come to perfect men." No. He said, *"till we all come to…a perfect man, to the measure of the stature of the fullness of Christ."* The Church, Christ's body, must imitate the Head. The Church must overcome its divisions through surrender to God's process of character development, which is modeled after our holy, righteous, Royal High Priest, Jesus Christ.

In the old order, the religious order, the Church was not willing to surrender all to Christ and obey Jesus, its Head. The Body was not willing to suffer for the sake of Christ and the gospel of the Kingdom. But now, during this current reformation of the Church, the saints are coming into the knowledge that we are as anointed as we can stand the pain of surrender, tribulation and suffering – components of the kingdom standard that leads to spiritual maturity. We are coming into the knowledge that our degree of pain, suffering and tribulation is relative to our individual purpose and kingdom assignment. But, as we surrender to the Will of God, we are poised to become one perfect man. *"Let each one remain in the same calling in which he was called"* (1 Cor. 7:20). *"For as the body is one and has many members, but all the members of that one body, being many are one body, so also is Christ…"For in fact the body is not one member but many"* (1 Cor. 12:12, 14).

The Church is being reformed, changed for the better, from the inside-out to become the true demonstration of the reality of the Kingdom of God for which the world longs for. In order to transform the Seven Mountains of Culture, controlled by the demonic world systems, we must not remain shortsighted. Instead, we must wholly follow the lead and move of Holy Spirit as He downloads into our spirit supernatural strategies from God how to rightly discern and pull down demonic strongholds. We will engage them through progressive prayer and intercession, interacting and working together with other saints within the community of the Body. *"For the weapons of our warfare are not carnal but mighty in God for pulling down strongholds, casting down arguments and every high thing that exalts itself against the knowledge of God, bringing every thought into captivity to the obedience of Christ"* (2 Cor. 10:4-5).

Morris Ruddick, founder of Global Initiatives Foundation says, "The goal is the progressive consciousness of God's presence that guides the community as a whole, and becomes the pathway through which the community is built and serves as a light on a hill. It is when the infectious reality of God's presence results in the unified community itself becoming spiritually contagious, that the attention of the surrounding community is attracted, being drawn into its sphere. Even in operation, it overwhelmingly challenges the gatekeepers of darkness." (Strategic Intercession Global Network, "UNLOCKED", August 12, 2014)

God's heart is for His people. There have been many church leaders who, over the years, have not had God's heart and His compassion for people. Some of these leaders began their ministry with a true heart for the people but lost their focus as they climbed to new heights of fame and fortune. They lost focus of their stewardship as managers who were faithful to carry out God's mandates on behalf of His people. They became obsessed with power, personal gain and influence instead of raising spiritual sons and daughters, training them to become commissioned, kingdom-level leaders.

Nevertheless, God has raised a remnant of commissioned, kingdom-level leaders all over the world who have His heart for people, and have accepted their kingdom assignment to take up positions of servant leadership in cities, regions and nations, mobilizing people that they train and equip for kingdom transformation, reformation and assignment. These are the kingdom leaders who have asked the Father to empower them with an anointing to solve people's problems. Servant leaders are problem-solvers; they become the solution.

These kinds of leaders know that they have been called, ordained, and sent forth to reveal the government of the King of God to the world. **God has required an extended time of intense preparation for this kind of servant leader.** It was not an overnight process. This level of leadership preparation comes with tests of love, faith, obedience, surrender, suffering for the sake of Christ, personal sacrifice, integrity, moral character and tests of stewardship (not an exhaustive list) tried in the fire of Holy Spirit purification to ensure that the earthen vessel is qualified to be an anointed cistern that others can connect to and draw from.

These servant-leader saints are distributors who are dedicated to using their unique gifts and anointing to serve the purposes of God. They make decisions inspired by Holy Spirit because they stay in the presence of God. God trusts them to represent His purposes. They are reformers because they take faith risks. Faith risk-takers become faithful success-makers. These reformers do what is unpopular, uncomfortable, and what seems foolish to everyone else. They see the end from the beginning – the completed version of something old being transformed into something new. These are the servant leaders who know their God. *"...but the people who know their God shall be strong, and carry out great exploits"* (Dan. 11:32).

In the current reformation of the Church, the third great awakening – the Kingdom Age Awakening – strategic-minded saints are being birthed who hear Holy Spirit and will allow Him to lead and guide them into their destinies. No longer focused on the immediate, short-term thinking that produced the stagnant religious church that went to sleep, the interdependent Church of the 21st Century is focused on developing long-term strategic plans for immediate action and deployment within the spheres of culture. The commissioned, kingdom-level leaders of this age of the Church's awakening, have become the catalysts for change, releasing to the people God's strategies for mobilizing and activating them as change agents, ready and anointed to transform atmospheres, environments, mindsets and cultures within the Seven Mountain Society. As one commissioned, kingdom-level leader/author has recently and poignantly stated:

"The Body of Christ knows more about the cultural spheres of influence than ever before, giving believers the opportunity to occupy key strategic and tactical positions in the economic, social, political, educational, business, governmental, and scientific power grids on planet Earth. We are more than 'observers' and we have an actual hand in the development of templates and transitional models that have a lasting effect on earth. Now we have possession of our 'Thrones' and the righteous influences that God has been waiting to release to usher in a new Earth!

"If the question is asked, 'What does God want to do next?' We reply with this: He wants us to know where He is NOW and where He will be NEXT. Today we have a stronger sense of His presence and we're more able to sense where He will be in the future because we are conscious of His presence. We follow Him onward to new places of influence in the Seven Mountains and the entire 'Mountain Range.' We are truly co-laborers in restoring the planet He so deeply loves. God wants us to be able to apply all that we've learned and all that we've become to usher in His complete and fulfilled purposes for planet Earth. Being sensitive to His presence and position is a key experience in knowing how to navigate the future.

"We've been tempered, tried and tested in the furnace of affliction and emerged with a new level of trust in God and with a new level of trust 'from' God. We are trusted to guard, steward and advance a greater measure of resources from God and from the Earth. We have a greater sensitivity to what is important to God and we'll stand watch as 'Sentinels' over the **interests of God** in the Seven Mountains." (Dr. Gordon E. Bradshaw, "2016 – The Year of the Sentinels!" GEMS Newsletter)

This is a dangerous time to be spiritually lazy! One of the end-time schemes of Satan has been to keep the saints of God busy doing good things, but not the God-thing. He wants to keep us busy doing what seems right to man, but not learning or obeying the voice of the Father in order to fulfill our kingdom assignments. This is called religion. As stated many times throughout this book, the fulfilling of a divine assignment requires spiritual maturity, commitment, loyalty and faithful devotion to God, which will always lead to advancement of His kingdom in the earth. And, advancing the kingdom begins with advancing people.

Apostle Paul says, *"Take the teachings that you heard me proclaim in the presence of many witnesses, and entrust them to reliable people, who will be able to teach others also. Take your part in suffering, as a loyal soldier of Christ Jesus. A soldier on active duty wants to please his commanding officer and so does not get mixed up in the affairs of civilian life… Think about what I am saying, because the Lord will enable you to understand it all"* (2 Tim. 2:2-4, 7; GNB).

In this season of God's great preparation of the Body of Christ for the endtime harvest of souls, the Church cannot afford to simply be saints – slumbering and sleeping with vessels that contain no oil. You see, the five foolish virgins were just as much saints as were the five wise virgins. What was the difference? **Spiritual maturity!** They had been processed and prepared by God with a readiness to will and to do God's good pleasure. The five foolish virgins had enough oil to *live in the kingdom,* but not enough to operate within next level assignments which require mantles of spiritual maturity for the *advancement of the kingdom.*

This is where the Church finds herself today. God is ushering the saints into next level advancement and new realms and assignments for supernatural manifestation and exponential increase and multiplication of resources for the fulfillment of our kingdom assignments. God knows that the saints must be fully committed and possess an abundance of His Word (Oil) for distribution to the unprepared world-oriented multitudes – unbelievers and faithless believers.

God is releasing supernatural manifestations through the saints – demonstrations of the Spirit and of power, convincing proof of the power of God's Spirit. *"And my speech and my preaching were not with persuasive words of human wisdom, but in demonstration of the Spirit and of power"* (1 Cor. 2:4); *"For the kingdom of God is not in word but in power"* (4:20). If you are a mature saint who is a servant leader, this reformation of the Church signifies the beginning of your times of fulfillment. All of your preparation to become commissioned, kingdom-level leaders has been leading you to and positioning you for such a time as this.

You are no longer a foot-soldier, getting beat up by the demonic technologies of the systems of the world. You are a horseman, who will ride with Jesus as a commander in the armies of heaven clothed in clean, white, fine linen. *"Now I saw heaven opened, and behold, a white horse. And He who sat on him was called Faithful and True, and in righteousness He judges and makes war…And the armies in heaven, clothed in fine linen, white and clean, followed Him on white horses"* (Rev. 19:11, 14).

You have been pruned, shaped and molded, shifted and sifted over the years. And it has all been leading you to this God-season – this kairos time where things that God has ordained should and must be done. At the same time, God is requiring a deeper love, faith, humility and Word-walk from you. The invitation of God's heart to you is for a deeper level of seeking Him; a deeper level of consecration; a deeper level of abiding in His presence; and, a deeper level of yielding, worship and praise. This is to keep you pure. You've entered a season of radical shifts, sudden transformation and instant alignment with the heart of God's plans and purposes.

God is shifting things in the earth that are easily shaken into their proper place, time, and rank so the saints can look and discover first things, excellent things which are the original things from the eternal mind of God manifested in the earth. **The eternal mind of God set in Heaven is meeting its appointed time in the earth.** *"THY WILL BE DONE, AS IN HEAVEN, SO IN EARTH"* (Luke 11:2, KJV, author's emphasis).

God's consuming fire is being released upon the saints, purifying and releasing us suddenly into this new season of awakening, where we're being reformed and refreshed through supernatural manifestations. What held us back in past seasons is being burnt away and Father is manifesting Himself as an all-consuming fire, initiating a deep level of refinement that will prepare and release the Body of Christ into this Kingdom Age glory. We will advance the Kingdom of God in the earth beyond what we've ever imagined. We will experience furtherance in the five-fold ministry ascension gifts of the Lord Jesus, and we will soar to heights and dimensions above what we've dreamed.

This is a fullness of time season – a season of no restraints to God to do what He has already ordained from before the foundation of the world. The saints must embrace the fact that God is with us. We cannot fail! Our faith in Jesus' finished work at Calvary has sealed our victory. *"It may be that the Lord will work for us.* **For nothing restrains the Lord** *from saving by many or by few"* (1 Sam. 14:6b, author's emphasis). God said that His plans would never fail, that He would do all He has intended to do from eternity, *"DECLARING THE END FROM THE BEGINNING, AND FROM ANCIENT TIMES THE THINGS THAT ARE NOT YET DONE, SAYING, MY COUNSEL SHALL STAND, AND I WILL DO ALL MY PLEASURE"* (Isa. 46:10, KJV, author's emphasis).

The glory of the Latter Rain, the outpouring of Holy Spirit is here! God is speaking to the commanders, the apostles and prophets, His servant leaders and revealing to them His secrets. *"Surely the Lord God does nothing, Unless He reveals His secret to His servants the prophets"* (Amos 3:7). This is a *KAIROS time and season – special times that God marks because He is releasing mantles, graces and the anointing for breakthroughs.* "To every thing there is a season, and a time to every purpose under the heaven" (Eccl. 3:1). In revelation knowledge terms: God has placed us on the earth and given us a divine assignment. Once we discover it, He gives us time (chronos) and we allow God to process us and develop us according to His Word for the seasons (kairos) – the opportune time to reap the harvests of heaven. GOD IS SPEAKING!

In His presence is where the saints will hear Him clearly and succinctly in supernatural high definition through Holy Spirit – the Satellite stream from the Kingdom of God beaming down to the Body of Christ everything about the kingdom, 24/7. My slogan for this is, **"All Kingdom – All the time."** As we stay tuned to kingdom activities at all times, there will never be a time where we will miss what God is releasing to Christ's body. We will receive Holy Spirit rhema and revelations of truth. This is the place of refreshing (spiritual energy and strength) and hearing God's voice. This is the time of refreshing that comes only from the presence of the Lord. God is empowering the Church for kingdom conversion. *"Repent therefore and be converted, that your sins may be blotted* *out, so that times of refreshing may come from the presence of the Lord"* (Acts 3:19).

This is the Church God has been waiting on. We are it! God is making this crystal clear to the Body of Christ. We cannot entertain a similar question asked of Jesus by John the Baptist, who found himself in a moment of doubt after his imprisonment. John sent a couple of his disciples to inquire as to whether or not Jesus was the One everybody was expectantly waiting for. John's circumstances had changed and he was having doubts as to whether or not Jesus was indeed the Messiah, even though he'd received a revelation from Holy Sprit that Jesus was indeed *"The Lamb of God who takes away the sin of the world!"* (John 1:29). That was in one season. In another season John had a question for Jesus, *"Are You the Coming One, or do we look for another?"* Jesus' response was based on the fact that He was conducting the business of the kingdom in demonstration by the power of Holy Spirit. The words and acts of Jesus were the evidence that Jesus was the Messiah and the kingdom had indeed come.

In a similar way, God has not made a mistake about the Church He has chosen. Therefore, He is not pacing His throne room in the third Heaven wondering whether or not He made the right choice to empower the 21st Century Church to convert the kingdoms of this world to the Kingdom of God. He is not looking for another. We are it. Remember, God said His counsel would stand and He would do all of His pleasure.

Like John the Baptist, many saints have had doubts as to their callings, assignments and destinies. But, God no longer wants you to doubt who you are in Him. You are a member of the victorious Body of Christ, and you need not look for another to replace you. You are it! You are the one God has been waiting for. You are a commissioned, kingdom-level servant leader with the delegated authority of God to represent His kingdom in the earth as a king and a priest. You are the reformer who God has awakened to transform the kingdoms of this world. You are a servant leader within the Body of Christ who God has found faithful and has designated you as an influencer of righteousness. You have accepted God's assignment for your life and He has given you the keys of David to unlock the power of the kingdom and lock up the powers of darkness. God has made available to you the mantle of misrah – the prevailing grace and governmental authority of Jesus to transform and reform people, places and things. You are the reformer who God has awakened to fulfill your kingdom assignment in accordance to Rev. 11:15.

Yes, Church, We are the one. We need not look for another because there is no other. God does not have an alternate plan. His counsel will stand. We are the Church God has patiently waited for. And I say to you, kingdom-level leaders, ARISE! Ready yourselves for the end-time revival that will reap the greatest harvest of souls the world has ever seen. We are about to be married! We are the bride of Christ. *"O my love, you are as beautiful as Tirzah, Lovely as Jerusalem, Awesome as an army with banners! "Who is she who looks forth as the morning, Fair as the moon, Clear as the sun, Awesome as an army with banners?"* (Song of Solomon 6:4, 10).

CHAPTER FIFTEEN

KINGDOM ENFORCERS: POSSESSING THE MENTALITY OF VICTORY

*"I was watching in the night visions, And behold, One like the Son of Man,
Coming with the clouds of heaven! He came to the Ancient of Days,
And they brought Him near before Him. Then to Him was given dominion and
glory and a kingdom, That all peoples, nations, and languages should serve Him.
His dominion is an everlasting dominion, Which shall not pass away. And His
kingdom the one Which shall not be destroyed...**But the saints of the Most High
shall receive the kingdom,** and possess the kingdom forever,
even* forever *and ever."* (DAN. 7:13-14, 18, AUTHOR'S EMPHASIS)

"But thanks be to God, who gives us the victory through our Lord Jesus Christ."
(1 COR. 15:57)

Led by His commanders, the apostles and prophets, God has raised an end-time army of kingdom enforcers. I'm sure that some of you who are reading this book may have questioned my focus on the apostles and prophets and the fact I have not discussed the role of the evangelist, pastor and teacher. Why is there so much focus on the apostles and prophets in this Kingdom Age Awakening of the Church? First of all, the apostles and prophets are the foundation of the New Testament Church of grace and truth (Eph. 2:20). Secondly, apostles and prophets are spearheads who lead the charge outwardly – outside the gate; outside the comfort of the four-walled church or the old order that saints have become accustomed to. Apostles and prophets are not relegated or restricted to the religious mountain; they are successfully infiltrating the other six, releasing the order and government of the Kingdom of God. Evangelists, pastors and teachers are the inner sanctity of the Body, whose focus is salvation and deliverance, nurturing the lambs, teaching them how to become sheep that hear and obey the voice of the Shepherd.

The end-time revival is so powerful that it moves beyond church sanctuaries. This revival will burn in the marketplace and other major venues within the cultures of society which happen to be outside of the four-walled church. Jesus is our example. *"Therefore Jesus also, that He might sanctify the people with His own blood, suffered outside the gate. Therefore let us go forth to Him, outside the camp, bearing His reproach. For here we have no continuing city, but we seek the one to come"* (Heb. 13:12-14). Jesus died outside the gate, an open reproach, excluded from social and religious acceptance. **Apostles and prophets are the commanders who have been commissioned to lead the charge outside of the religious mountain.** They are anointed with the mantle of misrah to renounce the demonic world system's approval and accept the reproach of Jesus. Why? We are looking for that continuing or eternal city established by God. Like Abraham, the father of our faith, we are waiting for the city which has foundations, whose builder and maker is God (Heb. 11:10).

By taking His stand outside the gate, Jesus became a first of firsts. Jesus was the first kingdom enforcer. As I mentioned in one of the previous chapters, Jesus was a revolutionary, who enforced the kingdom, *"Who for the joy that was set before Him endured the cross, despising the shame, and has sat down at the right hand of the throne of God"* (Heb. 12:2). The word **"enforce"** means to give force to: STRENGTHEN; to urge with energy; CONSTRAIN, COMPEL; to effect or gain by force; to carry out effectively (Merriam-Webster). Therefore, an **enforcer** is one who enforces or strengthens with energy that which he is providing the force to; to effectively carry out a mission that will constrain and compel by the use of force, in this case, the Kingdom of God. Jesus was the first to enforce the Kingdom of God in the earth. That is why He was a first of firsts. Apostles and prophets are the commanders who are leading the charge as enforcers to advance the Kingdom of God in the earth. As saints, you, too, are a kingdom enforcer in whatever realm your kingdom assignment happens to be in.

Apostle Paul gives us a good illustration of why apostles are spearheads, the enforcers who lead the charge outside the gate to strengthen the kingdom by constraint, compelling the demonic systems of the world to be transformed and reformed. It is a dirty job, but true apostles are anointed to carry it out successfully. They are the "hit men" of the Kingdom of God and they bear the reproach of society and the religious order. *"For I think that God has displayed us, the apostles, last, as men condemned to death; for we have been made a spectacle to the world, both to angels and to men. We are fools for Christ's sake, but you are wise in Christ! We are weak, but you are strong! You are distinguished, but we are dishonored! To the present hour we both hunger and thirst and we are poorly clothed, and beaten, and homeless. And we labor, working with our own hands. Being reviled, we bless; being persecuted, we endure; being defamed, we entreat. We have been made as the filth of the world, the off-scouring of all things until now"* (1 Cor. 4:9-13).

As an apostle, I certainly can relate to what Paul is saying. After nearly 25 years as an ordained minister, the majority of them as a full-time vocational minister living by faith, and five of them as a commissioned apostle, I stand witness that religion really despises the apostolic. As long as I was a part of the circle of cycles that religion is, I was tolerated. I was never celebrated because my ministry was very much apostolic. But, once I was commissioned as an apostle, even the pastors of churches that I'd established fellowship with, one by one, began to shut me out. Some tried to get me to "tone it down" and maybe I would be more readily accepted. Most of these pastors would grimace the entire time I was ministering to their congregation, especially if the theme was on living by faith or grace. Several times, I've had pastors and their congregations leave right in the middle of my message because, as I would learn, I was allegedly "preaching a loose gospel, giving the people a license to sin."

I had a decision to make. I could present a false humility and conform to their religious circle of pretending to honor God with their lips but their heart was far from it or I could leave the religious circle and trust God to elevate me into the realm of fellowship with true kingdom saints who would celebrate my kingdom status. Of course, I chose the latter. Jesus, the first apostle of apostles (Heb. 3:1) said, *"These people draw near to Me with their mouth, And honor Me with their lips, But their heart is far from Me. And in vain they worship Me, Teaching as doctrines the commandments of men"* (Matt. 15:8-9). 2 Tim. 3:5 says that in the last days people will be *"having a form of godliness but denying its power."* Paul says, *"Have nothing to do with such people."*

I tend to agree with Apostle Paul in that true apostles are *"fools for Christ's sake."* True apostles and apostolic leaders are dishonored by society and religion. I can relate to both. I know what it feels like to be poorly clothed, beaten down and homeless; I've been persecuted too many times to count and I've endured many services where I was belittled or looked upon as if I were nothing; being reviled, I blessed not by might nor by power, but by Holy Spirit because I chose to love and respect others in spite of how I was perceived or treated by them. Everybody is not going to like you, especially those whom you surpass as you begin to ascend into your kingdom assignment. *"But the Lord is with me as a mighty, awesome One. Therefore my persecutors will stumble, and will not prevail. They will be greatly ashamed, for they will not prosper. Their everlasting confusion will never be forgotten"* (Jer. 20:11).

This season of apostolic reformation is exposing people who are hungry for the presence of God. They want to experience His glory in greater dimensions. They are not bound by religion and legalism. They have a hunger for the Kingdom and the authority delegated to them as kings and priests unto God. These are the ones that will be used by God as commanders to lead His end-time army in the earth. These kingdom enforcers will be comprised of the many instead of the few, as was the form of the old church model, *"for there is no restraint to the Lord to save by many or by few"* (1 Sam. 14:6b, KJV). Many of the past moves of God have been led by the "few." But, in this kingdom awakening of the Church, God is using the many – no name, no fame, only credible and loyal servant leaders who genuinely express the heart of God.

No doubt, the New Testament Church has been extremely resilient. It has survived the centuries of the great persecutions; it survived the bureaucracy of the Middle Ages; and, it has survived the cultural movement of the Renaissance – all of this over centuries. Still, at the onset of the 21st Century, the Church was found slumbering, sleeping, and wagging its tail in anticipation of receiving God's best when it had not actually kept its half of the covenant. The Church still possessed a spirit of entitlement; and, like spoiled kids, too many believers were crying out to God, pitching fits and performing other shenanigans to get God to pay attention to them and give them what they wanted and desired, even if their lusts were out of His will and their motives completely carnal. The Church still had not refocused on its mandate to go into all the world and teach the gospel of the kingdom, making disciples of men, women and nations. The reason being is this is a kingdom mandate requiring servant leaders and not a statement of hope based upon religion and a selfish agenda.

There was not a sustained labor force of believers working in the harvest field of the world reaping souls. Many in the Body were working their own fields, focusing their affections on the external nature of man rather than the internal nature of Christ. But, God's counsel, His plans and purposes, shall stand. The 21st Century Church is the Body of Christ to be known as the end-time army of God. That's why **the Church will remember 2016 as the pivotal, acceptable year of the Lord's favor, the year of Jubilee,** the year of the "Shanah Shift," Rosh Ha-shanah 5776, which began in September 2015 according to the Jewish calendar.

The wind of the Ruwach is blowing times of refreshing onto the lives of the saints. We are seeing heaven and earth connect. Shanah is a Hebrew word that means to duplicate, repeat and to do again. The Shanah Shift is the beginning of this new season of kingdom awakening where God is shaking things from the perfect order of heaven onto the very shaky earth in order to remove those things in the earth that are shaky – that can be shaken. He is replacing them with things, God originals, which cannot be shaken. The Church can no longer be a collection of saved folk with no power. We are receiving a kingdom which cannot be moved! God is restoring His victorious kingdom Church with power and dominion. We are the Kingdom Enforcers! This is why the Body of Christ must possess the mentality of victory.

"The quickest way to lose a battle is to not have a mentality of victory" (Dr. G. E. Bradshaw, "Tongues of Fire: Bringing Your Axe to Battle. Pt. 2" – CD, Nov. 23, 2014). What a powerful statement. God's plan for every born-again human being is absolute victory. Through Jesus, God has given the saints grace and righteousness in order that we might reign as kings and have dominion on the earth. We were born again as winners – triumphant ones! Since we know what Jesus has done for us – destroyed the power of the devil; disarmed the wicked demon spirits; took the keys of death and hell from the devil; His resurrection made possible a resurrection in us, raising us from death to life; from defeat to victory – why is it that so many believers do not possess the mentality of victory?

Jesus has not left His Bride short-handed. He is the Head of the Body, and has supplied His Body with every spiritual weapon necessary to defeat Satan. But, we must know that we possess a spiritual war-chest, an arsenal of weapons that operate with pinpoint accuracy to obliterate the enemy. *"For this purpose the Son of God was manifested, that He might destroy the works of the devil"* (1 John 3:8). The power of Satan was broken by the death and resurrection of Jesus Christ, the Head of the Body who *"loved the church and gave himself for her… that He might sanctify and cleanse her with the washing of water by the word, that He might present her to Himself a glorious church, not having spot or wrinkle or any such thing, but that she should be holy and without blemish"* (Eph. 5: 25-27).

The intimacy of Christ's relationship to the Church is clearly evident throughout the New Testament. Jesus is "The Head" of the many members of the Body, which illustrate the Church as a vibrant, functioning entity, in which each believer has a unique role in its growth. Jesus is the Cornerstone of the Church, which attests to the foundational value of Christ upon which the Church is built. As the "Vine" of the Church, we (the branches) depend on nourishment, sustaining strength from the Vine for our growth. As helpless sheep, we trust the "Good Shepherd" to lead us from pasture to pasture, maturing us to the standard of the kingdom enforcers.

However, I must emphasize that no believer ever reaches this level of maturity if he does not learn to live by his faith. **Living by faith that is settled in the Word of God is the mindset of victory.** Believers cannot live in fear and expect victory. As saints, we have victory in life already won for us through Jesus' victory over Satan. We are more than conquerors and Jesus has overcome the world.

By now you might be asking yourself, "If the Church is all that, why aren't we seeing more miracles? Why aren't we doing greater works than Jesus did? But, I would submit to you that we are doing greater works and we're seeing many miracles performed. In Jesus' years of ministry, the global population was not anywhere close to what it is today. Plus, Jesus didn't have the technology that could reach them all, at the same time, wherever they were on the earth. Jesus was the power source of God on the earth, and He could only be in one place at a time. Yet, He changed the entire world.

But now, we will see exceeding great miracles; and the greater works that we are already doing will become more and more evident because of the "many" servant leaders that make up the end-time army of the Lord. Remember, God is using the many as opposed to the few. And, wherever we go, the power of Holy Spirit is with us to release the power and the glory of God to change nations.

What the old order of the Church lacked was proper servant leadership. True apostles and prophets were shunned. And, religion stripped the Church of her power. Religion is a stronghold which produces a mindset molded by rules, traditions and practices – "do's" and "don'ts" – concocted by men and adopted by the spiritually immature. Religion holds to a form of godliness that is void of power and lacks the delegated authority of God's power. It is empty, without obedience to the pure Word of God. Religion is restrictive; it places limitations on faith, and is insensitive to the voice of God. Satan uses religion as a means to keep the Church stagnant and void of power and dominion.

True apostolic and prophetic preaching is a weapon against the stronghold of religion. This is one of the reasons why believers with religious mindsets shun Holy Spirit illumination, revelation knowledge of the Scripture as taught by true apostles and prophets. As servant leaders, true apostles and prophets do not focus on themselves and their personal desires as much as they focus on pouring themselves into spiritual sons and daughters, training them and raising them to become commissioned, kingdom-level leaders – commanders – kingdom enforcers who occupy the frontlines of warfare, exemplifying the government of the Kingdom. True apostles and prophets confirm and strengthen the souls of disciples, equip them for their kingdom assignment, and build up the Body of Christ.

In this Kingdom Age of the Church's awakening, we are going to see God methodically put together an end-time army of mature saints. The many will lead the charge as opposed to the few. Credibility will trump celebrity. The youth of the world will make up the greater part of this army. Over the past eight years God has released commissioned faith warriors, tested in the furnace of affliction, trained and equipped to be launched and exposed during this kingdom age of awakening and reformation.

The Old Testament technology of using the "few" was initiated by God, as the Spirit of God had not come to dwell in the heart of mankind. In the Old Testament, the Spirit of God came on the kings, priests and prophets enabling them with supernatural ability and power to accomplish a task, fulfill a mission or defeat an army; then He would leave. However, we live under a better covenant built on better promises, and Jesus is its mediator. Holy Spirit, the supernatural power and ability of God, now dwells in our spirit; the same power God used to raise Jesus from the dead, and we are now the "many."

We are the Christian soldiers of the 21st Century, men and women of valor; mighty warriors; kingdom enforcers; an anointed people group that move in the higher realms of kingdom revelation and power. We are a fully mature army. Let's take a look at how God used Gideon to defeat the Midianites with only a "few" hundred men. Keep in mind what the Scripture says, *"There is no restraint to God to save by many or by few."*

Because the children of Israel did evil in the sight of God, He delivered them for seven years into the hands of the Midianites, an army of marauders, who constantly attacked Israel and raided their fields and granaries. When the Israelites cried out to the Lord because of the Midianites, the Angel of the Lord appeared to Gideon as he was threshing in small quantities in an inconspicuous place, hoping to finish quickly and avoid detection by the Midianites. *"And the Angel of the Lord appeared to him, and said to him, 'The Lord is with you, you mighty man of valor!'"* (Judges 6:12).

Of course, Gideon didn't feel like a mighty man of valor, and he certainly seems to have had doubts as to whether or not the Lord was with him. *"Gideon said to Him, 'O my lord, if the Lord is with us, why then has all this happened to us? And where are all His miracles which our fathers told us about? …But now the Lord has forsaken us and delivered us into the hands of the Midianites'"* (vs. 13). Sometimes you might feel like Gideon did. But, the Lord will say to you what He said to Gideon, *"Go in this might of yours, and you shall save Israel from the hand of the Midianites, Have I not sent you?"* (vs.14)

Like Gideon, you may feel overwhelmed by the magnitude of your kingdom assignment, and may even think of yourself as too weak or insignificant to accomplish such an arduous and daunting task (vs. 15). But, God has already established you in victory, for if you obey God even though you are afraid, He will give you further assurance as He did for Gideon. *"But if you are afraid to go down, go down to the camp with Purah your servant, 'and you shall hear what they say; and afterward your hands shall be strengthened to go down against the camp'"* (7:10-11).

We know the rest of the story. God delivered Israel by the hands of Gideon using the "few." Gideon started out with 32,000 men, but too many of them did not meet the standard of God's chayil army. In the end, only 300 men qualified as kingdom enforcers – those who showed correct military alertness. With these 300, God used Gideon to defeat the Midianites. The other 31,700 men were careless, unprepared and/or afraid. And, God wanted the glory.

In this Kingdom Age of the awakening and reformation of the Kingdom

Church, God is using the "many," an unstoppable force of kingdom commanders and servant leaders who have reached spiritual maturity and are now commissioned with delegated authority and power to be deployed into their specific theatres of battle. Armed by the God of the Angel Armies, we will have no fear of Satan or the demonically-driven world systems, but will represent the Kingdom of God as loyal, faithful servants who bring glory to God.

As a kingdom enforcer, you, too, are a mighty man or woman of valor and God definitely is with you. Many of you can relate to how Gideon felt, especially in light of what your current situation is or how long you've been dealing with a problem. And you've cried out to the Lord, and it seems like nothing is happening to turn your situation around. In times like these, you may not feel like the Lord is with you. But, thank God, your faith in His faithfulness is about what you know as opposed to what you feel. You must obey God in spite of your feelings.

Let's take a look at the word valor, because I think that it is one of the marks of the Lord Jesus that you and I carry in our body. The Hebrew word translated **valor** is *chayil (khah-yil),* which means a force, whether of men, means or other resources; an army, wealth, virtue, valor, strength: able, activity, band of soldiers, company of great forces, might, power, riches, strong, substance, valiant, war worthy (Strong's).

The Kingdom Age Church is the Chayil Army of God, a great warrior force marked by wealth, virtue, valor and strength. We are a company of great forces possessing might, power, riches and strong substance whether of men, means or other resources. As kingdom enforcers, we wear the chayil garments of the Lord in our body. These are the marks that certify us as commissioned, kingdom-level leaders. Apostle Paul said, *"From now on let no one trouble me, for **I bear the marks of the Lord Jesus"*** (Gal. 6:17, author's emphasis). The Greek word translated **marks** is *stigma (stig-mah),* which means a mark incised or punched for recognition of ownership, i.e., a scar of service (Strong's).

As the end-time Army of the Lord, the Church is being prepared for battle. We wear the scars of faithful, dedicated and committed service, and Father has marked us for recognition of ownership. We are His! And the Lord knows those who are His! *"Nevertheless, the solid foundation of God stands, having this seal: 'The Lord knows those who are His'"* (2 Tim. 2:19). **Jesus, the Cornerstone of the Church, has laid a foundation upon which the Church has been built; that foundation is solid and it will stand. The Lord knows those who are His kingdom enforcers – the Army of the Lord. And, we are led by the God of Chayil – EL CHAYIL!**

I was honored and blessed to have attended the 2016 Kingdom Enforcers Conference held in Mississauga, Ontario, Canada, hosted by Dr. Pat Francis – a Kingdom Enforcer of kingdom enforcers; a general of the Chayil Army of the Lord, whose ministry reflects the Kingdom of God in word and in deed. Through Dr. Francis, I received a greater revelation of chayil. I had studied the word before, but I had never gotten a revelation of EL CHAYIL and CHAYIL GLORY. There, I was introduced to the seven Chayil Pillars of her kingdom ministry: worship, wisdom, power, honor, favor, wealth, and influence, which describes kingdom enforcers' intent to grow like Jesus and with godly core values.

Dr. Francis writes: "The Bible describes the intentional growth of Jesus: *"And Jesus grew in **wisdom** and stature, and in **favor** with God and men"* (Luke 2:52, author's emphasis). Amplified, this verse can read, *"And Jesus grew in wisdom [understanding, revelation, sense, insight] and stature [**power, honor,** maturity respect], and in favor with God [**worship,** prayer, humility, obedience] and favor with men [prominence, **wealth, influence**]."* The words in bold form the CHAYIL pillars." (Dr. Pat Francis, *ALTARS TO OUR KING OF GLORY*, 2016, p. 188, Guardian Books, Canada)

The Chayil Army of the Lord is being mobilized for deployment with delegated authority from EL CHAYIL for successful completion of our kingdom mandate. I believe we've entered the time frame of "the fullness of the Gentiles." *"For I do not desire, brethren, that you should be ignorant of this mystery, lest you should be wise in your own opinion, that blindness in part has happened to Israel **until the fullness of the Gentiles has come in. And so all Israel will be saved"*** (Rom. 11:25-26, author's emphasis).

God is reforming the Body of Christ in this Kingdom Age Awakening so that the Church can reform the peoples and nations of the earth. God is shaking heaven's righteous pattern down to the earth to bring correction to the perverse systems of culture that exists prior to Jesus' return. Already, the world is experiencing more and more uncertainty in its financial markets. And, those who trust in their wealth will panic and be overcome by terror because great fear will overtake them. *"And because lawlessness will abound, the love of many will grow cold"* (Matt. 24:12). The instability of world systems is part of God's shaking and dismantling those things that can be shaken or are shaky. God is using foolish things to confound the wise. And, He will use the Church to reform people and nations.

Kingdom enforcers will be the "sought out" ones, for they will be master problem-solvers who use the wisdom of God to manifest the righteousness of God. Times like these will be the Church's greatest opportunity to converge upon the mountains of culture, transforming and subduing the nations for the Kingdom of God. *"For you see your calling, brethren, that not many wise according to the flesh, not many mighty, not many noble, are called. But God has chosen the foolish things of the world to put to shame the wise, and God has chosen the weak things of the world to put to shame the things which are mighty…that no flesh should glory in His presence"* (1 Cor. 1:26-27, 29).

During these times, people of all nations who would normally run to psychics, psychiatrists and other mediums for instruction, counsel or advice, will have to seek God's servant leaders for the God-solution to their problems. There will be a famine of hearing the words of the Lord (see Amos 8:11), not only for unbelievers, but also for weak or immature Christians. Those who have become addicted to prophecies – running from one prophet to another to get a word from the Lord instead of getting to know their Father intimately for themselves — will also find themselves in this situation. Commissioned, kingdom-level leaders will be sought out, for they will solve problems in alignment with the Word of the Lord.

In this Kingdom Age Awakening of the Church, God is challenging His saints to a deeper level of commitment of studying His Word and receiving a Holy Spirit revelation of it. Spirit-filled words spoken out of the mouth of a believer by faith will release the demonstration of the Spirit with power! Jesus said, *"The words that I speak to you are spirit, and they are life"* (John 6:63); *"He who believes in Me, as the Scripture has said, out of his heart will flow rivers of living water"* (John 7:38); *"For out of the abundance of the heart the mouth speaks"* (Matt. 12:34).

God wants the saints to be full of His Word and revelation, so that we can be cisterns of His Word to the multitudes in the time of the famine of the word of the Lord. God is speaking to commissioned, kingdom-level leaders who dare to commit to Him in loyal, faithful devotion. He is speaking to His servant leaders, giving us His God-language on how to comfort anybody in any situation because He has comforted us (see 2 Cor. 1:4). As servant leaders we will be sought after as we provide the Word of God to the weary to refresh them.

God wants to teach the saints knowledge, and give us wisdom and understanding through His Word – God speaking to us Holy Spirit-filled words that will keep our spirit man full of the Word, so that we will be able to cause those who are weary from a lack of hearing God's Word to be refreshed in it. **This is the refreshing – God speaking!** *"Whom will he teach knowledge? And whom will he make to understand the message? Those just weaned from milk? Those just drawn from the breasts? For precept must be upon precept, precept upon precept, Line upon line, line upon line, Here a little, there a little. For with stammering lips and another tongue* **He will speak to this people, To whom He said, 'This is the rest with which you may cause the weary to rest,' and, "This is the refreshing"'** (Isa. 28:9-12, author's emphasis). Yes, darkness and destruction shall cover the earth. But, *"the earth will be filled With the knowledge of the glory of the Lord, As the waters cover the sea"* (Hab. 2:14).

Get ready saints. The Shanah Shift is on NOW! The wind of the Holy Spirit is blowing and shifting the Church into her proper order, time and rank so that the original plan of God for Christ's Body can be displayed through us. The greatest outpouring of the Holy Spirit is at hand. This is global revival time! Refreshing! Relief! God is manifesting heaven upon the earth. Commissioned, kingdom level leaders – commanders – servant leaders and kingdom enforcers are anointed to change the world – to subdue the Seven Mountains of Culture and sit on our earthly thrones as the kings and priests that we are unto God.

We will shift the culture of the demonic systems of the world from the inside-out through revelation knowledge of the Word of God. Yes, we live in a time where the youth of the world are stuck in a generation where "loyalty is just a tattoo, love is just a quote, happiness is a myth, lying is the new truth, and being fake is a lifestyle." Nevertheless, we will teach, train and become spiritual parents to young children, adolescents and young adults, empowering and equipping them to become kingdom-level leaders and kingdom enforcers, commissioned by God for success and completion of their kingdom assignment. We are anointed with the Spirit of God to preach good tidings to the poor; to heal the brokenhearted; to proclaim liberty to the captives; to open the prison doors to those who are bound; and, to proclaim the acceptable year of the Lord (Isa. 61:1-2).

This is a great time to live – a great time to abide in the Presence of the Lord – and to walk in our faith that is settled in the Word of God which has provided us with victory through Jesus Christ. We are indeed more than conquerors. God loves us, and we have faith in the love of God toward us. We are delightfully married to the Lord Jesus; we are indeed the redeemed of the Lord; and we shall be called Sought Out, A City Not Forsaken (Isa. 62:12).

The world is getting ready to see the glory of the Lord like never before. The glory of God is upon the Church. And, God is raising the Church to be the light by which the world is drawn to His Light. So, arise Kingdom-level leaders! Shine! *"For behold, the **darkness shall cover the earth,** And deep darkness the people; But **the Lord will arise over you,** And **His glory will be seen upon you.** The **Gentiles shall come to your light,** And **kings to the brightness of your rising.** Lift up your eyes all around, and see: **They all gather together, they come to you; Your sons** shall come from afar, And **your daughters** shall be nursed at your side. **Then you shall see and become radiant, And your heart shall swell with joy; Because the abundance of the sea shall be turned to you, The wealth of the Gentiles shall come to you"*...I, the Lord, will hasten it in its time"* (Isa. 60: 1-5, 22; author's emphasis).

It's reformation time! God is raising commissioned apostles and prophets who have been processed and developed with present-truth revelation from Holy Spirit; they possess the delegated authority of the King of kings to function with power; they have the capacity to suffer for the sake of Christ and the gospel; they are spiritual parents who possess the character qualities of perseverance and kingdom conduct. These kingdom enforcers are the "hit-men" who, through apostolic and prophetic authority, attack and obliterate the rebellious spirit of religion. These servant leaders exercise the power and demonstration of the Spirit to teach, train and equip the saints with the laws and principles of Kingdom government and life. *"For this reason I will not be negligent to remind you always of these things, though you know and are established in the present truth"* (2 Pet. 1:12). *"But the Helper, the Holy Spirit, whom the father will send in My name, He will teach you all things"* (John 14:26).

The apostles and prophets – the commanders of the Kingdom Age – will operate with authority and function with power. Kingdom authority is the authority of the King's word, and *"where the word of a king is, there is power."* They will understand the authority they possess as ambassadors to the King of kings. God is with them. They are mighty men and women of valor who do not love their lives to the degree that they neglect the advancement of the Kingdom. These kingdom enforcers know Him and the power of His resurrection, and the fellowship of His suffering. And, they are willing to be conformed to His death. Like Paul, they say, *"That I may know Him and the power of His resurrection, and the fellowship of His sufferings, being conformed to His death"* (Phil. 3:10).

These kingdom enforcers possess the mentality of victory and are wired with a spirit of perseverance. They are resilient as they face the difficulties and challenges of refocusing the mindset of the saints toward the kingdom and ousting the religious spirit of a false humility. They understand that perseverance is the place where miracles are manifested. Just ask Apostle Paul. *"Truly the signs of an apostle were accomplished among you **with all perseverance,** in signs and wonders and might deeds"* (2 Cor. 12:12, author's emphasis). *"Praying always with all prayer and supplication in the Spirit, being watchful to this end **with all perseverance** and supplication for all the saints"* (Eph. 6:18, author's emphasis). *"But you have carefully followed my doctrine, manner of life, purpose, faith, longsuffering, love, **perseverance,** persecutions, afflictions…what persecutions I endured. And out of them all the Lord delivered me"* (2 Tim. 3:10-11, author's emphasis).

Kingdom enforcers function in kingdom conduct, which is built on covenant. The kingdom covenant is a covenant established upon love, faith, honor, obedience and humility. Kingdom enforcers understand the government of the Kingdom, *"For the kingdom of God is not eating and drinking, but righteousness and peace and joy in the Holy Spirit. For he who serves Christ in these things is acceptable to God and approved by men"* (Rom. 14: 17-18).

They are spiritual parents who raise sons and daughters who can also reflect their spiritual parents and leave their legacy of faith to succeeding generations. These kingdom enforcers – commanders – have embraced their calling to cover their sons and daughters and lead them into the presence of God as they teach, train, equip, commission and deploy them into their theatre of kingdom assignment as leaders, witnesses and commanders. "Presently the church is in transition. We are moving from the Church Age into the Apostolic Father-Son Kingdom Age." (Dr. Mark Kauffman, *"Fathers and Sons,"* in *Aligning With the Apostolic*, Vol. IV, General Editor Dr. Bruce Cook, 2013, p. 17, Kingdom House Publishing, Lakebay, WA).

The Kingdom of God is a government of increase, peace, order, judgment, and justice that is established forever. God never intended for succeeding generations of believers to re-invent the wheel and start over at zero. His will is for spiritual sons and daughters, commissioned servant-leaders, to benefit from the revelation of preceding generations so that the Church is established in present truth and continues to learn. God is currently restoring the Church, feeding it fresh manna. He's pouring new wine into new wineskins. He is restoring the position and authority of the apostles and prophets as the foundations of the New Testament Church of grace and truth. "Building Christ in the Body is true apostolic travail" (Kauffman).

The third great awakening of the Church has begun. This reformation will ensure that the saints possess the mentality of victory. The word translated **victory** in the Greek language is **nike' (nee-kay).** It means conquest, the means of success. It also means to subdue: conquer, overcome, prevail, triumph, to get the victory (Strong's). The Hebrew word translated **victory** is *teshuwah* (*tesh-oo-aw*). It means rescue, deliverance, help, safety, salvation, and victory

(Strong's). **Mentality** is one's way of thinking (mindset); one's predisposition; the preponderant likelihood of acting in a certain way, inclination or tendency (Merriam-Webster).

God is the possessor of all victory, since He alone possesses every component of victory. He is the God of all faith, and He possesses every component of what victory entails and looks like. And, since He upholds all things by the word of His power (see Heb. 1:3), God's Word is a sustained faith that holds the entire creation together just as He spoke it. It can never fail. Therefore, God possesses a mentality of victory. God is a Kingdom Enforcer! Hence, our example of possessing the mentality of victory comes from God, *"For whatever is born of God overcomes the world. And this is the victory that has overcome the world – our faith"* (1 John 5:4).

Commissioned, kingdom-level leaders, kingdom enforcers of the Kingdom Age, will possess the mentality of victory. Spiritual battles were lost in the old order, as many Christians were corralled by self-righteousness and the attainment of celebrity status rather than credibility before God. But, this great move of God will manifest the Chayil Army of EL CHAYIL! Get ready to see the most magnificent manifestations of EL CHAYIL'S power and glory ever recorded in the history of the Church. The glory released into the atmosphere produced by the global wildfire revival will fill the earth as the waters cover the sea (Hab. 2:14).

The Church will embrace the new 21st Century apostolic model of the servant leader. God is going to use the "many" no-name apostles and prophets mightily. The apostles and prophets will be the spearheads – the commanders – who will diligently heed their call as the foundations of the Church. They will be the spiritual parents of the kingdom enforcers who know how to fight as warriors, and who possess the mentality of victory. Most importantly, the Church will press forward with a great faith that will cause demonic activity to explode, obliterating them in the spirit realm with the name of Jesus.

Rise up Church and take your rightful place as the Bride of Christ who comes to the wedding without spot or wrinkle, holy and blameless, walking with royal confidence, and having possession of the kingdoms of the world. She comes to the wedding as a kingdom enforcer with the mentality of victory. She has matured into the perfect standard of the kingdom. She has been processed, developed, trained, equipped, transformed, transitioned and reformed – "From Footmen to Horsemen!" She has become the Body of Christ comprised of commissioned, kingdom-level leaders!

"Let us be glad and rejoice and give Him glory, for the marriage of the Lamb has come, and His wife has made herself ready" … *"Come, I will show you the bride, the Lamb's wife"* (Rev. 19:7; 21:9). *"O my love, you are as beautiful as Tirzah, Lovely as Jerusalem,* **Awesome as an army with banners!** *"Who is she who looks forth as the morning, Fair as the moon, Clear as the sun,* **Awesome as an army with banners?"** (Song of Solomon 6:4, 10; author's emphasis). SHE IS THE VICTORIOUS CHURCH OF THE KINGDOM AGE!!!

THE 21st CENTURY CHURCH IS ANOINTED TO CHANGE THE WORLD!

I am blessed of the Lord to be an apostle of Jesus Christ, sent forth to proclaim the gospel of the Kingdom of Heaven, and to share with you about commissioned, kingdom-level leadership and the process that leads to spiritually mature saints who discover their kingdom assignment and submit to the teaching, training and equipping that God requires in order to meet the standard of the kingdom.

The process toward spiritual maturity begins when you can reflect the vision of what God has seen and said concerning you and your kingdom assignment in His mind of eternity. *"Where there is no vision, the people perish"* (Prov. 29:18, KJV). Otherwise we can abuse or miss our purpose because we have no revelation of it from God. God said, *"For I know the thoughts that I think toward you, says the Lord, thoughts of peace and not of evil, to give you a future and a hope"* (Jer. 29:11). God reflects about you! The thoughts that God thinks about you are the image of your life as it should be. And, you must see what God sees about you so that He can invoke the process towards that end. *"'Jeremiah what do you see?' And I said, 'I see a branch of an almond tree.' Then the Lord said to me, 'You have seen well, for I am ready to perform My word'"* (Jer. 1:11-12).

It is my heart's desire that, all over the world, members of the Body of Christ understand what servant leadership is all about. As ministers of reconciliation, believers must understand exactly what it is God has called us to do. And, our standard must be in alignment with the Kingdom of God and not with the evil kingdoms and systems of the world. Kingdom greatness takes on the nature and character of the King, which encompasses all things good. As believers, we carry out the godly actions and teach others the good news about Jesus Christ and the government of Heaven. In the same way, greatness as it is defined in alignment with the evil systems of the world, will also partake of the nature and character of Satan.

Jesus said to His disciples, *"'You know that the rulers of the Gentiles lord it over them, and those who are great exercise authority over them. Yet it shall not be so among you; but whoever desires to become great among you, let him be your servant. And whoever desires to be first among you, let him be your slave – just as the Son of Man did not come to be served, but to serve, and to give His life a ransom for many'"* (Matt. 20:25-28). Nevertheless, many believers have allowed Satan to deceive them, through their lustful desires to be great, into developing evil standards according to the systems of the world.

Let's take a look at the life of Jesus. *"Most assuredly, I say to you, a servant is not greater than his master; nor is he who is sent greater than he who sent him. If you know these things, blessed are you if you do them"* (John 13:16-17). When we look at the life and ministry of Jesus, we see a man who never wrote any books; yet, the book about Him is the number one seller in the world. Jesus never conducted any seminars or workshops; never had a CD/DVD ministry, radio ministry, television ministry or a ministry over the many social networks on the world-wide-web. Yet, Jesus obtained godly notoriety. Jesus never started a church. He never set out to build a ministry; instead, Jesus built people.

Jesus was a Wise Master Builder of servant leaders, kingdom commanders and kingdom enforcers. Jesus built relationships. Over the three and a half years of His earthly ministry, Jesus infused the 12 with knowledge of the kingdom. They were His disciples (learners, pupils, imitators) whom He called apostles. Jesus became their spiritual father. He spent quality time teaching, training and equipping them to be "sent ones" – commanders who were given authority and power over all the power of the enemy. But, even after this, one of them betrayed Him.

If we are going to emulate our Master, *"the servant is not great than his Lord,"* greater works must be performed today. Not because we can come up with something Jesus didn't already do, but because we have greater resources. Holy Spirit dwells in all believers and we also have state of the art technology at our disposal to reach almost anyone in the world at any time. More than that, we have the anointing of Jesus Christ collectively to *"come to the unity of the faith… from whom the whole body, joined and knit together by what every joint supplies, according to the effective working by which every part does its share, causes growth of the body for the edifying of itself in love"* (Eph. 4:13, 16).

In less than four years, Jesus changed the entire known world. The Church also has as her mandate to change the world toward the pattern of the Kingdom of God. However, if she is to do that, she must operate in the level of authority and power delegated to her as kings and priests unto God, and ambassadors for Christ. I'm not talking about emotionalism; I'm not talking about people getting worked up for the moment because of a high-spirited service but have no power to sustain their passion. Members of the Body of Christ must understand and learn how to properly acquire a kingly anointing. A king's anointing must be kingly.

Let's take a look at how Jesus, the King of kings, got anointed. Jesus was not a wimp. Jesus was not some yellow-back, passive person running around in lacy pajamas singing "skip to the lou, my darling." No! Jesus was a revolutionary for the Kingdom of Heaven. You can't be a wimp and go into the Temple overturning the tables of the money exchangers, driving them out with a whip of cords.

You can't be a wimp and look religious folk (Scribes, Pharisees and Sadducees) in their eyes and call them hypocrites, vipers and white-washed sepulchers. Jesus was a revolutionary. And, the Church of the 21st Century must take on the nature and character of a revolutionary, individually and collectively. After the day of Pentecost had fully come, the apostles also became revolutionaries for the Kingdom of God. The people said of Paul and Silas, *"These who have turned the world upside down have come here too"* (Acts 17:6).

Prior to Jesus' baptism, you don't see any miracles performed; you don't see any eyes opened; you don't see any deaf ears unstopped; you don't see any people being fed. You see no miracles prior to Jesus getting anointed. The anointing Jesus needed to fulfill His earthly kingdom assignment was given to Him by His Father, Who was well pleased with His Son's exhibition of faith in, and obedience to, His Word. Jesus said, *"The Spirit of the Lord is upon Me, Because He has anointed Me … "* (Luke 4:18). Luke again tells us that the Father is the giver of the King's anointing, *"how God anointed Jesus of Nazareth with the Holy Spirit and with power, who went about doing good and healing all who were oppressed by the devil, for God was with Him"* (Acts 10:38).

Apostle John lets us know that God supernaturally bestows His anointing upon His "sent ones." *"And He who sent Me is with Me. The Father has not left Me alone, for I always do those things that please Him"* (John 8:29). Jesus gives us a major requirement for acquiring God's anointing: "I always do those things that please Him." *"You are My beloved Son; in You I am well pleased"* (Luke 3:22).

The author of the book of Hebrews gives us further understanding relative to the requirement of obedience prior to receiving or acquiring the anointing. *"Though He was a Son, yet He learned obedience by the things which He suffered"* (Heb. 5:8). Adversity produces maturity. The Greek word translated **suffered** is **pentho (pen-tho),** which means to experience a sensation or impression, usually painful (Strong's). Like Jesus, as you go through the process toward spiritual maturity where God releases upon you His kingly anointing, Holy Spirit will lead you into many experiences of life, many of them painful, which will test your capacity to yield to and obey God.

While you are experiencing these tests of your faith, God gives or bestows upon you an enabling to go through the tests as you obey His instructions. Having succeeded in going through the experiences which test your commitment to God, you will emerge having learned more about God and His divine nature and character. You will emerge more anointed than you were before you were led into the painful experiences of life that tested you. You are as anointed as you can stand the pain of your experiences; and, your painful experiences are relative to your kingdom assignment.

To this end, Paul writes, *"No temptation has overtaken you except such as is common to man; but God is faithful, who will not allow you to be tempted beyond what you are able, but with the temptation will also make the way of escape, that you may be able to bear it"* (1 Cor. 10:13). When you yield to God's will, He makes a way for you to endure the temptations, tests, and painful experiences of life which come to teach you faith and obedience. His *"making a way to escape"* is His endowment or enabling of His supernatural ability on you to push through any experience of life. It is His "Super" on your "natural" that gets the job done.

Chapter 4 of the Gospel according to Luke, verse one, says that Jesus was full of the Holy Spirit. That is true. Yet, Jesus had not been fully anointed. **Tests of obedience come before acquiring the anointing.** Remember, the child was born; but the Son was given (see Isa. 9:6). **The anointing is not earned; it is given.** As you make deeper levels of commitment to God, He tests your loyalty to His Word in the crucible of fiery trials in order to prepare you for the destiny He's divinely ordained for you before He created the world. After Jesus was baptized in the Jordan by John the Baptist, He was full of the Holy Spirit. Then Jesus was driven by the Holy Spirit into the wilderness. What was His purpose? It was to teach Jesus how to be victorious over Satan by obeying and speaking the Word of God by faith. Also, once Jesus passed this test, God would anoint Him with supernatural power.

Now let me tell you a little about the wilderness. The wilderness is not a very pleasant place to be. The Greek word translated **wilderness** is *eremos (er-ay-mos)*. It means a desert, desolate, solitary, lonesome place (Strong's). Jesus was in this type of environment for 40 days – reminiscent of the 40 years Israel wandered in the wilderness. But, where Israel, who represents a type of Christ in the Old Testament, wandered and failed because of their disobedience, Jesus fulfilled and accomplished God's will because of His obedience.

During His stay in the wilderness, Jesus fasted. And, each day the devil tempted Him. But, the thrust of the devil's temptation did not occur until the 40 days were ended, and Jesus was hungry. Satan took this opportunity to tempt Jesus, when the Lord was exhausted and weak from not having eaten anything for 40 days. The devil proceeded to tempt Jesus in the three major temptations of man: 1) lust of the flesh, 2) lust of the eyes, and, 3) the pride of life (1 John 2:16). But, even in His weakened, most vulnerable state, Jesus countered each temptation of the devil with God's Word.

Satan thought that he was so smart in quoting Scripture. But, he could not perceive the eternal effect of God's Word. God's Word is for all time – past, present, and future. God's Word is powerful. By faith, Jesus spoke God's Word in obedience, and He was immediately a candidate for God's grace. Paul writes, *"And He said unto me, My grace is sufficient for you, for My strength is made perfect in weakness"* (2 Cor. 12:9). *"Now when the devil had ended every temptation, he departed from Him until an opportune time. **Then Jesus returned in the power of the Spirit** to Galilee"* (Luke 4:13-14, author's emphasis). Jesus was fully anointed! Not only was He full of the Holy Spirit but He was also full of power – supernatural authority and ability.

Jesus reveals this supernatural ability when He confirmed the Words written of Himself in Isa. 61:1, *"The Spirit of the Lord God is upon Me, Because **the Lord has anointed Me** to preach good tidings to the poor; **He has sent Me** to heal the brokenhearted"* (author's emphasis). Jesus spoke to the people with the authority and power of God, letting them know that He was anointed to *"heal all that were oppressed of the devil."* His anointing enabled Him to preach the acceptable year of the Lord, relative to God's Kingdom agenda. What Jesus was saying that day is, **"I am anointed to change the world and bring it under the authority of the Kingdom of Heaven."**

This same kingly anointing that has the power to change the world and subdue the cultures of nations is available to the Church today, and Holy Spirit is beckoning the Body of Christ to receive this supernatural endowment through the process of spiritual maturity. Jesus had to grow up. Therefore, His Body has to grow up, increasing in wisdom and stature, to a perfect Bride, to the measure of the stature of the fullness of Jesus Christ. *"Now then, we are ambassadors for Christ, as though God were pleading through us: we implore you on Christ's behalf, be reconciled to God"* (2 Cor. 5:20). This is true of the Church today. If the Church is to fully accomplish her mandate to preach the gospel of the kingdom to all nations and people, advancing the Kingdom of God in the earth, she must endure the process toward spiritual maturity.

In this book, I have tried to communicate through personal experiences – many of them painful – the process which transforms believers from footmen to horsemen. It is a process of spiritual maturity that leads to the manifestation of commissioned, kingdom-level leaders, kings and priests, commanders, servant leaders, and kingdom enforcers. Spiritual growth happens when you trust God completely and obey the process of growth He has chosen for you. The process is relative to your kingdom assignment.

The truth of the matter is that, not many people are willing to go into labor in order to reap the harvest of lost souls. I implore you to take a stand for advancing the Kingdom of God. The real price of success lies with the need to persevere in doing things God's way. The trophy is never given to someone who does not complete the task. Saints, we have kingly-anointed power to change our communities, our states, our nation – the world, and give a new vitality to the faith of Jesus Christ. We must be able to get those who have lost faith in the Church to see that **Jesus was not a coward. He dealt with the hurts of humanity amid the glow of the Divine. He had compassion for human hurts. He was anointed to deal with the problems of the poor.**

This same anointing is available to the Church today. And this should be where we get our inspiration to prepare and go out into the fields of the world as commanders – kingdom enforcers – who reap the end-time harvest through the demonstration of the Spirit with power and subdue the mountains of cultures, opening the heavens for Jesus' return. We are the victorious 21st Century Church, and we are commissioned, kingdom-level leaders anointed by God to change the world! *"Who is she who looks forth as the morning, Fair as the moon, Clear as the sun, Awesome as an army with banners?"* She is the victorious Church of the 21st Century!

ABOUT THE AUTHOR

Dr. James Brewton is Founder and Senior Pastor of Community Empowerment Ministries, Inc., located in Estill, South Carolina, in partnership with Global Effect Movers & Shakers Network (GEMS) – Dr. Gordon E. Bradshaw, President. He is a founding father of the Allendale County Transformers (ACT), a collaboration of personnel representing every segment of community life, whose mandate is to transform the current mindsets and environments from poverty and complacency to one of activity, achievement, and growth, for community and economic success.

Dr. Brewton has been a minister of the Gospel of the Kingdom for over 24 years, 18 of them in full-time vocational ministry, and has served as Chaplain for the Allendale County (S.C.) Sheriff's Department and advisory member of the Sheriff's Task Force on Gang Violence. He has served as coordinator of several community activities for youth, involving recreation and other forms of social networking.

Currently he serves on the Board of Directors for Allendale County First Steps. He is the "Goodwill Ambassador" for the GEMS (Global Effect Movers and Shakers) Network, and a member of the Network's SCOPEVision Group and Tactical Application Commission (TAC). In addition, Dr. Brewton is a member of KCIA (Kingdom Congressional International Alliance) and serves on the Advisory Council. He is leader of the KCIA Executive Strategic Intercession Team, a member of the Commission on Cultural and Social Reformation, and is a Goodwill Ambassador for the Golden Rule International awarded by the Interfaith Peace-Building Initiative of the United Nations.

Dr. Brewton is a commissioned apostle and ordained bishop, and an apostolic advisor to several leaders, organizations and corporations locally, nationally and internationally. He received a bachelor's degree in History and a master's degree in Public Management from Florida A&M University. The Doctor of

Divinity degree was conferred upon him in 2013 by Hope Bible Institute and Seminary, South Bend, Indiana.

He is the author of two other books: *A Slave of Circumstance* and *Back Porch Meditations, Holy Spirit Revelations.* He and his wife, Margie, reside in Allendale, South Carolina.